COMPLETE
Pastrywork
TECHNIQUES

COMPLETE
Pastrywork
TECHNIQUES

I NICOLELLO

Foreword by Emile Lefebvre

Hodder & Stoughton

LONDON SYDNEY AUCKLAND TORONTO

The publishers wish to thank West Herts College (Cassio campus) for supplying all the ingredients and, in particular, Mr David Wells, Head of Department, for permission to use the facilities. Thanks also go to the three assistants, Cesare Caianiello, Scott Callow and Richard Shields for their help in preparing the dishes. Finally, the publishers would like to express their appreciation to Roddy Paine and Martin Ball for the photography.

British Library Cataloguing in Publication Data
Nicolello, Ildo
    Complete pastrywork techniques
    I. Title
    641.8

ISBN 0340 55147X

First published 1991

Typeset by Wearside Tradespools, Fulwell, Sunderland
Printed in Hong Kong for the educational publishing division of Hodder and Stoughton Ltd, Mill Road, Dunton Green, Sevenoaks Kent by Colorcraft Ltd.

CONTENTS

PREFACE

My object in preparing this book in the form of a manual is not to write a treatise on 'patisserie'. It is an art form as much as a science, and over the years my love for this art has taken me down many avenues. Cookery, with all its mysteries, derives from traditions world-wide, and the painstaking dedication of some individuals with the extraordinary flair and imagination to achieve the best possible results from the ingredients available to them.

My recipes and methods are clearly written to help develop an understanding of basic and original, new and old ideas. This understanding will enable even the inexperienced to learn the skills of patisserie, which can seem so difficult. Text and illustrations cover up-to-date recipes, and concise methods explaining how to produce dishes with ease and confidence.

This book will be a valuable reference for today's aspiring young patissier (pastemaker), particularly essential for students taking the City & Guilds 706/1, 2 and especially the 706/3 Pastry Examination. It will also be a useful guide for the busy chef and chef patissier, for anyone who desires sound knowledge in pastrywork, or just for those who are interested in pastry making.

My introduction to the delights and mysteries of this art was through my father, a patissier with experience in prominent London West End hotels, in the twenties and thirties. As an apprentice and with the guidance of my brother, I learned to develop the skills and application of creative work. I acknowledge the value of his help and wisdom.

He also deserves to be complimented for his well-acclaimed book, *Basic Pastrywork Techniques*, widely used in colleges and by patissiers everywhere.

My 35 years of practical experience began with four years of sound training at the Park Lane Hotel, Piccadilly, under the great chef, Monsieur Perrin. The next move was to the Piccadilly Hotel as commis pâtissier. After this, I enjoyed the responsibility of being chef patissier in the large hotels of Bournemouth. I have been lecturing on patisserie for the last 25 years and feel confident of being able to demonstrate the art of my profession.

During the task of writing this book, it has been my good fortune to have received help, encouragement and advice from many of my colleagues and friends. I gratefully acknowledge their assistance.

First and foremost, my dear wife, Maureen, for her tremendous endeavour and assistance, spending many hours typing and helping to bring together the text. I have to thank my brother, Lidio, for his expert advice and suggestions, kindly given throughout the writing of this book. Also Mr David Wells, Head of Department, Food Industries, West Herts College, Watford, for his kind co-operation over the use of the college facilities to produce the photographs. Mr Gerard McVeigh AHCIMA, FIBB, MCFA(CG), ACF, Cert Ed Senior Lecturer at the college of Business Studies, Dept of Catering, Belfast. I am extremely grateful to Gerry, for advice and contribution on the theory of yeast, to the text. Mr Graham Salter, CFA, ACF, City and Guild 706/3 (Hons) Senior Lecturer in Food

Technology, at West Herts College; I particularly thank Graham for his co-operation and for his section in the text on Ice Carving – in these days a very rare skill to be found. I am sure Graham's work will help many to improve their skills and knowledge in this difficult area. The Association Culinaire Française, as a committee and regional representative; I thank the President, Monsieur C. Mercier, the secretary Dr Rev. P. Miln and particularly Monsieur Emile Lefebvre for support and encouragement.

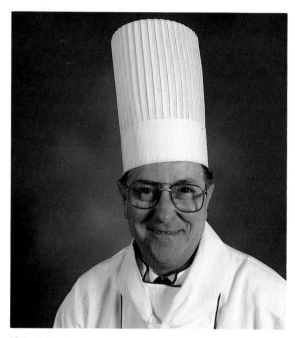

Ildo Nicolello, FEWMCS, ACF, NCFA (CG) Cordon Culinairé Lacam

FOREWORD

At last, a pastry manual that has been compiled by a professional patissier, expert in both hotel and retail production.

Mr. Nicolello is a dedicated teacher and has set out the wealth of his knowledge and experience in a clean and precise manner with clear and easy references and photographs and although this book is intended primarily for patissiers, I am sure that many other chefs will find it of immense value.

When I left school I learned the hard way by serving my apprenticeship in France. No reference books were available other than those which gave only recipes with no explanation as to method and procedure and everything that I learned I had to record myself for future reference. Mr. Nicolello's book would have been invaluable and would have saved me many a sleepless night recording the day's tasks.

This book has been written with students in mind, but even the most advanced craftsmen will undoubtedly find it a mine of information.

An enormous amount of thought has gone into the comprehensive selection of items which covers all the basic skills required by budding patissiers, and the analysis, theory and science of bakery materials are set out with great clarity. This is of the utmost importance, for without an understanding of basic component, the scope of their use in baking procedures is limited.

Precise quantities and consistency must always be the major factor in the preparation of confectionery, bakery and pastry work and these can only be achieved by adhering to well-balanced formulas. Mr. Nicolello is meticulous in his explanations.

As a retired senior lecturer at Westminster College for thirty years, I would say that this is the essential reference book for all students, particularly for those taking examinations in City and Guilds 706/1, 706/2 and 706/3 Pastry, parts 1 and 2.

E.J.P. Lefebvre C.O.N.M.
(Chevalier dans l'Ordre National du Merit)
Président d'Honneur de l'Association Culinaire Française de Grande-Bretagne
Président d'Honneur de l'Académie Culinaire de France Filiale de Grande-Bretagne

INTRODUCTION

■ *LA BRIGADE DE LA PÂTISSERIE*

The pastry chef (le chef pâtissier) is responsible for all hot and cold sweets for lunches, dinners and functions. Production in the patisserie includes:

    All cold buffet work
    Sweet trolley
    Ice cream dishes
    Pastries
    Petits fours
    Kitchen requirement, such as: vol-au-vents, cheese straws, etc.

The patissier in a large hotel or other establishment is in charge of all the sections in the patisserie and also works together with the head chef (chef de cuisine) on planning menus, functions, staff rota, ordering of commodities, etc.

The baker (le boulanger) is responsible for the production of all breads and main flour products, covering of pies, lining of flans, morning goods, etc.

The puff paste worker (le tourier) deals with all pastes and all products from each of the pastes.

The confectioner (le confiseur) requires great skill and experience. He produces many artistic items, such as: pulled sugar, chocolate, pastillage work, cake decoration, confits, petits fours, etc.

The ice maker (le glacier) produces various dishes in which ice cream is the main ingredient, such as: sorbets, water-ices, bombes, soufflés, coupes, omelettes surprise and even ice carving.

The duty chef (le chef de garde) is responsible for running the patisserie when most of the brigade are off duty, mainly in the afternoon and evenings.

The relief chef (le chef tournant) takes on responsibility from other chefs de parties, on their days off duty.

The assistant chef (le commis) most chefs de parties are assisted by a commis. They are usually capable of taking charge of the partie if it should be necessary.

The apprentice (l'apprenti) is learning the trade and is moved to each of the parties to gain experience and knowledge of all the sections.

■ FATS AND OILS

Butter

This is defined in the Food and Drugs Act 1984 as 'the substance made exclusively from milk with other preservatives, and with or without the addition of colouring matter'.

Butter is produced by agitating ripened cream to separate the globules of milk-fat and butter; the method is known as 'churning'. The globules of fat are formed into granules then worked into a spongy mixture. This is then drained, the liquid is removed until a homogeneous mass, butter, is formed. Colour can then be added to improve the appearance, also salt for flavour and keeping qualities.

By law butter must contain at least 80% milk fat, not more than 2% solids other than fat, and not more than 16% water.

Butter must be kept under favourable conditions, as it tends to become rancid due to the decomposition of the glycerides.

Margarine

This is a product specially designed to substitute butter. It consists of animal fats, vegetable fats and oils, with the addition of colouring matter. It is absolutely essential in the production of margarine that all ingredients are pure and fresh.

Margarine was invented by a French chemist, Mège-Mouriés, in the middle of the 18th century, for a competition developed by Napoleon III to produce a fat that would resemble butter to feed the army. He produced a fat with a pearly appearance, and it is from the Greek word for pearl (*margaron*) that margarine got its name.

Oils such as ground nut, fish oils, coconut, palm kernel, oleo oil are used for manufacturing margarine. Vitamin A and D, vegetable colouring and brine are added. A quantity of fat-free milk is pasteurised and added to the fats and oils, the mixture is then chilled and emulsified until it has reached the correct consistency and texture.

In some products a small amount of butter is blended in – no more than 10%. Lecithin or some other emulsifying agent and colour are added.

Lard

Lard is a fat obtained from the pig, mainly the part surrounding the kidneys. It is separated from the fatty tissues by melting. Lard when exposed to the air gradually becomes rancid. When prepared, it should be immediately run into sterile containers, not touched by hand and kept in a cool place, until ready for use.

Lard can be mainly used by the patissier as a shortening agent in making hot water paste for raised meat and fish pies.

Shortening

Originally an American invention, shortening is an adulterated 'compound lard'. Shortening now consists of hydrogenated animal or vegetable oils and 100% fats. This emulsified white fat possesses good creaming properties; it is used in small portions with margarine and butter in cake mixes, with the advantage of producing an improved crumb texture in the cake.

Vegetable oils

All vegetable oils are refined in the same way as fats. They have a low melting point and a liquid consistency even at normal temperatures. They are used in cheap quality cakes and for frying, but they have no creaming properties.

Vegetable oils can be obtained from olives, almonds, groundnut, cotton, corn, sesame, rape, coconut, palm kernel, and palm.

Suet

This is the hard fat encasing the heart or embedded in the loin of the bullock or sheep. It is removed from the tissues, chopped finely, and used for making steamed puddings and mincemeat.

■ MILK AND CREAM

Milk

> *Content:* Water 7%; Carbohydrates 5%; Protein 3%; Mineral salts and vitamins 1%; Fat 4%.
>
> *Retailing units:* ⅓ pt, ½ pt, 1 pt, 1 ℓ
> *Wholesale units:* 1 gal., 5 gal., 10 gal., 20 gallon churns

Milk is a food of high nutritional value. It contains the water soluble vitamins B1 and B2. The important minerals in milk are calcium and phosphorus. It also contains fat vitamins A, D, and E.

Pasteurised milk is heated to 72 °C, held at that temperature for 15 seconds, then cooled to at least 4.4 °C, this will destroy any harmful bacteria.

Homogenised milk is treated and forced through very fine holes to break up the fat globules. These become evenly distributed throughout the milk and will not separate to form a cream layer.

Sterilised milk is first homogenised, then bottled and heat treated. It will keep for seven days or longer.

Dried milk is either sprayed – forced at pressure through a vent hole to fall in powder form in a heated chamber, or it is skimmed by rollers – process-poured over hot rollers to dry and be scraped off.

Milk should be used on the same day of purchase. Always store in a covered container to protect it from dust, insects and germs, also from absorbing flavours from other foods. Always store in the refrigerator.

As milk is an ideal medium for the growth of micro-organisms, its bacteriological condition is of great importance. Very rigid standards are laid down by law for the handling of milk and milk products.

Contaminated dairy products can cause tuberculosis, typhoid, diphtheria, scarlet fever. All containers and utensils used for the preparation of milk must be sterilised in boiling water before use.

Dairy cream

Andrew Boorde wrote 'crayme is eaten more for a sensual appetyte' – words recorded over 400 years ago, which suggest that cream is consumed simply because it tastes nice. Cream is still a very popular product, used to enhance the enjoyment of food – in flavour and enrichment. It is also a versatile one – an ideal body-builder for foam products, such as mousses, bavarois, ice creams, fruit fools, or can be used just as an accompaniment.

Developments in food-processing technology have led to improvements in the quality and types of cream available today. Differences in fat content, heat treatment and the way in which creams are sold and packaged have considerably widened the choice of cream available.

WHAT IS CREAM?

The Cream Regulations 1970 defines cream as 'that part of milk rich in fat which has been separated by skimming or otherwise, and which is intended for sale for human consumption'. The fat content of cream is higher than that of the milk or water content.

Cream, like milk, is basically an emulsion of fat in water. The butter-fat globules are dispersed in a medium of skimmed milk containing protein, lactose, minerals and some vitamins.

The production of cream

Traditionally, the milk is left to stand for about 24 hours, the cream rises and is then skimmed from the surface. The modern commercial method is much more efficient and extremely rapid. The cream is separated by centrifugal force in a mechanical separator, under very strict hygienic conditions.

The separator consists of spaced conical plates and works much like a spin-drier. As the bowl spins round at high speed, the cream, which is lighter than the milk, flows towards the centre and the milk is diverted towards the outside. The cream is then cooled to 4.5 °C.

The skimmed milk is heated to a temperature of between 72 °C and 80 °C, to destroy any harmful bacteria. It is then cooled to less than 5 °C and used to produce other milk products, for example, cottage cheese.

Heat treatment of cream

Cream which has been pasteurised, sterilised, ultra-heat treated or is untreated must be described as such on the label. This is a legal requirement of the Cream Regulations 1970. Regulations also came into operation in November 1983, which include statutory specifications for heat treatment.

PASTEURISATION
Pasteurisation destroys any harmful microorganisms which may be present in cream and improves keeping quality, without affecting the nutritional value or flavour of the cream. The heat-treatment is carried out by:
(a) heating cream to at least 63 °C for not less than 30 minutes; or
(b) heating cream to at least 72 °C for not less than 15 seconds; or
(c) heating cream to any other time and temperature combination which has an equivalent effect to (a) and (b).

It is then cooled to 4.5 °C and pumped into tanks ready for packaging in bottles or cartons and sealed with metal foil caps.

HOMOGENISATION
In this process the cream is forced through a tiny orifice under considerable pressure. This breaks the butter-fat globules into a smaller, uniform size and ensures an even distribution through the cream. Homogenisation thickens the cream and increases its viscosity.

STERILISATION
Sterilisation destroys any viable microorganisms and their spores. Cream to be sterilised is first homogenised, filled into the containers in which it is to be sold, hermetically sealed and sterilised by:
(a) heating to 108 °C for not less than 45 minutes; or
(b) heating to any other time and temperature combination which has an equivalent effect to (a).

ULTRA-HEAT TREATMENT
This heat treatment destroys any pathogenic or non-pathogenic bacteria, but due to the short duration of the heating process, the cream retains a flavour similar to pasteurised cream. The cream is first homogenised, then heated to 132 °C for one second and cooled immediately. It is then packaged in foil-lined containers.

Types of fresh cream

Half cream may be called 'top of the milk' or coffee cream. It is ideal for pouring over fruit or cereal, or used in coffee.

Single cream is another pouring cream which does not have sufficient fat to whip. Its uses are as for half cream.

Whipping cream is ideal for whipping. It should whip to more than twice its original volume. It can be used for piping.

Double cream is slightly homogenised. It has a very rich texture. It will whip, but unless used for piping on gateaux etc., the whipping texture can be improved by adding a little milk.

Double cream extra thick is heavily homogenised and so will not whip successfully. It is served with puddings, sweets and on fruit.

Double cream 'extended life' is usually stored in glass bottles or jars. It may be described as 'long keeping' or 'extended life' cream. This cream is heated to 82 °C for 15 seconds, then cooled. It is homogenised, filled into bottles which are vacuum sealed and then heated in the bottle to 115 °C for 12 minutes, in a similar way to pasteurisation, but the cream has a longer life, and will keep for two to three weeks in the refrigerator.

Clotted cream is a thick cream with a nutty flavour and is golden yellow in colour.

MINIMUM LEGAL FAT CONTENT (BY WEIGHT)

Clotted cream	55%
Double cream	48%
Whipping cream	35%
Whipped cream	35%
Sterilised cream	23%
Sterilised half cream	12%
Single cream	18%
Half cream	12%

FACTORS EFFECTING THE WHIPPING OF CREAM

- (i) The fat content of cream
- (ii) Availability of free protein
- (iii) Temperature at which the cream is whipped
- (iv) Viscosity of the cream
- (v) The type of whisk used (a balloon whisk is recommended)
- (vi) The addition of sugar

(vii) The size of the fat globules

It is important that all equipment used, and the room in which the cream is to be whipped, should be cool (8 °C).

Once the cream has been treated, attempts should be made to whip it when it is 24 hours old. This increases the viscosity of the cream and improves its whipping properties. This is known as 'ageing the cream'.

■ WHEAT AND FLOUR

There is evidence that thousands of years before Christ, man used wheat as food. Bronze tablets dating from the 9th century AD depict the grinding of wheat and making of bread in Asia. In Egypt, tombs along the Nile River contain ancient murals which show wheat planting and harvesting, the grinding of flour and making of bread. In 1948 archaeologists uncovered an ancient village in Iraq. In the ruins they found two different kinds of wheat similar to those grown today.

Wheat found in the excavation of ancient cities often appears carbonised as though the husk had been removed by heat. Heating or parching the grain makes the glumes easier to rub off. Other cereals, corn, rice, and perhaps varieties of early wheat, could be popped like what we know as popcorn. The moisture inside the hard outer coat would turn to steam in the heating process to explode grain glumes.

Wheat is still eaten in primitive forms in many parts of the world. Similar crude tools and instruments to those used all those thousands of years ago, can still be seen in use today.

Choice of flour

So many foods today contain wheat it is often an unnoticed part of our diet; bread, of course, is the most familiar wheat product. There are many different types of flour one can purchase. When the recipe requires flour, the question arises, does choice of flour make much difference to baking? Definitely, yes. The right flour, plus practical skill, will give you the best results every time.

Flours vary in composition and, broadly speaking, are defined according to their rate of extraction and the type of wheat from which they are milled.

Wholemeal or wholewheat flours are 100% extraction. The flour contains the whole of the wheatgrain (including bran and germ) with nothing added or taken away.

Wheatmeal or brown flours usually contain 85–90% of the wheatgrain.

White flour usually contains 72–74% of the wheatgrain, although lower extraction rates can be produced.

Wholemeal and brown flours give variety, flavour, and colour to baking in speciality bread. Baked goods made with flours with a high proportion of bran and germ have a limited rise and closer texture than those made with white flour. To bake goods with a more open texture and of a lighter colour, replace half the total weight of whole or brown flour with white flour.

Baking characteristics

A protein present in the flour, glutenin, when combined with water forms gluten. The following experiment demonstrates how gluten works in the production of bread.

DIRECTIONS

Make a dough from 60 g of flour, and two tablespoons of water. Knead until smooth, then soak the dough ball in a basin of cold water for at least half an hour. Gently squeeze and knead the dough under a dripping tap until the starch is washed out. What remains is the gluten. The texture will be similar to chewing gum; it will stretch like elastic.

When the gluten ball is baked at 230 °C for 20 minutes the water inside is converted into steam which expands, blowing up the gluten into a balloon, by forming air pockets inside. Upon further baking the gluten sets and becomes light and crisp like a starch-reduced roll. When bread dough is baked the gluten in the dough is blown up and sets in exactly the same way. It is the gluten framework which forms the structure of the loaf, cake or pastry.

The quality and quantity of the gluten produced by a flour are both important. A tough gluten is hard to blow up, while a soft, sticky gluten blows up easily but collapses quickly. For the best quality bread a good elastic gluten is needed, which will blow up into large balloons but which will hold its shape until set by the oven heat.

The quantity of gluten is important because gluten absorbs water. Wheat grown in North America and Russia tends to have a higher protein content and hence more gluten-forming proteins than weak wheats grown in the UK and Europe. A strong flour made from such wheat yields a large quantity of gluten and will therefore have both high rising and high water-absorbing properties. Goods which should have a large volume and a light open texture, such as bread, are therefore baked with strong flour.

Gluten is toughened by:
Salt – if this is forgotten the bread will be sticky.

Acidity – lemon juice in puff pastry, and sour milk in scones.

Handling – mixing and kneading.

Gluten is weakened by:

High levels of other ingredients such as fat and sugar.

Wholemeal germ, brown germ, brown flours.

Old or badly stored yeast; enzymes in malt.

STRONG FLOUR

Yeast goods must be well-kneaded or beaten to develop the gluten structure, which ensures retention of the gases produced in the fermentation.

Shortcrust pastry and cakes require less tough elastic gluten. Care should be taken to handle as little as possible, to achieve a lighter finished product.

SOFT FLOUR

Add a little extra starch, i.e. cornflour or rice flour – approximately 80 g per kilogram of flour used. This gives a short texture, and flat finish.

Where possible only purchase a good quality flour; cheaper flours may look white, but they contain powdered bran which will spoil the quality of the gluten and will produce poor results in baking.

By varying the ingredients in the mix, handling and baking, the gluten in the dough can be toughened or weakened to produce the required texture.

SELF-RAISING FLOUR

This flour is generally produced from normal or general-purpose flour, chemicals are then added, to act as aerating agents. It is mainly prepared for shops and supermarkets as it is most suitable for household cooking, such as scones, victoria sponges and steamed puddings. No fermentation occurs in the products made, therefore no ripening of the gluten is needed. For this reason a medium or a weaker grade wheat is used, either Australian or soft European. The minimum amount of carbon dioxide released during the baking process is 0.4%. This will guarantee a sufficient rise in the finished product, suitable for normal home baking.

HIGH RATIO CAKE FLOUR

This is mainly manufactured for high quality flour confectionery, and is especially suitable for large quantity cake making which carries a high percentage of sugar content, and the traditional sponge and cake mixes made by 'all in' methods.

These flours are milled from soft wheats to a very fine particle size. They should possess a good colour and low ash content.

■ HERBS AND SPICES FOR THE PATISSERIE

Cultivation of herbs for culinary purposes dates back to the 'Iron Age'. The methods we use today for growing cereals and plants, including herbs, were used two millenia ago.

The Romans were the first to bring herbs with them to this country, although they were mainly used for medicinal purposes. Rich land owners and monks soon developed methods of growing them, recording detailed listings of 70 suitable herbs for cooking and describing whether seed, flower, bud, leaf, stalk, or root and how they were best prepared: raw, chopped, steamed or blanched.

The Egyptian merchants prospered in the spice trade. The monopoly of the eastern traders was broken by Marco Polo, the Venetian, who travelled thoughout the East and Asia between 1270 and 1293. It was from this period that medieval cooks increased the uses of spices in cooking, despite the cost.

It is important to store herbs and spices separately from each other, as individual tastes vary.

HERBS

Herbs	Origin	Uses
Angelica	Northern European	Crystallised for decorative purposes. Rice dishes, mousses and bavarois.
Anise/Aniseed	North America Europe	Seeds: Use whole or crushed, in breads, apple pies, fruit fools, jellies. Flower: mix with fruit salad, cheese cakes. Leaf: use as garnish, chopped in fruit salad, chestnut purée, meringue dishes.
Borage	European	Flowers can be crystallised. Chopped in fillings, crème pâtissiére, sweet ravioli, pastries.
Lovage (Seed)	European	Seeds are crushed and used in breads, liqueur to flavour rice dishes, stock syrups, milk puddings, custards.
Bay leaf	European	Place in rice storage jar to flavour rice.
Elecampane	European	Roots are crystallised. Used in petit fours. Chopped in rice dishes.
Lavender	European	Jellies, sauces, fruit fools, cheese cakes. Flowers can be crystallised.
Lemon Balm	European	Sauces, jellies, fruit fools, mousses, cheese cakes, custards.
Mint	European	As lemon balm.
Bergamot/Bee Balm	North American Indian tribe's drink	Jellies, sauces, junkets.
Sweet cicely/Myrrh	North American European	Seeds used in fruit salad. Chopped in ice creams and apple pies. To flavour chartreuse liqueur. Leaves are chopped for fruit tarts and omelettes and to reduce the acidity when cooking rhubarb, gooseberries, blackcurrants.
Marigold	European	Cheese cakes, omelettes, fruit salads.
Marjoram or Oregano	European	Savoury dishes: pizzas, quiches, flans.
Dill	European	Seed: apple pies, biscuits and breads.

SPICES

Spices	Origin	Uses
Allspice	West Indies and South America	Rich fruit cakes and puddings, honey cake (traditionally Jewish).
Star anise	Mediterranean coast	(Aniseed flavour). Sponges, small cakes, rice dishes.
Caraway	European	Small cakes and sponges, rye breads, biscuits, sauces.
Cardamon	India and Sri Lanka	Baked goods, honey cakes, boiled sugar petit fours, sweet omelettes, soufflés.
Cinnamon	Indonesia, China, Vietnam	Small cakes, fruit cakes, apple strudel and charlotte, stock syrups, compotes.
Cassia	Sri Lanka	As cinnamon.
Coriander	Holland, Romania	Apple pies, fruit cakes, sponges, biscuits, sauces.
Cloves	Zanzibar, Island of Pemba	Fruit puddings, apple dishes.
Ginger	China, Africa	Rich fruit cakes, puddings, biscuits and petit fours.
Nutmeg (nut covered with mace)	Malaya, Mauritius, Caribbean Islands	Milk puddings, junkets, rich fruit cakes and puddings.
Vanilla	America, Mexico, West Indies, Java	Cakes, puddings, sauces, biscuits, stock syrups. Place in sugar storage jars to flavour sugars.
Saffron	Spain	Cakes and biscuits.
Sunflower	European	Seeds: sprinkle on cakes and breads. Dipped in caramel for petit fours and praline.
Elder	European	Flower: the bunch can be dipped in batter and served as garnish with fruit fools or served with a sauce. Fruit: can be used in syrups.
Poppies	European	Sprinkle on breads, biscuits, cakes.
Parsley	European	Savoury dishes: pizzas, quiches, flans.
Rosemary	European	Flower can be crystallised. Pounded with sugar and mixed with cream. Added to fruit purees. Leaf: to flavour savoury dishes. Sprinkle on breads.
Roses	European	Flowers: remove the heels, sprinkle on fruit salad. Add to apple and cherry pies, ice creams and sorbets. Crystallise and use for decoration.
Ennel	European	Seed: sprinkle on breads.
Thyme	European	Chopped in fruit salads. Savoury dishes. Sprinkle on breads.
Violet (sweet)	European	Flowers can be crystallised for decoration. Eat raw in fruit salads. Make stock syrups.

■ NUTS FOR THE PATISSERIE

Botanically, 'nuts' are recognised as hard and dry shelled fruits such as walnuts or hazelnuts and normally cracked to extract the edible section.

For the confectioner, nuts are used for decorative purposes and also for flavour. They are highly nutritious, with a very high proportion of fat and protein but very little carbohydrate. Most nuts are imported and are

NUTS

Nuts	Origin	Uses
Almond (*Amygddalus communis*)	Southern Europe, Israel and California	Widely used in confectionery. Almonds may be obtained whole, half, split, filleted or ground. Used for decoration, mixed in cake making, pastes and marzipan production.
Brazil nuts (*Bertholletia excelsa*)	Brazil	Petits fours and nut pastes.
Coconut (*Cocos nucifera*)	West Indies, Pacific Islands, Japan	At maturity, the milk is extracted, the flesh removed and dried to produce various forms of desiccated coconut: shredded, coarse, medium or fine. Oil and fat, extracted from the coconut, used in the manufacture of margarines and vegetable butters. Desiccated coconut deteriorates rapidly. Use in rotation.
Peanut (*Arachis hypogaea*)	Africa, China, India, USA	Contains 40% oil. Used for making vegetable fats and acts as a form of stabiliser. Known as 'ground nut', it is widely used as a cheap substitute for ground almonds and cooking oil.
Hazelnuts/Filberts (*Cryllus avellana*)	Wild in most parts of Europe, can be cultivated	Contains 60% coil. Hazelnuts used on the continent for confectionery items such as nougat, japonaise and biscuits. If mixed in conjunction with wheat and rye flour will produce good bread. Deteriorates quickly. Purchase in small amounts.
Pistachio nuts (*Pistachio vera*)	Mediterranean regions	Skin removed by blanching in boiling water and rubbing between the fingers. Pistachio nuts are expensive and mainly used for decorating high class confectionery work, and some ice creams.
Walnuts	Black walnut – America White walnut – Asia and cultivated in England	Used in confectionery work, cakes and for decoration. Fancy breads.
Chestnuts	Grown all over Europe	Very low fat content but high in starch. In confectionery, mixed with creams; in pure form, or crystallised (marrons glaces), for decoration or petit fours.

cleaned and shelled in this country. Because of the high percentage of fat content, they are liable to go rancid rapidly. It is essential to store only the minimum amount, preferably using a sealed container and placed in a cool, dark and dry place. Always use in rotation.

■ LIQUEURS

Every liqueur possesses an individual flavour and texture. Standard and quality are essential to facilitate use in the patisserie. Liqueurs are either alcoholic tinctures or distillates of fruits, herbs and spices. Alternatively they are prepared by blending concentrated fruit juices and oils with alcohol and sugar. The patissier can make effective use of liqueurs, by carefully blending with flavoured syrups, about 50% liqueur to stock syrup, to soak sponges, swiss rolls and torten bases. They may also be added to fondant dips and petit fours. Alternatively the aroma will enhance the flavours of mousses, bavarois, fruit fools, compotes of fruits, ice creams and sorbets. A

small quantity (100 g per l), can be added to the basic recipe, with the mixture slightly cooled, to avoid dissipation.

Liqueurs are made in one of 3 ways – the first two of which are discussed below.

Distillation; infusion; manufactured flavours.

Distillation (the hot system). Consists of soaking the chosen fruit, herb or seed in strong alcohol, diluting and re-distilling slowly at moderate heat so that the flavours diffuse into the distillate, which is then sweetened and coloured. By this process the liqueur produced is always clear. The flavouring ingredients are literally distilled with the spirit.

Infusion (the cold system). The ingredients are soaked in alcohol, which is then sweetned and filtered. It is applied to aromatic plants from which not only the full freshness and fragrance, but also the colour is required. This process is used for fruits, plants, seeds and leaves, many of which contain essential oils that cannot be diffused by distillation, but which must enter into the flavour.

LIQUEURS

Liqueur	Origin	Description	Some recommended uses
Anisette	France or Holland	Apricot flavour	Compotes, fruit fools, gâteaux and tortens.
Abricotine	France or Holland	Apricot flavour	Compotes, fruit fools, gâteaux and tortens.
Aquavit	Denmark	Caraway flavour	Crème pâtissiére, jellies, rice dishes, cheesecakes.
Benedictine	France	Fecamp cognac	Crème pâtissiére, fruit fools, pancakes.
Calvados	France	Apples	Apple flans, charlottes, apple pancakes, compotes.
Chartreuse	France	Oranges and lime	Mousses, bavarois, jellies.
Cherry Brandy	France Holland	Brandy with cherries	Crème pâtissiére, pancakes, gâteaux and tortens.
Cointreau	France	Skins of oranges	Bavarois, mousses, soufflés, sorbets, ices, gâteaux and tortens, petit fours.

LIQUEURS

Liqueur	Origin	Description	Some recommended uses
Creme de Cassis	Dijon France	Flavour black currants	Mousses, bavarois, jellies, sorbets, ice creams.
Creme de Cacao	France	Flavour chocolate	Gâteaux and tortens, truffles, ganache.
Creme de Menthe	France	Mint flavour green	Sorbets, ice creams, petit fours, pastries, coupes, sauces.
Curacao	West Indies France	Orange	Mousses, bavarois, soufflés, gâteaux and tortens, cheesecakes.
Grand Marnier	France	Orange flavour (cognac/alcohol)	Soufflés, gâteaux and tortens, compotes, pancakes.
Kirsch	Alsace	Cherries	Gâteaux and tortens, compotes, soufflés, coupes, bombes, sauces.
Kummel	Germany	Caraway seeds	Gâteaux and tortens, coupes, sorbets, soufflés, sauces, rice dishes, pancakes.
Kahlua	Mexico	Coffee	Soufflés, sauces, rice dishes, pancakes.
Maraschino	Italy	Cherries	Coupes, sorbets, ice creams, pancakes, soufflés, sauces and cheesecakes.
Parfait Amour	France	Flavoured with violet/vanilla	Mousses, bavarois, petits fours, pastries, soufflés.
Royal Mint Chocolate	England	Chocolate mint liqueur	Mousses, bavarois, petits fours.
Sambuca	Italy	Made from elderberry flower	Petits fours, pancakes, soufflés, fools, cheesecakes.
Strega	Italy	Herb liqueur	Compotes, fools, petits fours.
Tia Maria	Jamaica	Coffee flavour Rum liqueur	Pancakes, mousses, fools, bavarois, cheesecakes.

■ SAFETY IN THE PATISSERIE

Avoiding accidents

KNIVES

1 Learn the safest way to use knives.
2 Use the corrrect knife for the job.
3 Always cut on a good, flat, stable board – never into the palm of the hand.
4 It is much safer to work with a sharp knife rather than a blunt one.
5 Ensure knives do not have greasy handles.
6 Do not leave knives protruding over a working surface.
7 Carry knives point downwards, blade inward and parallel to the body.
8 Never gesticulate with a knife (or any other utensil).
9 Never put knives (or glasses) into the washing-up sink.
10 When washing or drying knives, always wipe with the edge away from the hands.
11 Set aside a drawer for knives – try not to mix them with other utensils.

TINS

1 Always use an efficient tin-opener – fixed

in position if possible.

2 Keep the tin-opener blade sharp, as there can be a danger from metal shavings.

3 Cut round the lid completely. Remove the lid with a blunt instrument. Place lid back in tin before throwing away.

MACHINES

1 Always read manufacturer's instructions to use machinery correctly. There are no short-cuts to safety.

2 If the machine has to be
   (a) cleaned
   (b) opened to remove an obstruction
   (c) reloaded
   The golden rule is: Switch off motor, switch off current, *then* rectify the fault.

3 No person should be involved with any machine until they have been trained to use it.

4 Never leave a machine unmanned and in motion.

5 All machines with rotating blades must have safety guards.

6 Keep hair and clothing neat and tidy so that it does not get caught in moving machinery.

CROCKERY

1 Do not handle broken crockery – sweep it up with a dustpan and brush.

2 Discard any chipped or cracked crockery and place in a paladin bin.

3 If glass breaks near food, report this at once in case the food is contaminated.

BURNS AND SCALDS

1 Wear special cooking sleeves, when necessary, to protect arms.

2 Sensible shoes and correct uniform should be worn at all times.

3 Use good, strong, dry oven cloths or gloves.

4 Never leave a burner ignited when not in use. 'ON' must be written on electric solid tops when in use.

5 When opening an oven door bend your knees (not your back), to prevent hot air burning your face.

6 Tins containing hot liquid must be carried safely. Never carry more than three-quarters full. Ensure low cupboards or oven doors are kept closed. Use a trolley for transporting large pots or pans from one area to another.

7 Do not let saucepan handles protrude over the edge of the cooker, or over another flame or heat ring.

8 Never leave saucepan lids on top of the cooker. Keep the top of the cooker free from grease.

9 Never leave utensils in food when it is on top of the cooker (whisks, wooden spoons, etc.).

10 Never reach over anything that is steaming – keep kettles and boiling pans at the back of the cooker.

11 Always ensure that food is dry before immersing in hot fat and that the fryer is not over full. Be especially careful when using the fish fryer. Keep arms covered with the armlets provided. Never leave a lighted fryer unattended.

12 Always stand behind the steamer door when opening it. Open it slowly, letting out a little steam at a time.

13 Never store any vessel higher than eye level unless it is turned upside down.

14 Never put hands into a sterilising sink, or try to rescue any object that has fallen in it. Always use special baskets provided. Lower beakers into hot water at an angle to allow air to escape.

15 When packing transported meals, pack handles outwards. Write 'S' on the outside edge of small box tins and 'E' on any empty tins.

REACHING
1 Only reach as high as is possible with both feet on the ground.
2 Do not climb or balance on anything other than steps used in stores.
3 Never carry unduly heavy weights alone. Ask for help.

FLOORS
1 Always keep floors free from water, grease, food, mats, utensils and stores.

FURNITURE
1 Do not stack furniture too high.
2 Always remove furniture in pairs.
3 Always use a trolley where possible for moving both tables and chairs.
4 Report any broken pieces or catches at once.

ELECTRICAL EQUIPMENT
1 Defective electrical equipment must not be used until it has been seen by an electrician.
2 Plugs, switches or wall sockets must not be touched with wet hands.
3 Always switch off and remove plug from any electrical equipment being cleaned.
4 If another member of staff receives an electrical shock, switch off the current before attempting further help. If this cannot be done use a wooden or rubber object to remove the source of the shock.
5 Keep cooking equipment free from grease – surface grease increases the risk of fire.

GAS EQUIPMENT
If you smell gas:
1 Try to detect the leak – it may be an unignited gas jet.
2 *Never* strike a match.
3 Open windows and call the emergency gas service.

Training must be given to any members of staff detailed to light gas fire equipment.

Report any accident at once. Report anything that you see which could cause an accident.

Fire drill

It is important to familiarise oneself with fire precautions, to know the locations of fire extinguishers, blankets, and hoses, and to know how to use these items. It is also necessary to know the safest method of dealing with a person on fire (as well as those suffering asphyxiation or severe electric shock).

IN EVENT OF A FIRE
1 Raise the alarm.
2 Call for help. Report to the person in charge.
3 Attack the fire if at all possible (staff only).
4 Evacuate the guests and staff.
5 Evacuate the building yourself.
6 Report to the designated assembly point.

IF YOU HEAR THE FIRE ALARM
1 Report to the person in charge.
2 Staff should inform and evacuate the guests.
3 Leave the premises quietly.
Do not use lifts as means of exit.
Do not run or panic. If possible, stop others running or panicking.

Classes of fire

There are *several* types of fire, which are as follows:

Class A   are combustion of:
glowing embers
wood
papers
textiles

Class B   are caused by burning of:
liquids
oils
fats
paints

Class C   are caused by escaping gases.

Class D   are caused by electrical faults.

Extinguishers

Seek appropriate training, to familiarise yourself with the use and handling of extinguishers designed for the different types of fire that could occur. Never handle the extinguishers without this information. Likewise, do not let untrained personnel tamper with the extinguishers. Remember that extinguishers have to be constantly maintained.

■   FOOD SAFETY AND HYGIENE

1   *Increased awareness in matters relating to food hygiene, the control of unfit food.*
Tighter controls on unfit food and food which is not of the 'nature, substance or quality demanded' by the purchaser, are proposed. The aim will be to permit certain enforcement powers of the Food Act 1984 to apply to *possession for sale* as well as *sale* itself, so that regulations will apply before the goods are put on sale. New enforcement measures will be introduced to strengthen existing powers so that food suspected of being unfit can be detained by enforcement officers. This is still under investigation.
2   *An understanding of possible new legislation and its likely effects on the catering industry.*
Under the recent introduction of registration of food premises, regular inspections of premises by Local Authority Environment Health Officers will be carried out, with the penalty of deregulation a possibility if the premises do not meet required hygiene standards. The implications are that the catering industry will have to take food hygiene seriously or risk being put out of business, and that Local Authorities will be more 'enforcement orientated' than advisory. Lack of resources will prevent Local Authorities having the time or staff to advise on how to get it right – as with the Health and Safety Law. The onus will be on the food business owner or manager to be aware of the law and follow the regulations, or risk prosecution or closure should ignorance prevail.

Food poisoning

This unpleasant illness usually occurs within 36 hours of eating contaminated food. The symptoms of food poisoning usually include one or more of the following:
abdominal pains
vomiting
diarrhoea
nausea
headache
dehydration
The symptoms can last 1–7 days. They are generally the result of the body ridding itself of poisons.

Food poisoning by the listeria bacteria causes somewhat different symptoms, usually flu-like symptoms, meningitis, septicaemia, and in pregnant women it can cause miscarriages and stillbirths.

SALMONELLA
(Approximately 1000 different types.) This is the commonest cause of food poisoning in the British Isles. It is responsible for 80–90% of all notified poisoning outbreaks. *Salmonella* can be present in untreated milk and cream, and some eggs. Symptoms usually include nausea, vomiting, diarrhoea, abdominal pains, possibly accompanied by headache and fever. The onset of symptoms can be within 6–72 hours after eating, but is usually

12–36 hours after eating.

Contamination is carried from food to hands, utensils, work surfaces (which in their turn can contaminate other surfaces), and in food which is not reheated correctly or not returned to the refrigerator.

CLOSTRIDIUM PERFRINGENS

This can be present in soil, humans, animal excreta, in raw meat and poultry and in other foods including dehydrated products.

Contamination is caused by spores of bacteria which lie dormant in the food, soil and dust, and which are capable of withstanding heat and dehydration. They are then activated by cooking to germinate and multiply to the large numbers necessary to cause illness.

STAPHYLOCOCCUS AUREUS

This can be present in normal healthy skin, nose and throat or septic sores in food handlers.

Contamination is caused by infected hands directly onto cooked foods. The bacteria, although destroyed by normal cooking, produces a heat-resistant toxin. Once contamination occurs in certain made-up or prepared dishes, reheating or even thorough cooking will not destroy it.

Hygiene in handling eggs

The highest standards of safety and hygiene in the patisserie are rightly expected of the modern patissier. This section therefore contains the requirements for safe and hygienic working practice both within the pastry room and through to service. These are the guidelines advised by the Department of Health.

SALMONELLA IN EGGS

Recently there has been some public alarm concerning eggs and *salmonella*. Eggs are used in the manufacture of ice creams, mousses, bavarois and other egg dishes. However, they must be pasteurised prior to manufacture *to kill any harmful bacteria*.

HYGIENE RULES FOR HANDLING RAW SHELL EGGS

Recent concern has highlighted the need to eliminate food poisoning risks from this source. For this reason the rules for handling raw shell eggs are covered, to ensure any contaminating bacteria within the eggs themselves are rendered harmless. The temperature which should be achieved during the preparation and service of those recipes involving the use of eggs has been specified. Where necessary recipes and/or preparation methods have been modified to ensure that these temperatures can be achieved.

1 Eggs should be obtained from a reputable supplier.
2 Eggs should be stored in a cool, dry place, preferably under refrigeration.
3 Eggs should be stored away from other raw foods which may contaminate them, for example, raw meat.
4 Stocks should be rotated – first in, first out.
5 Cracked eggs should not be used.
6 Hands should be washed before and after handling eggs.

HYGIENE RULES FOR EGG DISHES

1 Preparation surface, utensils and containers should be regularly cleaned and always cleaned between the preparation of different dishes.
2 All recipes in which raw egg is used must involve a heating or cooking stage. The minimum temperature achieved during cooking must be 70 °C, which must be maintained for at least one minute. Alternatively, pasteurised egg may be used as a recipe ingredient.

3 Egg dishes should be consumed as soon as possible after preparation or refrigerated at a temperature of 5 °C or less, if not for immediate use.
4 Re-heating of eggs should be avoided.
5 Egg dishes to be eaten cold should be refrigerated at a temperature of 5 °C or less.
6 Egg dishes to be eaten hot should be held at or above 63 °C.

Food preparation and food handling

In small units with limited work space, it may be necessary to use work-tops for more than one purpose. In this case, the working surface will need to be changed, i.e. by using a preparation board, and both surface and board should be thoroughly cleaned and dried between each use. Wiping with a cloth is not enough. Use one work top for one purpose only. For example, food such as sandwiches and pastry should not be prepared on surfaces previously used for those which need further cooking, such as raw meat.

Use entirely separate utensils and chopping boards for raw and for cooked food. (These can be colour-coded so that red utensils and chopping boards indicate raw food.) Raw and prepared food should also be stored or refrigerated separately. Where this is not possible cooked food must always be stored *above* raw food.

Keep all preparation surfaces clean and dry at all times. Food must not be placed where there is any risk of contamination from any source.

Use a digital probe thermometer for temperature testing, wipe the probe and immerse it in sterilant after use.

For tasting food use disposable spoons once only. Keep food covered until it is needed – do not leave it lying around un-covered, or in a warm room, but in correct storage conditions.

No filling containing milk or eggs, having been cooked in the pastry, should be re-heated, except as part of a properly planned and controlled service. If food must be re-heated, use a reheating method that ensures that 70 °C is reached as soon as possible, for example by using forced air circulation ovens, steamers, infra-red units, or microwave ovens. In a microwave oven food is heated from the centre outwards, so ensure that the outside of the food reaches 70 °C.

Cleaning in the patisserie

A detailed cleaning schedule must be followed. All ancillary equipment should be kept off the floors and stored on suitable racks.

It is absolutely essential that signs of pest infestation of any type must be reported immediately to a superior. Live animals must not be allowed to come in the pastry room or into contact with any food.

Cleaning equipment, materials and chemicals must be stored in a cleaners' room or cupboard which includes a sluice sink. Cleaning chemicals are poisonous and must never be left or stored in the operational part of the Catering Department. Training should be taken to understand and use the cleaning agents; only approved cleaning agents should be used. Always wear rubber gloves, protective clothing and footwear, and eye goggles when using caustic substances.

All structural surfaces less than 2.5 metres above the floor must be cleaned at weekly intervals; floors and work surfaces must be cleaned daily. If pressure-cleaning equipment is used for deep cleaning, all food preparation surfaces and equipment should be removed or covered and cleaned afterwards. Disposable paper cloths must be used for wiping and drying surfaces and equipment. Dish cloths and tea-towels must *not* be used for this purpose.

Special attention must be paid to corners and junctions between wall and floor, and behind and under fixed equipment. Mops should be washed and wrung out after use and stored in a mop drying rack. Mops should not be left standing in water or disinfectant solutions.

Water for buckets or machines should be obtained from the cleaners' room sink, not from sinks in the pastry room. Buckets and machines must be emptied into an outside gulley or sluice sink.

Personal hygiene

Food poisoning bacteria can live in the human and animal gut without any sign of disease. These germs can be excreted with the faeces and toilet paper does not prevent contamination of the hands.

Other sources of food poisoning bacteria are throat or nose infections, boils, styes and septic sores. Germs can spread not only through direct contact, but also by coughing and spitting.

Hands have many cracks and crevices where germs can live and multiply; they can easily transfer harmful bacteria from food to food or from surface to fingers to food. The hands and fingernails should be scrubbed thoroughly before handling food or equipment. Various infections and bacteria can be transferred to the fingers and spread to food which other people will eat. Also the scalp can be dirty or infected with dandruff which will be transferred to food via the fingernails. Fingernails should be kept short and clean. Do not use nail varnish or wear earrings or finger rings (except plain wedding rings),

because nail varnish can chip off, jewellery could drop into food.

Hand basins should not be used for food or food equipment – they are for hand washing only. Equally, do not wash hands in food sinks, or let others do so.

disposable paper towel, or a hot air drier.

Hand basins should not be used for food or food equipment – they are for hand washing only. Equally, do not wash hands in food sinks, or let others do so.

Keep cuts, grazes, and septic sores covered with blue waterproof dressings. This prevents cuts becoming infected which makes them slow to heal; infected wounds can produce bacteria which cause food poisoning. Blue dressings can be seen more obviously if lost.

The fingers can be contaminated by bacteria from the nose and throat. A sneeze contains millions of bacteria, some of which can cause food poisoning – always use a paper handkerchief.

If hair is long, tie it back, cover with a net and wear a protective hat.

Food handlers must always wear clean protective clothing and keep clean their cloths, tea-towels, etc., as these materials soon become dirty and germ laden and will transfer bacteria to the hands each time they are used. Washing the hands in hot soapy water for several minutes is the only acceptable method of keeping hands clean.

PROTECTIVE CLOTHING

Food handlers must always wear clean protective clothing. Jackets should be close-fitting at the wrist, or the sleeves should be rolled up above the elbow, to avoid risk of entanglement with machinery.

Outdoor and protective work-wear clothing should not be stored together; receptacles for soiled laundry should be available in all changing areas. Work clothing should not be used for any other purpose.

WORKING WITH FOOD

1 Do not cough or sneeze over food.
2 Do not touch your nose, teeth or ears.
3 Do not lick your fingers.
4 Do not scratch your head, ears or any part of your body.
5 Do not smoke near your work place.
6 Do not wipe your hands on an apron or cloth.
7 Do wear the proper, clean, protective clothes.

LIST OF RECIPES

11 SOUFFLÉS

12 BAVARIAN CREAMS

13 MOUSSES

14 TRIFLES

15 JELLIES

16 COLD CHARLOTTES

17 YEAST GOODS

PASTES

SHORT PASTRY, *PÂTE BRISÉE*

The sense of the word 'short' in pastry work, means it is friable; the texture should not be in the least leathery or tough. Most fats will accomplish the required texture to varying extents. All fats will reduce the extensibility of gluten, according to the amount used and the method of production. Butter is added for flavour and to improve the quality of a product.

Moistening agents are also used; in most recipes, water is added – if omitted the paste will not combine and will crumble.

Eggs are also used in some recipies, especially when a rich and high quality paste is required.

It is advisable to prepare the paste in advance, preferably the previous day. It should be stored well-wrapped, in the refrigerator, to prevent a crust forming. Trimmings should always be added to a fresh batch to avoid wasting, but take care not to over mix trimmings with fresh pastry.

For the best results, follow these rules:
1 Ensure that all necessary equipment and working surfaces are perfectly clean, and check the freshness of the ingredients.
2 Make sure all ingredients are at room temperature (21 °C).
3 Break eggs into a bowl before starting the production of the paste.
4 Sugar must be dissolved in the liquid used or creamed with the butter. Granulated sugar must be avoided, as it will caramelise during baking to produce

dark brown spots on the surface, and will have a hard, crunchy appearance, so spoiling the completed item.
5 A pinch of salt added to the flour will enhance colour and flavour.
6 It is important to allow the shortpaste to stand in a cool place before rolling out.
7 Only roll out the amount of paste required at one time for each item.
8 Use a minimum amount of flour for dusting purposes.
9 Always keep the paste covered during storage, to avoid discoloration and crusting.
10 Shortpastes and shortpaste products, baked or at the raw stage, can be frozen or kept in the refrigerator for up to three days if protected from the air.

There are two methods of mixing shortpaste:

1 *Rubbing-in* Cut the butter into pieces onto sieved flour, rub the two ingredients with tips of the fingers until the butter is evenly distributed (an appearance of small particles like breadcrumbs is achieved – avoid over mixing).

Any liquids used, should be added in one go, to avoid the dough becoming tough, elastic and greasy.

2 *Creaming* Cream the butter and sugar together until a light texture is obtained, any liquids are then added gradually to the creamed mixture, until an emulsion is developed, before adding the flour. This is usually considered the most suitable method for obtaining a paste with a delicate texture and less shrinkage, whilst baking.

Moulding paste, *Pâte à foncer* (rubbing-in method)

Flour (medium grade)	500 g
Salt	2 g
Butter	250 g
Water	1 ½ dl

Sieve the flour and salt onto a clean working surface. Rub in the butter and shape into a bay, add the water. Gradually mix the dry ingredients into the water, mix to form a smooth paste. Avoid over mixing.

Use for baked jam roll, jam and treacle tarts, baked apple dumplings, Cornish pasties, Quiche Lorraine.

Shortpaste (rubbing-in method 1)

Flour	500 g
Salt	2 g
Eggs	2
Castor sugar	50 g
Butter	250 g
Water	25 g

Sieve the flour and salt onto a clean working surface. Rub in the butter and shape into a bay, add the eggs, water and sugar. Gradually draw in the dry ingredients and mix to form a smooth paste. Avoid over mixing.

Shortpaste (creaming method 1)

Butter	250 g
Water	100 g
Salt	2 g
Flour	100 g
Flour	400 g

Cream the butter and first flour together on a clean working surface. Gradually add the water, until a light emulsion is obtained. Add

the remaining sieved flour and salt. Avoid over mixing.

Shortpaste (creaming method 2)

This paste, with the extra butter content, is specifically prepared for covering of fruit pies.

Butter	275 g
Castor sugar	50 g
Eggs	2
Flour	500 g
Salt	2 g

Cream the butter, sugar and little of the flour, to form a light emulsion. Gradually add the eggs. Mix in the sieved flour and salt. Avoid over mixing.

Shortpaste (rubbing-in method 2)
(For covering fruit pies)

Flour	500 g
Salt	2 g
Butter	275 g
Castor sugar	50 g
Eggs	2
Water	25 g

Sieve the flour and salt onto a clean working surface. Rub in the butter and make a bay, add the eggs, sugar and water. Gradually draw in the dry ingredients and mix to form a smooth paste. Avoid over mixing.

Sweetpaste, *La pâte à sucre or pâte sucrée*

Castor sugar	125 g
Butter	250 g
Eggs	2
Flour	500 g
Salt	2 g

Cream the butter and castor sugar to a creamy

texture. Add the eggs gradually and continue creaming until a light emulsion is obtained. Add the sieved flour and salt. Mix to form a smooth paste. Avoid over mixing. Store in the refrigerator, leave to rest before using.

Use for fruit flans, Bakewell tart, lemon meringue pie, fruit tartlets and barquettes.

German paste or sweet almond paste, *Pâte allemande*

Flour	1.25 kg
Butter	750 g
Ground almonds	180 g
Castor sugar	250 g
Egg yolks	4
Water	4 ml

Cream the butter and half the flour to a creamy texture. Separately beat the yolks and sugar, gradually add to the first mixture. Finally, add the remaining flour and ground almonds. Avoid over mixing.

This paste is very soft when first made, and is ideal for piping. It is most suitable for jam tarts, Linzer tart, torten bases and biscuits for petit fours.

SUET

Suet is a hard fat encasing the kidneys and situated around the flanks of cattle and sheep. It consists of tiny globules of fat, surrounded by membranous bags. It is extensively used in making boiled puddings and mincemeat. Finely chopped particles of suet, in a dough, partially boil during the cooking process and create steam. Aeration in the dough is then brought about by the expansion of the pressurised vapour produced by the heated suet. Suet is now prepared on a large scale in shredded form, dry and free from skin.

Suet paste, *Pâte à la grasse de boeuf*

Flour	500 g
Salt	10 g
Water	3 dl
Chopped suet	250 g
Baking powder	10 g

Sieve the flour and salt together onto a clean working surface and mix in the prepared suet. Shape into a bay, pour in the water, draw in the dry ingredients and mix to form a pliable paste. Leave to rest in the refrigerator for at least 20 minutes before use.

It is advisable to produce only the amount of suet paste likely to be required at one time, as suet paste deteriorates rapidly.

Use in steamed jam rolls, steamed fruit rolls, steamed fruit puddings, steak and kidney pudding.

PASTA

Pasta is a dough made from durum wheat semolina, water and often eggs. Pasta is shaped in various ways and is sometimes flavoured. It is sold dried or fresh, ready to cook in boiling salted water. It can be served with a sauce or garnish, or used in *gratins*.

Durum wheat is grown in Italy, the Mediterranean, the Middle East, Russia, North and South America. It is a hard wheat, high in gluten, which is ground into semolina. It is believed that pasta was invented in China 6 000 years ago, and that 700 years ago the explorer Marco Polo introduced pasta into Italy from China. In fact the first known reference to pasta can be traced to Sicily, in the Middle Ages, when the island was under Arab domination. It has been a basic food in Italy for many years, particularly in Naples and Rome, before Catherine de Medici introduced it into France.

Pasta is made by kneading semolina with water (2–2.5 litres per 10 kg, adding various other ingredients if desired), eggs, flavouring, vegetable purees, etc., then shaping it. Flat pastas are rolled out with rollers into thin sheets that are cut into various shapes with a punch, a stamp or some other suitable machine. The drying is an important operation, care must be taken to ensure that the pasta will mature and keep well.

Ready-made pasta should be boiled in salted water for 8–10 minutes, until just tender. Fresh pasta must be brought to the boil and allowed to simmer gently for 2–3 minutes (al dente), then removed and refreshed.

Pastas made with wholewheat and buckwheat are richer in vitamins and minerals with more dietary fibre than other pastas.

An average individual portion of pasta – about 60 g – provides 230 calories. With a little butter, tomato, grated parmesan cheese (providing proteins, fats, carbohydrates, vitamins, and fibre), pasta makes a well-balanced meal.

Fresh pasta can be frozen successfully.

Noodle paste, *Pâte à nouille*

Strong flour	*1 kg*
Salt	*10 g*
Egg yolks	*18–20*
Eggs	*5*
Milk	*150 g*
(Serves 10)	

Sieve the flour and salt onto a clean work surface and shape into a large bay. Pour into the bay milk, eggs and the yolks, gradually pull in the flour and mix to form a firm, but pliable dough. Divide into smaller pieces and store in polythene bags, and allow to rest for at least 30 minutes.

Roll out each piece of paste paper thin. (This is best achieved by rolling the paste folded, using dusting flour. It will improve

the extensibility of the rolled paste.) Brush off the surplus flour and hang the paste to dry slightly on wooden handles. When partly dry the paste can be folded into three, using a little dusting flour to prevent from sticking. Cut into strips to the size required. Allow strips to dry completely, by spreading out in a large tray, or replacing on the wooden handles.

Noodles	Cut into 5 mm strips
Lasagne	Cut into 10 mm strips
Canneloni	Cut into 8–10 cm squares

Step-by-step production of noodles

Noodle tomato paste, *Pâte à nouille de tomate*

Strong flour	1 kg
Salt	10 g
Egg yolks	16–18
Eggs	5
Tomato purée	100 g
(Serves 10)	

Proceed following the same method as above, adding tomato purée at the same time as the eggs. A few drops of red colour can be added if desired but it is normally not needed.

Noodle spinach paste, *Pâte nouille à l'epinard*

Strong flour	1 kg
Salt	10 g
Egg yolks	16–18
Eggs	5
Spinach purée	100 g
Grated nutmeg to taste	
(Serves 10)	

Proceed following the same method as plain noodles, adding the previously prepared, cold spinach purée and grated nutmeg at the same time as the eggs. (Spinach purée can be prepared by bringing fresh spinach to the boil, cooking until just tender, draining well and passing through a fine sieve or a liquidiser.)

Because of the extra moisture used in the production of these pastes, extra egg can be added until the correct consistency is attained.

Lemon, orange or black colouring can be used in these pastes, but should be added with care and attention to quantity.

Ravioli paste, *Pâte à ravioli*

Flour	500 g
Salt	10 g
Egg yolks	2–3
Olive oil	1 dl
Warm water	3 dl

Produce the ravioli paste in the same way as the noodle paste, adding the oil and warm water together. (The warm water is important as it will assist in stabilising the gluten in the flour, giving the dough a smooth and firm texture.) Wrap in a polythene bag and rest for at least 30 minutes.

33

Step-by-step production of ravioli

roll the second rolled-out paste over a rolling pin and lay over the prepared one, avoiding air pockets forming. Using an upside-down 1½ cm square cutter, press each filled area to seal the filling. Cut through the seal, using a wheel cutter or a knife, to divide each ravioli.

Left overs can be used for the filling. The quantities given will be sufficient for 24 ravioli.

Filling A
Minced cooked meat (chicken, beef, pork, veal, or combination of all)   500 g
Eggs, well beaten   2
Chopped parsley
Nutmeg, pinch
Salt and pepper, to taste

Filling B
Minced cooked meat (chicken, brains, mozzarella cheese, chopped spinach)   500 g
Nutmeg, pinch
Salt and pepper, to taste

(Any suitable desired ingredients that can be mashed can be used as filling, such as herbs, onions, shallots, sausage meat, chicken livers, mushrooms, garlic, any cooked fish.)

CAPPELLETTI
Pinch two opposite corners of the ravioli together, to seal, and fold over another corner, to resemble a cap. Allow to dry thoroughly before cooking.

TORTELLINI
Proceed as for ravioli, cut using a 2 cm cutter into round shapes instead of square.

AGNOLOTTI
Proceed as for ravioli using larger shares of filling and an 8 cm cutter. Agnolotti are much larger and usually served 3–4 per portion with plenty of liquid, chicken stock, gravy or soup.

Roll the paste paper thin, using ground rice or fine semolina for dusting. (This paste should not be folded for rolling.) Divide the rolled paste in two, one half slightly larger than the other. Place the smaller piece onto a clean cloth or greaseproof paper.

Using a paper cornet or piping bag, pipe the filling in hazelnut-size rounds onto the rolled paste at regular intervals, about 3½ cm apart. Egg wash in between the filling rounds,

▦ PUFF PASTE, *PÂTE FEUILLETÉE*

Many attempts have been made to discover the origins of puff paste. The most likely explanation is that of the commis, who forgot to rub in the butter while producing a batch of bun dough. He then tried adding the butter in lumps, and failed. He then rolled the dough to hide the lumps of fat, which eventually resulted in the product rising in a different way than originally intended.

Puff paste is a dough interleaved with butter or tough pastry margarine, folded while rolling to give hundreds of layers of fat, which will rise during baking in a layered or laminated structure.

Three methods are known for successful production of puff paste: (1) French; (2) Scotch (rough puff); (3) English.

French method

The paste is rolled out to the shape of an open envelope, with four angles pointing out from a thick, square centre. The fat is placed in the centre and sealed in by bringing the four angles to the centre. It is then rolled as described on page 37 (full puff paste).

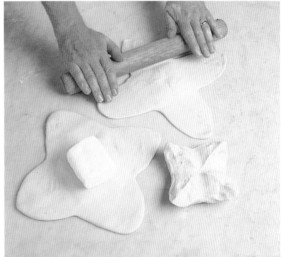

Step-by-step French puff pastry

Scotch (rough puff) method

A quick method of producing puff paste, but not ideal as the process can be messy.

The fat is added to the flour in small lumps, water and acid is then added to the bay and the whole mixed together, maintaining the fat more or less intact. Again the dough is rolled as described on p. 37.

English method

Out of three methods of incorporating the fat into the folds, this seems to me to be the most

practical. The paste is rolled into a rectangular shape, the fat is placed over half of it, the other half of the paste is then folded over, resulting in two layers of paste and one of fat. It is then rolled following the method described in full puff paste. It will be noticed that if the paste is turned six times, hundreds of layers of fat will be formed:

1st turn	$1 \times 3 = 3$ layers
2nd turn	$3 \times 3 = 9$
3rd turn	$9 \times 3 = 27$
4th turn	$27 \times 3 = 81$ (¾ puff paste)
5th turn	$81 \times 3 = 243$
6th turn	$243 \times 3 = 729$ (full puff paste)

Note: An extra turn will result in 2,187 layers of fat. At this stage the paste will not give adequate rise, especially if butter is used.

Aeration in puff paste

Gluten is an insoluble protein hydrated in the ratio of one part protein to two parts water. The steam generated during baking results in the expansion. As the fat is heated, it boils and produces steam, forcing the thin layers of paste to expand and to blister; the protein coagulates, becomes rigid, and forms the laminated structure. To produce enough steam to make the paste rise the oven temperature must be very high – 215 °C–230 °C.

Flour: Strong grade flour should be used; the gluten must be resilient and elastic to stand the manipulation involved in building up a laminated structure. Only a strong gluten will be resilient enough to produce and maintain sufficient volume in the oven.

Butter: It is important that the butter is fairly firm, to facilitate the building of the structure. In warmer seasons it may be necessary to use it straight from the refrigerator. The use of butter in puff paste will impart a good flavour and will produce quality products.

Tough margarine or *pastry margarine:* This contains little or no salt and very little water. It has a tough plastic texture, enabling it to withstand the rolling and folding procedure. Pastry margarine is toughened by the addition of stearin or oils; the emulsion is then converted to a solid form by pouring into cooling drums, serviced by ice-cold brine. The mixture is then scraped off and passed through kneading machines to smooth out the texture.

Lemon juice: A few drops of juice added to the water when making the paste helps to stretch the gluten, making it more malleable during the rolling procedure.

Salt: This is added to improve the flavour, but it also helps to bind the gluten and to enhance the colour while baking.

Water: Cold water must be used (and a very little yellow colour can be added if desired). The quantity of water may vary according to the strength and absorption properties of the flour. The dough should have a manipulable texture and should not stick to the table – the minimum flour only should be used for dusting purposes.

Full puff paste, *Pâte feuilletée*

Strong flour	500 g
Salt	10 g
Butter	50 g
Cold water	3 dl
Lemon juice, teaspoonful	
Butter or tough margarine	450 g

Sieve the flour and salt onto a clean working surface and rub in the first 50 g of butter.

Make a bay shape. Pour the water and lemon juice into the bay, then gradually draw in the flour. Mix to form a firm pliable dough, working well until the dough becomes elastic in texture and free from the table. Kept covered, to prevent from crusting, allow to rest for at least five minutes.

Using a little dusting flour, roll the paste to a rectangular shape and arrange the butter, which should have the same consistency as the dough, on one half of the rolled-out dough. Fold over the remaining dough, to entirely cover the fat, seal the edges. Leave paste to rest for a short time to reduce its springiness.

Roll the folded dough out to about twice its length. Fold into three, starting with the end furthest away. Repeat the process of rolling and folding once more, then allow to rest for at least 20 minutes, well-covered with either a dry then a wet cloth, or a polythene bag. Repeat four times making six turns in all. Rest the paste again for 30 minutes minimum after the fourth turn.

Quick puff paste, *Feuilletage rapide*

Sometimes called threequarter puff paste. For this method only threequarters of the amount of fat is used to flour, and the paste requires only four turns, instead of six.

Main uses:

(Kitchen and larder) vol-au-vents, bouchées, fleurons, pailettes, sausage rolls, dartois, pie covering, boeuf and salmon en croûte.

(Pastry) pithiviers, bande aux fruits, jalousie, dartois, palmiers, mille feuilles, Eccles and Banbury cakes, allumettes glacées, mince pies, cornets à la crème, chausson.

SWEET PUFF PASTE

Fruit bande, Bandes aux fruits

Puff paste	250 g
Crème pâtissiére	3 d
Fresh fruit	
Apricot glaze	
(Makes 10)	

A completed fruit bande

Roll the puff paste to approximately 30 cm in length and 15 cm wide. Cut two strips of about 2½ cm wide. Place the remaining, larger paste on a lightly greased baking tray with the two strips upright on either side, egg wash the tops, place the bande to rest in the refrigerator for 30 minutes. Bake in the oven at 210 °C until dry and the edges have risen evenly. Place on a cooling tray.

Spread some crème pâtissiére on the base, about 10 mm thick. Arrange the chosen fruit, in slices, on top. Glaze with boiled apricot glaze. Serve on silver dish lined with a doily.

Almond slice, *Jalousie d'amande*

Puff paste	500 g
Raspberry jam	75 g
Frangipane	200 g
Egg-wash	
Icing sugar	
(Makes 10)	

Roll out the puff paste to approximately 28 cm. Cut across the middle leaving one strip 13 cm wide the other 15 cm. Place the narrower strip on a lightly greased baking tray, egg wash the edges, spread the jam in the middle, pipe the frangipane on top of the jam.

Fold the other strip of rolled paste over lengthways, using a large knife. Make cuts all the way through. Unfold and place on top of the frangipane, seal the edges, egg wash the top, allow to rest in the refrigerator for 30 minutes. Bake in the oven at 210 °C until risen and dry. Remove from the oven, generously dust over with icing sugar, replace back in a very hot oven to glaze. Place on a cooling tray. Serve on an oval silver dish with a doily.

SAVOURY PUFF PASTE, *FEUILLETAGE SALÉ*

Sausage rolls

Puff paste (fresh or trimmings)	800 g
Sausage meat	500 g
Egg-wash	
(Makes approximately 50 rolls)	

Roll the puff paste to about 2½ inches thick, maintaining a tidy square or rectangle. Form the sausage meat into rolls, using a little flour, to lengths about the width of a chipolata. Egg wash the paste all over and arrange the sausage strips at one end of the paste, about 3 cm from the edge. Fold the edge over to seal in the sausage meat, forming a flat ridge at the side. Make an incision along the top. Cut along the ridge and repeat the process with another strip of sausage until the rolled out paste is finished. Cut rolls into approximately 6 cm lengths.

Egg wash the cut rolls, place the pieces onto a lightly greased baking tray, allow to rest for at least 20 minutes before baking at 220–230 °C.

The glaze can be improved by giving a second coat of egg wash just before baking. The size of each roll can be altered as desired. Sausage rolls are mainly served as cocktails and at buffet services.

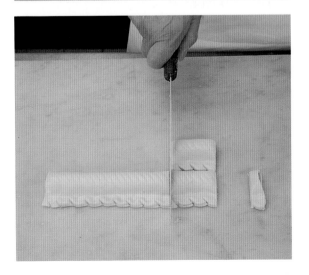

Step-by-step sausage rolls

Fleurons

Puff paste (fresh or trimmings)	500 g
Egg-wash	
(Makes approximately 60)	

Roll out the puff paste to 2½ mm thick. Using a 6 cm plain or fluted cutter, cut crescent shapes, about 3½ cm wide. Place them onto a greased baking tray, egg wash. Allow to rest for a minimum of 20 minutes, then egg wash again. Bake at 225 °C to 230 °C, until light brown in colour.

Use as garnish for unglazed fish dishes.

Cheese straws, *Paillettes au parmesan/ fromage*

Puff paste trimmings	500 g
Grated Parmesan cheese	100 g
Egg-wash	
Salt, cayenne pepper to flavour	
(Makes approximately 100)	

Roll out the puff paste to 2½ mm thick, maintaining a tidy square or rectangle. Egg wash generously all over, sprinkle heavily

Cheese straws

with grated Parmesan, salt and cayenne pepper. Lightly dust the surface with flour, fold the rolled paste over and cut into 5–6 mm wide strips.

Using one strip at a time, hold one end with the palm of the left hand and twist the other end with the right hand. Place the strips onto a very lightly greased baking tray, sealing down the ends onto the tray.

Allow to rest for at least 20 minutes before baking at 120–130 °C. Cut into pieces while still hot, about 8 mm long, before removing from the tray.

Use for cocktails, buffet services, garnish for consommé.

Vol-au-vents

Vol-au-vents are puff pastry cases, which can be filled with either a sweet, or served as entrée with a savoury filling. They may be round, oval, petal or any other shape and size. For very large pieces it is easiest to cut the paste with a knife dipped in hot water, maybe using a template of cardboard, or flan rings.

> Puff paste   2 kg
> Egg wash

Vol-au-vent surrounded by a variety of alternative shapes

Roll the paste to about 5 mm thick, cut out rounds using a plain or fluted cutter, 7–8 mm in diameter. Place half of the rounds onto a lightly greased tray, lightly egg-wash and cut a smaller ring half-way through each round, in the centre, which will be removed when baked.

Place the remaining rounds on a work surface and with a smaller cutter cut out the centres, forming rings. Egg-wash the pieces on the baking tray, place the rings on top, egg-wash again.

Allow the prepared pieces to rest for at least 30 minutes, before baking at 220 °C, to a light brown colour.

Remove from the tray and immediately scoop out the inners, keep the lids for replacing on top when filled.

Bouchées

Roll the puff paste about 4–5 mm thick and cut out circles with a 5 cm plain or fluted cutter. Place the cut pieces onto a lightly greased baking tray, lightly egg wash and with a 3 cm plain cutter, cut half-way through the thickness of the paste. Allow to rest for at least 20 minutes.

Bake at 220–230 °C, while hot remove the centres and keep the lids for replacing when serving.

Bouchées and petites bouchées

PETITES BOUCHÉES
Proceed as for bouchées using a 3–4 cm cutter for the outside and 1½–2 cm for the centres.

Cornish pasties

Cornish pasties were originally the meal carried in the pocket by Cornish miners who were unable to take an ordinary meal into the mines.

The proportion of meat present in the pasties must comply with the current regulations, i.e. not less than 12½% of the total weight of the pastry.

Shortpaste or puff paste trimmings	750 g
Diced steak (small)	500 g
Potatoes (raw)	150 g
Salt and pepper to taste	
Onion	50 g
Water	50 g
(Makes 8)	

Place the diced meat into a bowl, add the diced onions and peeled potatoes diced in small cubes, add the salt, pepper, water, mix together.

Roll out the paste 3–4 mm thick, cut out rings about 15 cm wide. Using a rolling pin, stretch each ring to a slightly oval shape. Egg-wash all over, place a small amount of the prepared filling in the centre of each. Fold the paste over to seal in the filling and crimp the edge, egg-wash over both sides and place them onto a lightly greased baking tray, in a standing position. Allow to rest for about 20 minutes. Bake at 204 °C, to a golden brown colour. Cornish pasties can be eaten hot or cold.

Other vegetables can be added to the filling, for example, peas, carrots, parsnips.

CHOUX PASTE

Choux paste is an elastic paste achieved by scalding flour, fat and water. Baked choux items are extremely light. The aeration of this paste is achieved partly by mechanical means, but mainly by the expansion of steam generated by the fat and water.

Choux paste

These quantities will produce approximately 50 éclairs or 100 profiteroles.

Butter	125 g
Water	3 dl
Castor sugar (optional)	50 g
Strong flour	250 g
Eggs	7–8

Bring to the boil the butter, sugar and water, using a saucepan sized so that the water comes half-way up the side. When thoroughly boiling, remove from the heat and immediately add the previously sieved flour (a pinch of salt can be added if unsalted butter is used or if the paste is to be used for savouries). Mix in the flour using a wooden spatula, return to the heat to gelatinise the flour and to fully absorb the remaining liquid. Allow the mixture to cool slightly for a few minutes (do not allow to get completely cold).

Add the broken eggs one at a time, mixing in each before adding the next. The amount of eggs absorbed will vary according to how long the water is boiled, to the strength of the flour, and to the size of the eggs. The completed paste must have a creamy soft texture, maintaining a stable shape when piped. Bake all items at 204 °C, until dry, and with a rigid structure which is capable of supporting their shapes when cold.

Note: All pâte à choux items have to be thoroughly cooked, as if under-cooked, they will collapse.

Before baking each pastry can be egg-washed, and scored with a fork to eliminate any trapped air pockets.

Volatile or *Vol* is the name given to ammonium carbonate. This is used in some baked items (biscuits and soft cakes, including choux paste and cream buns) and mainly steamed buns; it gives an attractive cracked top. Vol also assists in the aerating of the choux paste, as a strong alkaline it produces carbon dioxide when heated.

Vol gives off an odour while baking, but this will disappear when cooled, and will not flavour the cooked item.

HOT WATER PASTE, *PÂTE À L'ANGLAISE*

(For raised pies)

Flour (medium grade)	500 g
Salt	15 g
Lard	200 g
Water	4 dl
Eggs	2

Sieve the flour and salt on greaseproof paper. Boil the water and the lard, add the sieved flour and immediately stir the mixture using a wooden spatula. Remove from the heat and keep warm. Use as required.

The term 'raised pie' is applied to a meat pie, the paste shell of which is raised on a wooden block, or using pie moulds. The paste will keep soft, as long as it is warm, and while being handled; it sets to a hard biscuit like shell when it cools, before the minced and spiced meat is placed in it.

Raised pies are used for pork, veal and ham, and game; they are not used for fruit.

2 OPEN TARTS, FLANS AND PIES

Bakewell tart, *Tarte à la frangipane*

This is a very easy and popular dish. It can be served either as a sweet or as a tea cake, although it was originally known as a pudding. It was invented accidentally 100 years ago, when the chef of the Rutland Hotel of Bakewell was instructed to produce a tart as the sweet of the day. Unfortunately, or fortunately, he was uncertain of what to do with the eggs and butter so he decided to roll out the puff paste, line a flan ring, and mix all the other ingredients together as a filling. Apparently the customers were so impressed with the new sweet that it became a regular item on the menu.

Bakewell tart used to be made with cakecrumbs, from left-overs. Our recent pastry chefs have glorified the recipe by introducing ground almonds, instead of cakecrumbs.

Sweetpaste (p. 30)	200 g
Raspberry jam	50 g
Frangipane (p. 134)	300 g
Apricot jam	20 g
Fondant	20 g

Line a 20 cm flan ring as described in apple flan (p. 48). Line the base of the flan case with raspberry jam, pipe the frangipane evenly on top. Bake in a moderate oven, 204 °C, to a light brown colour, with the frangipane evenly cooked throughout. Allow the tart to settle on a cooling tray, then brush the surface with boiled apricot jam. When set, lightly brush with soft, warm lemon-flavoured fondant. A neat trellis pattern can be formed on top, using the left-over trimmings, if desired.

The tart can be served as a sweet on a silver dish covered with a doily, or cut into approximately 10 portions and served for afternoon tea.

Belgium tart, *Tarte Belge*

Puff paste trimmings	200 g
Raspberry jam	100 g
Frangipane	200 g
Boiled raspberry jam	
Thinned-out fondant	

Roll out the trimmings thinly, place in a greased, deep baking tray or swiss roll tin,

A bakewell tart and the main ingredients

allow to rest for 10 minutes. Spread raspberry jam on the base and fill with frangipane, smooth the top, neatly arrange fine strips of the same trimmings to form a trellis pattern. Allow to rest, bake in the oven at 180 °C until the frangipane is cooked and has a firmish top.

Brush all over with boiled raspberry jam, allow to set and to cool. Brush all over with thinned-out, lemon-flavoured fondant. Cut to requirement (about 10 portions). This tart can be used as a sweet or cut into lozenge shapes for afternoon teas.

Linzer tart, *Tarte linzer*

Castor sugar	200 g
Butter	200 g
Egg yolk	2
Egg	1
Ground almonds	300 g
Cake crumbs	300 g
Flour	50 g
Ground cinnamon	10 g
Raspberry jam	300 g

Cream the butter and sugar together to a light creamy texture, gradually add the eggs a little at a time, until well blended. With an 8 mm piping tube, line the inside of a large, greased flan ring (20 cm), or two small ones. Reserve some of the paste for the top. Spread the base evenly with raspberry jam. Pipe a fine trellis pattern on top, brush with boiled and strained apricot jam. Serve on a doily-lined silver dish.

LINZER TART WITH FRUIT, *TARTE LINZER AVEC FRUIT*
Proceed as for Linzer tart, filling the tart with fruit instead of jam. Peaches, pears, pineapple, apples, cherries, apricots, etc., can be used.

APPLE LINZER TART, *TARTE LINZER AUX POMMES*
Proceed as for Linzer tart. Instead of jam, half-fill the flan with fine slices of eating apples. Pipe frangipane on top to nearly fill the tart. Bake as before. When settled, brush with boiled apricot jam.

Brittany tart, *Tarte Bretagne*

Shortpaste	200 g
Ground almonds	50 g
Prunes	100 g
Cream or milk	5 dl
Castor sugar	150 g
Eggs	4
Prunelle or cognac	50 g
Nutmeg	

Line the flan ring with the shortpaste, allow to rest for 20 minutes. Prepare an egg custard, boiling the cream, adding to the eggs mixed with sugar, and liqueur. Place the ground almonds in the base of the flan case, arrange the sliced prunes on top, pour in the prepared egg custard, sprinkle with grated nutmeg. Bake in the oven at 204 °C, until the egg custard has set. Serve hot or cold.

Tarte tatin

Shortpaste	200 g
Eating apples	750 g
Butter	60 g
Granulated sugar	150 g
Zest of 1 orange	
Zest of 1 lemon	
Calvados liqueur	100 g

Line the flan ring with shortpaste, allow to rest for 20 minutes. Peel the apples, slice into quarters and mix with the sugar, add the zest of orange and lemon, allow to stand for 20 minutes. Clarify the butter in a large plat sauter, add the apple mixture, cook at a high temperature, until the sugar has caramelised, add the liqueur. Allow to cool. Partly blind-bake the flan case, add the filling, return to the oven to complete the baking. Serve hot or cold with crème monté.

Lemon meringue tart, *Tart au citron meringue*

Sweetpaste	200 g
Filling (lemon curd):	
Castor sugar	150 g
Butter	50 g
Lemons	5
Cornflour	30 g
Egg yolks	4
Water	3 dl
Top (meringue):	
Egg whites	4
Castor sugar	150 g

For the flan case: Line the flan ring as in apple flan (p. 48), place into the refrigerator to rest, then line the inside with greaseproof paper. Fill with baking beans, bake in the oven at 204 °C, until paste is nearly coloured, remove the beans and return case to oven to complete the baking and dry out the inside.

For the filling: Zest the lemons using a grater and extract the juices. Dissolve the sugar in the lemon juice and zest. Use half sugar and lemon mixture for dissolving cornflour in a bowl, the other half bring to the boil. When boiling, whisk in the diluted cornflour add water and bring back to the boil. Remove from the heat, using a wooden spatula quickly stir in the egg yolks, return to the heat and allow to just thicken. Pour immediately into the flan cases, leave to cool.

For the meringue: Whisk egg whites (using a scalded bowl) until stiff, gradually whisk in the castor sugar to form a firm meringue,

avoid over mixing. Pipe the meringue onto the prepared cooled curd, using a piping bag and star tube. Dredge the top with castor sugar and return to the oven to brown the surface. Serve on doily-lined silver flat.

Golden syrup tart, *Tart au sirop d'or*

Shortpaste (creaming method, p.30)	200 g
Golden syrup	500 g
Breadcrumbs (fresh and white)	100 g

Line a 20 cm flan ring using the same method as for apple flan (p. 48), allow to rest for at least 20 minutes. Bring the syrup to the boil, remove from the heat, mix in the served breadcrumbs using a wooden spatula, allow to cool. Pour into the prepared flan case. Roll out the paste trimmings thinly and cut into 5 mm strips, arrange on top of the prepared tart in a trellis pattern. Bake at 204 °C. Serve on a doily-lined silver dish.

Pear tart bourdaloue, *Tarte au poire bourdaloue*

Shortpaste	200 g
Crème pâtissiére	500 g
Pears	8
Flaked almonds	
Icing sugar	
Poire Williams	

Line a 20 cm flan ring with the shortpaste, place aside to rest for 20 minutes. Poach the pears until cooked, but firm. Prepare the crème pâtissiére, flavoured with Poire Williams liqueur. Bake the flan case blind, to a light brown colour, 1/3 fill with the flavoured crème pâtissiére, allow to set. Arrange the poached pears on top, coat completely with more crème pâtissiére, sprinkle flaked almonds on top, dredge with icing sugar.

Place under the salamander to colour the top. Serve hot or cold, with apricot sauce flavoured with Poire Williams.

■ FRUIT TARTS

Dutch apple tart, *Tarte Hollandaise aux pommes*

Shortpaste	220 g
Cooking apples	500 g
Castor sugar	200 g
Cinnamon (optional)	20 g
Sultanas	100 g
Butter	50 g
Lemon (zest)	1

Dutch apple tart

Roll the paste into a circle about 3 cm larger than a 20 cm flan ring, insert into the greased flan ring, form a lip in the inside of the ring, roll the rolling pin over the top to cut off the surplus paste, fold into the remaining paste and reserve for the top. Place the lined flan onto a clean baking tray. Allow to rest. Wash, peel and core the apples, slice into pieces about 1 cm thick.

Heat the butter using a plat sauter, add the cinnamon, sugar, zest and allow to cook to a light caramel, add the sliced apples. Continue cooking for a few minutes to bind all the apples with the caramelised sugar. Allow to cool.

Place the prepared apples into the lined flan case. Roll out the remaining paste to a round large enough to cover the tart, fold into four and cut out a pattern, and unfold. Dampen the edges of the flan case with water, place the rolled ring on top, press the edges to seal and to cut off the surplus paste. Water-wash the top, sprinkle liberally with castor sugar. Allow to rest for 10 minutes, longer if possible. Bake at 204 °C, to a light brown colour. When nearly baked, remove from the oven, remove the flan ring, egg-wash the sides of the tart, replace back into the oven to glaze. Serve hot or cold on a silver dish with a doily. Serve with semi-whipped fresh cream or sauce anglaise.

APPLE TART, *TARTE AUX POMMES*
Proceed as for Dutch apple tart omitting the cinnamon and sultanas.

MIXED FRUIT TART
Proceed as for Dutch apple tart, using 350 g of cooking apples. Add 150 g of other fruit (e.g. blackcurrants, cherries, raspberries, blueberries) after caramelising and before placing the fruit into the lined flan case.

PLUM TART, *TARTE AUX PRUNES*
Proceed as for mixed fruit tart, putting 50 g of white breadcrumbs into the base of the flan cases before adding the fruit.

Follow the same procedure for the following tarts:
Gooseberry tart, *Tarte aux groiselles*
Rhubarb tart, *Tarte à la rhubarb*

Greengage tart, *Tarte à la reine claude*
The breadcrumbs help to absorb moisture from the fruit produced while cooking. Complete as for Dutch apple tart.

■ FRUIT FLANS, *FLAN AUX FRUITS*

'Flan' is the French word for 'mould', but it has come to mean an open tart filled with an egg custard mixture (and completed in various ways). Flans were originally brought to Europe by the Romans. They mainly consisted of a lined tin or ring, filled probably with a mixture of spicy meat and vegetables.

Apple flan, *Flan aux pommes*

Sweetpaste	*200 g*
Cooking apples (for purée)	*500 g*
Eating apples (top)	*500 g*
Egg (for egg-wash)	*1*
Sliver of lemon or clove	*1*
Apricot jam (for glazing)	*200 g*

Procedure for apple purée: Wash the cooking apples, slice into large pieces and cook in plenty of water until soft and tender. Drain and pass through a sieve, place back into the saucepan. Add a sliver of lemon or a clove (or both) and boil gently over a low heat until a thick purée is attained. Allow to cool.

Step-by-step apple flan

Procedure for flan: Using the prepared sweet-paste (p. 30) roll out a round large enough for a 20 cm flan ring, allowing for the depth as well as the width of the ring. Roll the paste over the rolling pin, and unwind over the greased flan ring, mould into the ring, make a border with the paste, cut off the surplus by rolling a rolling pin over the top. Raise the rim to a tidy edge, crimp as desired. Place the lined flan onto a clean baking tray and half-fill with the prepared apple purée. Decorate the top of the purée with slices of (peeled) eating apples. Allow to rest for 10 minutes, place in the oven at 204 °C. Bake to a very light golden colour. Remove from the oven, remove the flan ring, egg-wash the exposed sides, return to oven to complete baking. The rims of the apples should be slightly browned, to give an attractive baked appearance. Alternatively the flan can be flashed under the salamander to brown. Place onto a cooling wire. Glaze with boiled and strained apricot jam or flan glaze. Serve on a serving dish lined with a doily.

Note: Avoid over baking the flans, as the paste will harden on cooling, and will be very difficult to serve, as well as unpalatable to the customer. It is not compulsory to egg-wash the outside of the flan whilst cooking, but egg-wash does improve the appearance.

Flan Alsacienne

Sweetpaste as for apple flan	
Cooking apples	750 g
Castor sugar	60 g
Egg custard:	
Eggs	1
Castor sugar	15 g
Milk	1 ½ dl
Vanilla pod	
Egg-wash	

Prepare the flan as for apple flan, using half the apples for purée, the remaining slices for the top. Bake at 204 °C. When almost cooked, remove from the oven and carefully pour the egg custard (p. 70) over the top. Return to the oven to complete the cooking. Serve on a dish lined with a doily.

Various fillings for fruit flans

The following should be placed in the base of the flan, prior to decorating with the specified fruits:
Apple purée and sliced fruit = apple flan.
Breadcrumbs = plums, gooseberries, rhubarb.
Crème pâtissiére and fruit = strawberries, raspberries, bananas, blackcurrants. (Flan case to be baked blind.) Frangipane and sliced fruit = apricot, peaches, pears, pineapple.

Fruit flan with rice, *Flan au riz avec fruits*

Line the flan with sweetpaste, bake blind. Half-fill the base with rice condé. Arrange chosen fruit on top and glaze.

Egg custard flan, *Flan au lait*

Line the flan with sweetpaste and fill with egg custard (p. 70). Sprinkle the top with nutmeg. Bake at 204 °C. Egg-wash if desired.

■ SAVOURY FLANS

The following proportions will be sufficient for two 20 cm flan rings, or about 10 portions. Individual tartlets can be produced using the same filling serving two per portion, using 20 tartlet moulds. Savoury flans and tartlets can be served at cocktail parties, cold buffets, or as starters.

Cheese flans, *Tartes au fromage*

Moulding paste (p. 30)	*400 g*
Cheddar or Gruyere cheese	*150 g*
Nutmeg	
Cream	*3 dl*
Milk	*3 dl*
Eggs	*3*
Salt	*10 g*

Grease the flan rings and place onto a clean baking tray. Divide the paste in half, roll out to about 25 cm in diameter, insert the paste into the rings, mould in, and make a ridge all round, cut off the surplus paste. Raise the paste rim higher than the rings, crimp the edges. Place both flans into the refrigerator to rest for about 30 minutes. Put cheese into both flan cases. Fill with the prepared egg mixture, grate the nutmeg on top. Bake at 204 °C, until firm but springy to the touch. Serve hot or cold.

QUICHE LORRAINE
Proceed as for cheese flan adding julienne slices of ham and steamed onions.

MUSHROOMS QUICHE LORRAINE, *QUICHE LORRAINE AUX CHAMPIGNONS*
Proceed as for quiche lorraine adding steamed mushrooms.

COURGETTE AND TOMATO FLAN, *TARTE AUX COURGETTES ET TOMATES*
Follow the procedure for cheese flan, adding steamed slices of courgette and tomato on top of the cheese.

SOFT MUSSEL FLAN, *TARTE MOELLEUSE AUX MOULES*
Proceed as for cheese flan, adding steamed onions and mussels.

CRAB AND CHEESE FLAN
Proceed as for cheese flan, adding flakes of crab meat to cover the top of the cheese.

Pissaladière

Brioche dough	*500 g*
Gruyere cheese	*100 g*
Anchovies	*50 g*
Black olives	*50 g*

Line two 20 cm flan rings with the brioche dough, leave to rest in the refrigerator for 10 minutes. Complete as for cheese flans, placing the anchovies on top half-way through the baking.

Cheese and tomato pizza

Brioche or bread dough	*500 g*
Tomato pulp	*200 g*
Mozzarella cheese	*500 g*
Oregano or thyme	
Salt and pepper	
Olive oil	
(Makes 10)	

Roll the dough to a large round thin disk, place in a greased 30 cm pizza pan. Make depressions in the surface, brush with olive oil. Spread the tomato pulp nearly to the edge of the ring. Sprinkle on the herbs, and lay the cheese in fine slices, again nearly to the edge. Salt and pepper to taste.

Bake in a hot oven at 230–240 °C, for approximately 15 minutes. It may be necessary to reduce the temperature and cook for a few more minutes, to dry the base of the dough well without burning it. Anchovies, sliced ham, tongue, prawns, slices of fish, crab meat, lobster meat, sausages, salami, peppers, or any other suitable ingredients may be used as a topping. Pizzas are named after the main ingredient used, for example, pizza d'anchois, pizza aux fromages, pizza au jambon.

FRUIT PIES

Sweet pie paste	750 g
Fruit	2 kg
Castor sugar	200 g
Water	

Cooking apples, rhubarb, cherries, black-berries, plums, greengages, blackcurrants, blueberries, or a combination of apples with one other fruit for example blackberries and apple pie, gooseberries and apple pie, plum and apple pie, etc.

(Makes 10 portions)

Prepare the sweet pie paste, either using the rubbing or creaming method. The creaming method will result in a friable, better eating quality, with less shrinkage.

Place the chosen fruit in two 20 cm pie dishes, making sure they are filled well above the rim of the dish.

Add the castor sugar. If using apples, two or three cloves can also be added. Pour in sufficient water to half fill the pie dish.

Roll out half the paste, sufficient to cover one pie, approximately 3 cm larger than the pie dish. Using a small knife, cut out a strip on the outer edge of the paste, 2 cm wide. Egg-wash the rim of the dish, place the cut strip on the rim of the dish. This is to produce a double thickness of paste round the edge of the pie, to even out the baking. Egg-wash the strip and place the larger paste on top. Press to seal.

Using a small knife crimp the edges. Egg-wash all over. Dredge with castor sugar and make a small hole in the centre, for the steam to escape while baking.

Allow to rest for at least 20 minutes.

Bake in the oven at 204 °C, to a light brown colour. With a small knife check that the fruit inside is cooked. Serve hot on oval serving dishes, with doilies, and pie frills and accompanied by custard sauce.

CHEESECAKES, *TOURTE AU FROMAGE*

Almond cheesecake (cooked)

Shortpaste (p. 30)	200 g
Cream cheese	500 g
Castor sugar	100 g
Ground almonds	50 g
Eggs	3
Lemon (zest and juice)	1
Cornflour	25 g
Double cream	25 g

Line two 15 cm flan rings with the shortpaste, allow to rest in the refrigerator for 30 minutes (on baking trays). Prepare the filling by mixing the cream cheese in a bowl and, using a wooden spoon, add the zest of lemon. Separately mix the eggs with the sugar and dilute the cornflour with the cream. Gradually add the eggs and sugar to the cheese and then using a small whisk mix in the diluted cornflour. Whisk until well blended.

Spread the ground almonds on the pastry bases, pour the mixture into flan cases and cook in the oven at 185–200 °C. To test that the cheesecake is fully cooked, insert a small knife into the centre – the knife should come out clean. Lightly brush the top with boiled apricot jam and sprinkle with roasted, nibbed or flaked almonds. Serve hot or cold on serving dishes lined with dish paper.

Sultana cheesecake (cooked)

Shortpaste	200 g
Butter	100 g
Castor sugar	75 g
Cream cheese	500 g
Sultanas	50 g
Grated lemon rind	1
Eggs	4
Wholemeal biscuits	6
Salt, pinch	
Nutmeg, pinch	

Line two 15 cm flan rings with the shortpaste, place on baking trays and allow to rest in the refrigerator. Cream the butter, sugar, salt and the lemon zest, then gradually add the eggs. Cream the cheese well in a separate bowl, add the creamed butter, fold in the sultanas and the finely crushed biscuits. Spread the filling in the lined flan rings and bake in the oven at 185–200 °C. The centre should be firm to the touch when cooked. Serve hot or cold on serving dishes lined with dish papers.

Fresh fruit cheesecake, *Sabayon technique* (uncooked)

Egg yolks	8
Lemon zest	1
Castor sugar	200 g
Lemon juice	1
Leaf gelatine	50 g
Liqueur of choice (optional)	100 g
Fresh fruit of choice	750 g
Cream cheese	500 g
Frech cream	5 dl
Cake crumbs or crushed biscuits	

Prepare two 15 cm torten rings, or soufflé dishes, with either: cake crumbs, sponge, or japonaise bases. Place slices of fresh fruit to cover the base. Soak the gelatine in cold water. Using a large mixing bowl over a bain-marie, whisk the yolks, sugar, zest and liqueur (if used), to a thick foamy texture. Warm the gelatine in a saucepan with the lemon juice, add to the whisked mixture and continue whisking until cold.

Whisk the cream, keep cool. Cream the cheese well and fold in the cold sabayon mixture, then fold in the whipped cream. Pour some of the mix onto the prepared bases, add more fruit, continue until the filling reaches the top of the ring. Place in the refrigerator to set.

Remove the torten ring, decorate the top with rosettes of cream and slices of the fruit used. Serve on serving dishes, lined with doilys.

Italian cheesecake, *Tiramisu I*

Mascarpone cheese	1 kg
Egg yolks	4
Eggs	4
Icing sugar	200 g
Cakecrumbs for the base	
Sponge fingers	200 g
Strong cold coffee	100 g
Tia Maria	100 g
Cocoa powder (unsweetened)	
(Makes 10)	

Whisk the yolks and eggs with the sugar over a bain-marie, to a light foamy texture. Cream the cheese and add the egg mixture. Continue whisking until light and creamy.

Prepare 10 serving glasses or bowls with cakecrumbs and soak the biscuits in the Tia Maria and coffee. Pour some of the mix into the dishes, add some of the soaked biscuits, add more mixture. Repeat until the glasses are full. Heavily dust the tops with the cocoa powder. Decorate with a rosette of cream and a small marzipan coffee bean.

Tiramisu (2)

Italian cheesecake, *Tiramisu 2*

Egg yolks	8
Castor sugar	200 g
Leaf gelatine	50 g
Juice of 1 lemon	
Tia Maria	100 g
Strong cold coffee	100 g
Mascarpone cheese	500 g
Fresh cream	5 dl
Sponge fingers	200 g
Sponge bases (1 cm thick)	2
Cocoa powder (unsweetened)	

Proceed by producing the Sabayon mixture and two 15 cm bases as for fruit cheesecake. Saturate the sponge bases and sponge fingers with the coffee and Tia Maria. Pour about 2 cm of the mixture over the bases, arrange a neat layer of the saturated sponge fingers on top. Repeat until the top of the ring is reached. Allow to set in the refrigerator. Remove the torten ring and heavily dust the top with unsweetened cocoa powder. Present on serving dishes lined with doilys.

3 AERATED GOODS

Chemical aeration

Over the last 200 years aeration of flour products, besides the use of yeast, has been a problem in terms of the texture and keeping qualities of cakes. Traditionally the only chemicals available for use were alum (potassium and aluminium) and 'pearl ash' (commercial potassium carbonate). Eventually carbonate of ammonia (known as vol), carbonate of magnesia, cream of tartar and sulphuric acid were tried. After further experiments the ordinary carbonate of soda was used with the acid substances just mentioned, mainly in the production of biscuits.

Ready-made baking powder was imported from America around 1850; this was known as 'German yeast'.

Baking powder

This is a mixture of substances, consisting of an alkaline and an acid, which when moistened and heated, produces a gas called carbon dioxide CO_2. When cooked the acids are practically tasteless. The alkali and acid used in correct proportion are harmless to human consumption. A mixture of 30 g of bicarbonate of soda and 60 g of cream of tartar produces an efficient home-made baking powder. This would be sufficient to aerate 2 kg of flour for making scones. It is very important to sieve the mixture at least twice, to obtain even distribution.

Means of aeration: Carbon dioxide (CO_2) is released when the baking powder is heated.

This, and the moisture produced, are trapped in the gluten network, in air cells previously created in the mixing. The gas expands as it is heated, mainly during the early stages of the baking procedure. Eventually the proteins in the cake coagulate, the structure becomes rigid. Baking powder helps to produce a pleasant colour, palatable appearance and a light digestible texture.

■ SCONES, *GALETTE AU LAIT*

Traditionally this is the English cake, and very popular all over the British Isles. Originally scones were baked on a griddle or 'girdle'. They were, and are, commonly used to replace bread, and potatoes were often added to make the flour go further. Even today in many farmhouses it is possible to find a little crane attached to the kitchen stove, with a chain to hook the griddle on. By this means the griddle can be raised to different heights from the fire, according to the degree of heat desired.

A peat fire was considered the best for cooking girdle cakes and scones, but as a substitute for a girdle a very thick frying pan was used, or even an iron plate.

The girdle was heated slowly, then well-floured before the scones were put on. The flour would be brushed off, and more added before cooking each fresh batch of scones. If the flour burns, the girdle is too hot and the flour must be brushed off, the girdle cooled and a little fresh flour added.

Plain scones

Flour	1 kg
Baking powder	75 g
Salt	5 g
Butter	200 g
Castor sugar	150 g
Milk	6 dl
(Makes 8×4 rounds)	

Plain scones

Sieve the flour, salt and baking powder together onto a clean surface. Rub in the butter, make a large bay, pour in the milk and sugar. Draw in the dry ingredients and mix to just form a paste. Avoid over mixing, as this will toughen the dough. Allow to lie for 15 minutes, covered with a cloth.

Divide the dough in 8 equal sections, make into balls, roll into a round shape, about 15 cm in diameter. Cut each piece in 4 and place, in rounds, on a lightly greased baking tray. Egg-wash over the tops, allow to rest for 25–30 minutes, egg-wash again and bake in the oven at 215–230 °C, until nicely browned. Place on a cooling tray when cooked. Scones can be served warm or cold, on the same day of production.

Individually baked: Scones can also be produced by rolling the dough on a floured surface to 2 cm thick and cut out using a round 5 cm plain cutter, placed on a greased baking tray, egg-washed, rested and baked as described above.

Sultana scones

Flour	1 kg
Baking powder	75 g
Salt	5 g
Sultanas	200 g
Butter	200 g
Castor sugar	150 g
Milk	6 dl

Follow the method for plain scones, adding the washed and dried sultanas to the rubbed flour and butter mixture, prior to adding the milk and sugar.

Wholemeal scones

Flour	250 g
Wholemeal flour	750 g
Baking powder	75 g
Salt	5 g
Butter	200 g
Castor sugar	150 g
Milk	6 dl

Sieve flour together and proceed as for plain scones.

Potato scones

Flour	500 g
Baking powder	75 g
Salt	10 g
Butter	200 g
Potatoes boiled and sieved	500 g

Sieve the flour, salt and baking powder onto a clean surface, mix in the potatoes. Allow the dough to rest for 10 minutes. Roll out to 2 cm thick, cut out using a 5 cm cutter, place on a greased baking tray. Egg-wash the tops. Rest for a further 10 minutes. Bake in the oven at 215–230 °C, to a brown colour. Serve hot and buttered.

Potato scones are best eaten within two hours of baking. It is not advisable to reheat – texture and flavour will be diminished.

■ CHEMICALLY AERATED BUNS
Raspberry buns

Flour	I kg
Baking powder	75 g
Salt	5 g
Butter	250 g
Castor sugar	200 g
Milk	5 dl
Eggs	2
(Makes 30–32)	

Follow the same method as for plain scones, add the eggs with the milk to the bay, form a smooth dough, avoiding over mixing. Measure into 120 g pieces, divide each piece in two. Roll into balls and turn over onto a flour-dusted surface. Flatten the balls lightly, make cavity in the centre of each. Using a paper cornet, pipe a small amount of raspberry jam into the cavity, draw the edges of the buns together, and entirely seal in the jam. Turn over the buns again on the surface, egg-wash, dip each bun in castor sugar, cut an incision across the top of each and place onto a greased baking tray.

Allow the buns to rest for about 20–25 minutes, bake at 215–230 °C. Place on a cooling tray when cooked and immediately cut an incision on the tops to show the jam.

Coconut buns

Flour	I kg
Baking powder	75 g
Salt	5 g
Desiccated coconut	200 g
Butter	250 g
Castor sugar	200 g
Milk	6 dl
Eggs	2
(Makes 32)	

Proceed as for raspberry buns adding the coconut to the rubbed flour and butter mix, prior to adding the milk and sugar. Ball up the buns, egg-wash and dip the tops in coconut, place on greased baking trays. Allow to rest for 20–25 minutes. Bake at 215–230 °C.

Caraway and cinnamon buns

Proceed as for coconut buns, adding 100 g of caraway seeds and 50 g of cinnamon powder to the flour (instead of the coconut) prior to rubbing in the butter. Sprinkle a few caraway seeds on the tops.

Chocolate buns

Proceed as for coconut buns, sieving 100 g of cocoa powder with the flour (instead of the coconut).

Coffee buns

Proceed as for coconut buns, substituting 50 ml of concentrated coffee for the coconut and adding it to the milk.

Rice buns

Proceed as for coconut buns adding instead 150 g of ground rice and dipping the tops of the buns in nibbed sugar.

Rock cakes

Flour	1 kg
Baking powder	75 g
Salt	5 g
Butter	250 g
Currants	250 g
Mixed peel	100 g
Eggs	2
Milk	5 dl
(Makes 30–32)	

Make the dough as for raspberry buns, incorporating the washed currants and mixed peel to the rubbed flour and butter mix. Roughly break off equal-sized pieces, place on a greased baking tray, egg-wash, sprinkle the tops with castor sugar. Allow to rest for 20–25 minutes, bake at 215–230 °C.

ALMOND BUNS
Proceed as for rock cakes, using 100 g of nibbed almonds in the rubbed flour and butter mix, instead of fruit. Egg-wash and sprinkle the tops with nibbed or flaked almonds.

LEMON BUNS
Proceed as for raspberry buns, using lemon zest rubbed into the flour and butter. A small amount of lemon curd can be added in place of the raspberry jam.

CHERRY BUNS
Proceed as for raspberry buns, adding 200 g of diced glacé cherries to the rubbed mixture, prior to adding the eggs and milk. Ball up, flatten down lightly, egg-wash and push half a glacé cherry into the centre.

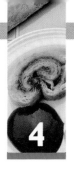

4 STEAMED PUDDINGS

One of the best methods of cooking puddings is to steam them. The same principle applies for both suet and sponge puddings. The action of the steam (water vapour), under varying degrees of pressure will produce a very palatable and digestible pudding.

A steamer should be available in most kitchens. It is an enclosed chamber, fitted with a pressure valve which controls the amount of water filling it and another valve that acts as an overflow for the pressure of steam produced. A steamer requires very little maintenance; regular cleaning and changing the water is essential.

The process of steaming has much in common with boiling at a temperature not exceeding 100 °C. Both methods of cooking have the advantages of preventing burning and retaining natural moistures. Puddings are covered during steaming to prevent water entering the mixture and making it soggy.

If a steamer is not available, steamed pudding can be made easily by the basic and very adequate method used before the steam cabinet was invented. The pudding basin is stood on a little trivet in a saucepan, with water only half way up the basin; more can be added as it boils away. The saucepan used must have a tight-fitting lid and should not be opened unless absolutely necessary. When the pudding is cooked, it is left to stand for a few minutes for the steam to settle, turned out onto a serving dish and served with the appropriate sauce.

Remember not to over-fill the saucepan, allow space for the pudding to expand. Attention to the following is required in the use of the steamer:

(a) Pressure control.
(b) Time control (if related).
(c) Sufficient water, prior to ignition.
(d) Releasing the steam pressure before opening the lid.
(e) Regular maintenance and cleaning, indicated by the manufacturer's recommendations.
(f) Ensuring correct cooking time.
(g) Lighting the steamer at least 20 minutes before putting in the puddings.

A selection of steamed puddings

Rich and solid steamed puddings are improved by long boiling; but puddings of sponge texture deteriorate with over-cooking and become dry.

Steamed sponge pudding

Butter	250 g
Castor sugar	250 g
Eggs	5
Fruit (if required)	150 g
Flour	250 g
Baking powder	3–4 g
Spice	2 g
(Serves 10)	

Well grease either two basins to hold 5 portions each or 10 individual dariole moulds. Cream the butter and castor sugar to a light creamy texture. Beat in the eggs a little at a time. Add the sieved flour and other dry goods, lightly mix together. Add the fruit, if required, fold until well blended, but avoid over mixing, as this will produce a heavy pudding with a tight crumb. Place into the steamer tray and cover thoroughly with greased greaseproof paper, place in the steamer. Steam for 75–90 minutes for the large containers and 50–60 minutes for the individual portions. Serve hot with the appropriate sauce.

CHERRY SPONGE PUDDING, *POUDING AUX CERISES*
Add 50 g of diced glacé cherries.

SULTANA SPONGE PUDDING, *POUDING AUX RAISINS*
Add 50 g of sultanas, use mixed spice.

CURRANT SPONGE PUDDING, *POUDING AUX RAISINS DE CORINTHE*
Add 75 g of currants, use mixed spice.

JAM SPONGE PUDDING, *POUDING À LA CONFITURE*
Cover the base of the mould with jam. Serve the pudding with jam sauce.

GINGER SPONGE PUDDING, *POUDING AU GINGEMBRE*
Add 50 g of finely chopped ginger and serve with ginger syrup sauce.

GOLDEN SYRUP SPONGE PUDDING, *POUDING AU SIROP D'OR*
Place sufficient golden syrup in each mould to cover the base. Serve with golden syrup sauce.

HONEY SPONGE PUDDING, *POUDING AU MIEL*
As for syrup sponge pudding using honey.

GOOSEBERRY SPONGE PUDDING, *POUDING AUX GROSEILLES*
Cover base of mould with fresh gooseberries, serve with custard sauce or sauce anglaise.

APPLE SPONGE PUDDING, *POUDING AUX POMMES*
As for gooseberry sponge pudding, using apples and mixed spice.

BLACKBERRY SPONGE PUDDING, *LE PUDDING AUX MÛRES*
As for gooseberry sponge pudding, using blackberries.

BLACKCURRANT SPONGE PUDDING, *POUDING AUX CASSIS NOIRS*
As for gooseberry sponge pudding, using blackcurrants.

■ STEAMED SUET ROLLS,
POUDING ROULÉ

Steamed jam roll, *Pouding roulé à la confiture*

Suet paste (p. 31)	750 g
Raspberry jam	500 g
(Serves 10)	

A steamed jam roll

1. Prepare the suet paste, allow to rest for 20 minutes.
2. Roll it out into an oblong shape, approximately 40 by 50 cm.
3. Spread the jam all over leaving one edge clear.
4. Roll up, sealing in the jam.
5. Place the roll into the greased sleeve moulds, if not available place into a clean cloth, fold the cloth and tie the ends.
6. Place the sleeve moulds or covered roll into the hot steamer and steam for 75–90 minutes.
7. When cooked remove from the moulds or the cloth, place onto a serving dish lined with dish paper. Serve hot with jam sauce, sauce anglaise or with a separate custard sauce.

Steamed almond roll, *Pouding roulé d'amandes*

Prepare the suet paste as described on page 31, adding 250 g of nibbed or flaked almonds to the flour mix. Roll the suet paste as for steamed jam roll. Roll out 500 g of marzipan slightly smaller than the paste. Brush the paste with boiled apricot jam and place the rolled marzipan on top, again brush with the boiled jam. Roll up sealing in the marzipan, steam as for jam roll. Serve on a serving dish lined with a dish paper and with a separate almond sauce.

STEAMED GOLDEN SYRUP ROLL, *POUDING ROULÉ AU SIROP D'OR*
Proceed as for steamed jam roll using golden syrup.

DALMATION ROLL or SPOTTED DICK
Proceed as for steamed jam roll. Omitting point 3. Add blackcurrants into the flour at the mixing stage.

STEAMED APPLE ROLL PUDDING, *POUDING ROULÉ AUX POMMES*
Proceed as for steamed jam roll, replacing jam with 750 g of diced apples, cinnamon, sugar and lemon zest.

■ SUET FRUIT PUDDINGS,
POUDING DE GRAISSE AUX FRUITS

Steamed apple pudding, *Pouding aux pommes*

Suet paste	500 g
Cooking apples	1 kg
Cinnamon sugar*	250 g
Cloves (optional)	4–6
*(250 g castor sugar, 100 g cinnamon)	
(Serves 10)	

Prepare the suet paste as described on page 31, allow to rest for 20 minutes. Wash, peel, core and slice the apples, 1 cm thick. Roll out the suet paste into a pocket shape and place into the previously greased pudding basin. Fill with the prepared apples, add the cinnamon sugar and cloves, a little water can be added for extra moisture (if desired). Trim off the surplus paste and roll to fit the top of the pudding, water-wash the rim of the basin and place the rolled paste on top, trim, smooth out the edge. Make a hole on top for the steam to escape. Place in the steamer to cook for 80–90 minutes, depending on the cooking quality of apples used. To make sure the apples are cooked, insert a small knife in the pudding, if cooked the knife should enter fairly easy. Remember that the pudding may have to be kept on a hotplate during service and the cooking will continue. Serve on a silver dish with a serviette, and with custard sauce separately.

Apple and blackberry pudding, *Pouding aux pommes et mûres*

Suet paste	500 g
Apples	750 g
Blackberries	250 g
Castor sugar	250 g

Proceed as for apple pudding adding blackberries.

Apple pudding St Omer, *Pouding aux pommes St Omer*

Suet paste	500 g
Eating apples	750 g
Ground almonds	100 g
Flaked almonds	50 g
Orange zest	1
Castor sugar	250 g
Cointreau	30 g

Line the basin as described in steamed apple pudding. Wash, peel, core and slice the eating apples, place the apples into a plat sauter and fry for a few minutes, add the sugar and orange zest, continue cooking until a light caramel is formed, add the ground almonds, stir well than add the Cointreau. Place the prepared mixture in the lined basin and complete as for apple pudding. Serve with sauce d'amande.

Individual steamed puddings can be made by using dariole moulds, and presented as a plated service, with appropriate coulis.

■ STEAMED BREADCRUMB PUDDINGS

Fruit dumplings, *Boulettes aux fruits*

Breadcrumbs	300 g
Flour	150 g
Suet	250 g
Baking powder	10 g
Castor sugar	150 g
Fruit (as required)	100 g
(e.g. currants, sultanas, glacé cherries, figs, dates, mixed peel, coconut)	
Grated nutmeg, pinch	
Eggs	4
(Serves 10)	

Mix together the breadcrumbs, flour, suet, baking powder, nutmeg and chosen fruit, make a large bay. Add the eggs and sugar to the bay, mix to dissolve the sugar. Gradually draw in the dry ingredients to form into a paste, do not over mix. Allow to rest for 20 minutes. For easy cooking the paste can be divided into two halves. Ball up, place into a greased basin, cover with greased greaseproof paper and steam for 90 minutes. Serve on a silver dish on a serviette with custard sauce separately.

Individual portions can be made by weighing up 60 g of the paste, balled-up and steamed on a greased tray.

Steamed orange or lemon pudding

Breadcrumbs	300 g
Flour	150 g
Suet	250 g
Baking powder	60 g
Castor sugar	150 g
Orange or lemon zest and juice	2
Eggs	4

Proceed as for fruit pudding, replacing the fruit with the grated zest and juice of either orange or lemon.

■ CHRISTMAS PUDDING, *PUDDING DE NOËL*

As the times change, and we change with them, certain traditions remain in a modified form which preserve the usages of the past. The good old-fashioned family dish, plum pudding, dates back to William the Conqueror, when his personal chef produced a particular meat stew using an earthen pot on Christmas day. Over the centuries herbs and plums were added, gradually the meat and plums were substituted with prunes and sultanas and the modern Christmas pudding evolved.

Christmas puddings need to mature after their first cooking, and are therefore better if prepared weeks or even months in advance, then removed from their containers, wrapped in greaseproof paper and stored in a dry and well-ventilated place.

Basic Christmas pudding

Flour	250 g
Suet	250 g
Mixed spice	50 g
Ground almonds	50 g
Breadcrumbs	200 g
Sultanas	300 g
Currants	300 g
Raisins	300 g
Mixed peel	200 g
Prunes	200 g
Apples	150 g
Oranges	2
Lemons	2
Footes sugar	200 g
Beer (dark)	3 dl
Eggs	3
Rum	20 g
Brandy	20 g
Sherry	20 g
(Makes 2 × 1.125 kg puddings)	

Wash and dry the raisins, sultanas, currants, and add the rum, brandy and sherry. Place in a sealed container, allow to stand for a couple of hours (preferably overnight).

Sieve all the dry ingredients onto a clean surface, add the suet, mix together and make a large bay. Place in the centre the soaked fruit and juice, make another bay and dissolve the remaining liquids with the sugar, add the eggs, and orange and lemon zest and juice. Pulling first the mixed fruit towards the centre, then the dry ingredients, continue mixing until well blended. Divide the mix equally and place in two well-greased pudding basins. Cover with greased greaseproof paper and steam for at least 6 hours. When cooked and cold, demould, wrap in clean paper and store in a dry place until required.

Before serving place the puddings into greased basins, cover, and steam for 2 hours. Serve hot on silver dishes accompanied with rum or brandy sauce made from a base of cornflour, egg yolks, or Sabayon method (see Sauces, p. 137) or with rum or brandy butter.

The Christmas pudding can also be flamed prior to serving, in front of the customer. For individual portions, the portions can be scooped out and moulded just before serving.

RUM OR BRANDY BUTTER

Cream together equal amounts of icing sugar and butter to a light texture, gradually add rum or brandy to taste. Pipe shapes onto trays lined with greaseproof paper and freeze until required, serve one piece per portion with the pudding.

Christmas pudding

5 MILK PUDDINGS, *POUDING AU LAIT*

Baked rice pudding, *Pouding au riz*

Rice (Caroline)	250 g
Milk	1 ℓ
Castor sugar	250 g
Butter	50 g
Sliver of lemon or grated nutmeg	
(Serves 10)	

Caroline rice is a short-grain rice, which makes it most suitable for puddings. It possesses a high percentage of starch, and will help achieve a good creamy texture.

Heat the milk and sliver of lemon in a saucepan with half the sugar (this is important, as if all the sugar is added at this stage, it will caramelise over the grains of rice preventing them from swelling). Rain in the rice, stirring occasionally with a wooden spatula, allow to simmer gently over the heat until the rice is fully swollen and has a creamy texture. Remove from the heat, add the butter and remaining sugar, stir gently at this stage to avoid damaging the cooked grain. Taste the mixture to check the flavour.

Pour the cooked rice into a dish, allow to stand for 10 minutes until a skin has formed, then glaze under the salamander to lightly brown the surface. Keep on a hotplate until ready for serving. Serve on an oval silver dish with a doily.

A variety of rice puddings can be prepared by adding dry fruits, such as dates, sultanas, raisins and figs.

Sago pudding, *Pouding au sagou*

Milk	1 ℓ
Castor sugar	250 g
Sago	250 g
Nutmeg to taste	
(Serves 10)	

Boil the milk, sugar and nutmeg in a saucepan. Rain in the sago, stirring continually with a wooden spatula to prevent it matting at the base. Continue cooking slowly, stirring occasionally, until it has a semi-transparent appearance. Pour into individual dishes, allow a skin to form on top then place under the salamander to glaze. Keep on a hotplate until ready for serving. Serve on an oval silver dish with a doily.

Semolina pudding, *Pouding à la semoule*

Milk	1 ℓ
Semolina	250 g
Castor sugar	250 g
Sliver of lemon	
(Serves 10)	

Boil the milk and sliver of lemon in a saucepan. Rain in semolina, stirring continually. Continue cooking very gently over low heat, until thoroughly cooked. Pour into individual dishes, allow a skin to form on top then glaze under the salamander. Keep on a hotplate until ready for serving. Serve on a silver dish with a doily.

SEMOLINA FRUIT PUDDING, *POUDING DE LA SEMOULE AUX FRUITS*

Prepare the semolina dish as above, do not glaze, decorate the top of the dish with any suitable fresh fruit. Glaze the fruit and pudding, with boiled apricot jam or flan glaze. When cold decorate the top with whipped cream, glacé cherries, angelica, almonds, etc.

PASTA MILK PUDDING

Proceed as for rice pudding using any type of pasta desired, sliver of lemon and grated nutmeg. Cook until the pasta or noodles are soft, pour into serving dishes, allow a skin to form on the top, then, glaze under the salamander.

Blancmange, *Blanc-manger à l'Anglaise*

Milk	1 ℓ
Cornflour	120 g
Castor sugar	150 g
Flavour to taste	
(Serves 10)	

Mix the sugar and cornflour together in a bowl, dissolve with some of the milk. Pour the rest of the flavoured milk into a saucepan, bring to the boil. Pour the mixture into the saucepan, whisk together stirring constantly. Cook for one minute then pour it into a suitable dish or dishes. Decorate when cold as desired. Blancmanges can be turned out of the mould or prepared individually in glass bowls or glasses.

Note that rosewater and orange-flower water are the most suitable flavouring agents in blancmange.

CHOCOLATE BLANCMANGE, *BLANC-MANGER AU CHOCOLAT*

Proceed as above, adding 250 g of grated or finely chopped chocolate couverture. The top can be decorated, when cold, with whipped cream and more grated chocolate.

FRESH FRUIT BLANCMANGE, *BLANC-MANGER AUX FRUITS*

Proceed as for blancmange, adding a suitable fruit or mixture of fruit, and naming the dish after the fruit used. Slices of fruit can be placed in the base of the dish and more on top to decorate. Ideal fruits for blancmanage are strawberries, raspberries, blackcurrants, redcurrents, cherries, bananas, kiwis and mangoes.

ALMOND BLANCMANGE, *BLANC-MANGER AUX AMANDES*

Proceed as for blancmange, boiling 120 g of ground almonds with the milk, then strain through a very fine strainer or muslin. Continue as before using the strained and flavoured milk. Decorate the top with whipped cream and glazed almonds.

LIQUEUR BLANCMANGE, *BLANC-MANGER AU LIQUEUR*

Proceed as for basic blancmange or the fruit recipe, adding 50 g of a chosen liqueur. A limited amount of colour can be used.

RIBBONED BLANCMANGE, *BLANC-MANGER À LA RUBANÉ*

Prepare various coloured and flavoured blancmanges, add one layer at a time, allowing each one to set before adding the next. When the mould is complete, allow to set and demould onto the serving dish. Decorate the top with whipped cream. Individual glasses prepared in this way can look very attractive and appetising.

Junket, *Lait caillé*

Originally this was made with pure cream, curdled with rennet and flavoured with rosewater, nowadays is made with milk.

Milk	1 ℓ
Castor sugar	50 g
Rennet essence	50 g
Flavour to taste	
Brandy (optional)	30 g
(Serves 10)	

Heat the milk and sugar in a saucepan until just warm, stirring to dissolve the sugar. Making sure the milk is just lukewarm, stir in the rennet essence and any flavour required (e.g. raspberry, strawberry, almond). Brandy or other liqueur can also be added. Sprinkle with grated nutmeg and chopped walnuts. Pour the prepared liquid immediately into a serving dish, place aside, in normal room temperature, until set. The junket can then be chilled, and served as required.

6 RICE DISHES

Riz à l'impératrice (top) with ananas créole (below)

Rice condé, *Riz condé*

Milk	1 ℓ
Vanilla flavour to taste	
Castor sugar	150 g
Rice (Caroline)	200 g
Eggs	2
Egg yolks	2
(Serves 10)	

In a saucepan bring to the boil the milk, vanilla flavour and half of the sugar. Rain in the rice and stirring continually allow to cook gently until the rice is creamy in texture. Remove from the heat and stir in the remaining sugar, eggs and yolks, return to the heat, until it just thickens. Pour the rice mixture into serving dishes (greased flan rings can be used on a serving dish, this recipe will be sufficient for two 20 cm flan rings). Allow to cool completely, then remove the rings and decorate the tops with the desired fruit, e.g. pears, peaches, pineapples or apricots. Glaze with boiled, strained apricot jam or flan glaze. When cold decorate with rosettes of whipped cream, glacé cherries, angelica or glazed almonds.

Riz à l'impératrice

Rice condé, half recipe	
Mixed or candied fruit	120 g ⎫ Salpicon
Kirsch	50 g ⎭ of fruit
Orange jelly	2 dl
Bavarois (vanilla) half recipe (p. 99)	
Raspberry coulis	3 dl
Whipped cream to decorate	
Orange-flower water (optional)	
(Serves 10)	

Line either a charlotte mould, or dariole moulds for individual portions, with orange jelly, place in the refrigerator to set. Prepare the cooked rice for the condé and the salpicon

of fruit, place both aside. Prepare the vanilla bavarois (p. 99). Ensuring both mixtures are cold, add the fruit to the condé, gently blend and fold in the bavarois. Pour the mix over the set jelly, to nearly fill the mould. Place in the refrigerator to set, about 30–40 minutes. Immerse the mould in warm water, just for a few minutes. Dry the bottom of the mould using a cloth and demould the Impératrice onto a clean silver dish or dishes. Pour the coulis round the base and decorate the top with whipped cream, glacé cherries and angelica.

Remember to avoid over-filling the moulds as this will make the demoulding difficult. Also keep the ingredients refrigerated as much as possible, between 1 °C and 4 °C. Use on the day of production.

RIZ À LA MALTAISE

Proceed as for riz à l'impératrice, using segments of 5 oranges instead of salpicon of fruit. Decorate with orange coulis and segments of orange.

Riz à la Palerme

RIZ À LA PALERME

Proceed as for riz à l'impératrice, using savarin moulds instead of charlotte moulds, and fill the centre with segments of fresh straw-berries. Bleed with strawberry coulis and strawberry liqueur. Decorate with rosettes of fresh cream.

RIZ À LA FEDERALE
Proceed as for riz à l'impératrice, using a charlotte mould, adding 150 g of blackcur-rants instead of salpicon of fruit. Complete by pouring blackcurrant coulis round the base.

BAKED RICE PUDDING
See milk puddings, page 64.

Ananas créole

Rice condé (p. 68) I recipe	
Gelatine	75 g
Cream	6 dl
Rose-flower water (optional)	
Pineapple (fresh)	I
Currants	
Orange-flower water (optional)	
(Serves 10)	

Prepare the rice condé and while still hot add the soaked gelatine (avoid over mixing as this might damage the rice grain). Place aside to cool. Whip the cream until just firm, but do not over-whip. Fold the cream into the cooled rice mixture, again avoid over mixing. Place the mixture onto an oval silver dish, and form the shape of half a pineapple. Allow to set in the refrigerator. Completely cover the top with segments of pineapple, and place a cur-rant in each of the cavities. Glaze with boiled and strained apricot jam or flan glaze. Place some strips of angelica at one end, to repre-sent the pineapple leaves.

Remember to keep the ingredients re-frigerated as much as possible, 1–4 °C. Use on the day of production.

Ananas créole can be made by two other methods:
1 Line bombe moulds with lemon jelly, fill with the rice mixture. When set demould onto a round silver dish, surrounded with segments of pineapple, glazed with boiled apricot jam.
2 Cut the top off a fresh pineapple and scoop out the middle. Dice the pineapple after removing the core and place aside to marinade in kirsch. Mix the marinaded pineapple with the rice mixture. Fill the pineapple shell with the rice mixture, re-place the lid and present on a dish lined with a serviette.

Apricot fritters, *Beignets d'abricots*

Fresh apricots	30
Rice condé half recipe (p. 68)	
Breadcrumbs	150 g
Eggs	
Flour	
(Serves 10)	

Wash the apricots, cut in half, remove stones. Reform the apricots with a spoonful of rice condé in the centre. Roll in the lightly beaten eggs, then breadcrumbs (paner anglaise). Fry in hot clean oil until golden brown. Drain well and serve on a napkin or dish paper, with a piece of angelica in each to represent the stalks. Serve hot with apricot sauce separ-ately.

7 EGG DISHES

For production of egg custard dishes the process of cooking eggs has to be well understood. Even a small amount of heat will thicken an egg. The use of a bain-marie is necessary to avoid the eggs from over cooking. The rule to observe is that the water in the tray should be at the same temperature as the egg custard in the cooking-pan.

Egg custard will coagulate at approximately 83 °C. As boiling point is 100 °C, this means that the egg dish does not have to be boiled to be cooked. Coagulation of egg white, which is almost completely protein, starts at approximately 58 °C. Coagulation of the egg yolk starts at approximately 68 °C. Coagulation of yolk and white together starts at 65 °C. If the temperature is maintained at or above the coagulation temperature, the custard shrinks and the liquid is squeezed out, giving the dish a curdled effect.

The following recipes are based on eggs weighing about 60 g.

Baked egg custard

Eggs	6
Castor sugar	150 g
Milk	1 ℓ
Vanilla flavour	
Nutmeg	

Boil the milk with the vanilla flavour, place aside to cool slightly. Whisk the eggs and sugar in a bowl, add the hot flavoured milk gradually, avoid frothing. Lightly butter two 20 cm pie dishes or soufflé dishes, nearly fill

with the egg custard, grate some nutmeg on top. Place dishes in a deep tray and half fill with warm water, place into the oven to poach and set, avoid over-cooking. Remove from the tray, serve hot with sauce anglaise (p. 135), and, if desired, compotes of fruits, separately. Alternatively, serve as crème vanille placing half strawberry on top per portion.

Flavours can be added to the egg custard, as for petits pots de crème (p. 72).

Bread and butter pudding

Egg custard	
Sliced bread or brioche	300 g
Melted butter	250 g
Sultanas	100 g
Nutmeg	
Castor sugar	

Bread and butter pudding

Prepare the egg custard as for baked egg custard. Remove the crusts from the bread, cut slices into triangles of four. Partly dip triangles in the melted butter, and arrange in the base of the pie dishes or soufflé dishes, with sultanas in between the bread slices. Half fill with the egg custard, allow to stand for 10 minutes for the bread to absorb the egg custard. Fill with the remaining egg custard, again allow to stand for a further 8–10 minutes, allowing the bread to float to the surface. Sprinkle with grated nutmeg. Place in deep trays half-filled with water and poach in the oven at 200 °C until set. Test with the point of a small knife, if set, the knife should come out clean. Sprinkle a little castor sugar on top. Serve hot with sauce anglaise, and, if desired, compote of fruit separately.

Queen of pudding, *Pouding reine*

Raspberry jam	100 g
Egg custard, 1 mix (p. 70)	
Finger biscuits	100 g
Egg whites	2 dl
Castor sugar	150 g
Raspberry jam	50 g
Apricot jam	50 g

Line the base of two 20 cm pie or soufflé dishes with half the raspberry jam, arrange the biscuits on top to cover the base. Pour the prepared egg custard over, just to cover, allow to absorb the moisture, then fill with the remaining egg custard. Place the dishes in deep trays half-filled with water and poach in the oven at 204 °C until set. When cooked remove from the trays and allow to cool completely.

Whisk the egg whites and sugar to a firm meringue, pipe over the custard to cover the surface, leaving an indented daisy pattern on top (6 or 8 petals). Place the dishes back into the oven to partly cook the meringue to a light brown colour. Using a paper cornet, alternately fill the petals with the raspberry and apricot jam. Serve hot or cold.

Floating island, *Île flottante*

Sponge cake	500 g
Apricot jam	200 g
Kirsch or maraschino	
Roasted almonds	
Pistachio nuts	
Sauce anglaise	
(Makes 10 individual portions)	

Line 10 dariole moulds or silver coupe moulds, with small rings of paper. Fill with sponge rings sandwiched together with apricot jam, add currants, roasted almonds, pistachio nuts, and moisten with stock syrup flavoured with kirsch or maraschino. Compress well into the moulds, then turn out onto trays lined with greaseproof paper. Dredge the tops with icing sugar. Prepare the sauce anglaise, flavour with kirsch or maraschino, pour about 1 cm into glass dishes, stand the prepared sponge on top of the sauce. Sprinkle with chopped roasted almonds and pistachio nuts. Serve hot or cold.

PRALINE FLOATING ISLAND, *ÎLE FLOTTANTE PRALINÉE*

Proceed as for plain floating island, using praline in the sponge, and mixing approximately 100 g into the sauce anglaise. Decorate the tops with caramel.

CHOCOLATE FLOATING ISLAND, *ÎLE FLOTTANTE AU CHOCOLAT*

Proceed as for plain floating island, using chocolate sponge flavoured with rum and chocolate sauce anglaise. Sprinkle grated chocolate on top just before serving.

The following egg custard dishes are prepared using the crème renversée method (p. 73). They are cooked and served in the same dish, so less eggs are required. The poaching procedure is the same.

Les petits pots de crème

PETITS POTS DE CRÈME VANILLE

Egg yolks	6
Eggs	2
Castor sugar	150 g
Fresh cream	1 ℓ
Vanilla flavour	
(Serves 10)	

Bring the cream and vanilla flavour nearly to the boil. Whisk the egg and yolks with the sugar, gradually whisk in the hot cream, avoid producing a froth. Pour into 20 small petits pots until almost full. Place in a deep tray half-filled with warm water. Poach in the oven at 200 °C, until set. Remove from the tray.

If served hot, pour a small amount of liquid cream on top. If served cold, petits pots can be piped with a rosette of fresh cream.

PETITS POTS DE CRÈME CHOCOLAT
Proceed as for petits pots vanille, adding 100 g finely chopped chocolate to the cream before heating.

PETITS POTS DE CRÈME CAFÉ
Proceed as for petits pots vanille, flavouring cream with coffee (to taste).

PETITS POTS DE CRÈME PRALINÉ
Proceed as for petits pots vanille, flavouring cream with crushed praline (to taste).

PETITS POTS DE CRÈME LIQUEURS
Proceed as for petits pots vanille, adding 50 ml of liqueur to the mix, just before pouring into the moulds. Name the petits pots after the liqueur used.

Crème brûlée vanille

Fresh cream	1 ℓ
Vanilla flavour	
Egg yolks	10
Eggs	2
Castor sugar	150 g
Icing sugar	
(Serves 10)	

Heat the cream with the flavour to nearly boiling. Whisk the yolks and eggs together, add the sugar and gradually pour in the milk, avoid frothing. Pour the mixture into two 15 cm buttered soufflé dishes, place in a deep tray, half-fill with warm water. Poach in the oven at 190 °C to set, test using the point of a small knife, which should come out clean if set. Remove from the tray, dredge with icing sugar, add a little cream to cover the surface. Glaze under the salamander to colour lightly. A small amount of double cream can be poured on top just before serving.

CRÈME BRÛLÉE AU CHOCOLAT
Proceed as for crème vanille, adding 100 g of finely chopped chocolate to the cream before heating.

CRÈME BRÛLÉE AU CHOCOLAT ET RHUM
Proceed as for crème au chocolat, whisking in 50 ml rum just before pouring into moulds.

CRÈME BRÛLÉE AUX FRAISES ET GRAND MARNIER
Prepare a plain mix as for crème vanille, flavouring with strawberry compound and Grand Marnier. Butter and line the soufflé dishes with slices of fresh strawberries. Fill with the prepared mix, poach as described in crème vanille.

Sabayon, *Zabaion* **or** *Zabaglione*

This Italian speciality is a hot, foamy, egg dessert made with a fortified wine. Poured into a tall glass and sprinkled with nutmeg, it nicely completes a simple one-dish meal.

It may be poured over fruit which has been cooked in a light syrup, or, for instance, a bed of strawberries previously well-soaked in brandy.

Egg yolks	6
Castor sugar	100 g
Marsala wine (enough to fill 6 half egg shells)	
(Serves 10)	

Place the yolks, sugar and wine in a scalded copper bowl, whisk over a bain-marie until thick. Never allow the mixture to boil after it has thickened. Pour immediately into the prepared glasses, filling nearly to the rim, and serve with a finger biscuit on the side. Sabayon can be served hot or cold.

Sabayon made with marsala is traditional, but it can be made with sherry, malaga, cognac or port.

Snow eggs, *Œufs à la neige*

Egg whites	10
Castor sugar	400 g
Milk	2 ℓ
(Serves 10)	

Using a deep tray on low heat, bring the milk, vanilla and a quarter of the sugar to the boil. Whisk the egg whites until firm, add the remaining sugar gradually, continue whisking to form a meringue. Using two spoons, make rock shapes (two or three per serving portion), place in the simmering milk. Allow the meringues to poach gently for about 10 minutes. Turn over and repeat the process to cook the other side. Using a perforated spoon

remove from the milk, place onto a clean cloth to drain well.

Serving method 1: Place the poached meringues into serving dishes. Using the cooking milk prepare a sauce anglaise (p. 135). Coat the meringues with the sauce, to cover completely. Sprinkle with roasted flaked almonds. Serve hot or cold.

Serving method 2: Prepare a sauce anglaise and pour about 1 cm into a serving dish, float the prepared meringues on top, sprinkle with roasted almonds. Serve hot or cold.

ŒUFS À LA NEIGE RÉJANES

Proceed as for œufs à la neige, placing half a poached apricot on top of each meringue, and finishing with apricot glaze. Serve with sauce anglaise separately.

■ MOULDED CREAMS, *LES CRÈMES MOULÉES*

Avoid using copper utensils when producing egg custard dishes.

Reversed creams, *Crème renversée*

Eggs	8
Castor sugar	100 g
Milk	6 dl
Cream	4 dl
Vanilla flavour to taste	
Whipped cream (to decorate)	
Crystallised violets	

Grease, sugar and line ten dariole moulds. Boil the milk with the flavour, place aside to cool slightly. Lightly whisk the eggs and sugar in a bowl, avoid frothing. Add the milk gradually, pour into the prepared moulds.

Place the moulds in a deep tray, half-fill with warm water. Place in the oven and cook at 200 °C, until the egg custard has set. Test by inserting a small knife, if clean when removed the custard is cooked. Place aside to cool.

Demould by releasing the skin from the mould, turn over, and with two fingers underneath, shake out the egg custard. Decorate with rosettes of fresh cream, and a small crystallised violet on each.

Cream caramel, *Crème caramel*

For the caramel:	
Cube or granulated sugar	150 g
Water	50 ml
For the custard:	
Eggs	8
Castor sugar	100 g
Milk	1 ℓ
Vanilla flavour	

Cream caramels

Saturate the sugar with the water in a small saucepan. Bring to the boil, wash down the sides of the saucepan, to stop crystals form-

ing. Continue boiling to a light caramel, the temperature should reach about 180 °C. Remove the saucepan from the heat, allow the colour to improve, shake in more water to soften the caramel. Pour into ten dariole moulds, to cover the base. Allow to set.

Boil the milk and flavour, place aside to cool slightly. Mix the eggs and sugar in a bowl, whisking lightly to avoid frothing, add the milk gradually, pour into the moulds. Place the moulds in a bain-marie, half-fill with warm water. Poach in the oven at 200 °C for about 40–45 minutes. Test by inserting a small knife in the centre, if clean when removed the custard is cooked. Remove immediately from the bain-marie, place aside to cool completely before serving.

Demould the cream caramels by releasing the skin from the mould, turn the moulds over with two fingers underneath, shake out. Serve on the same day of production in their natural sauce. Any caramel left over can be thinned out adding a little extra water and poured over the caramels before serving.

Crème beau-rivage

Egg custard: as for crème renversée.

Croquante:

Granulated sugar	120 g
Water	1 dl
Hazelnuts (skinned)	75 g

Saturate the sugar with the water, bring to the boil. Continue boiling to a light caramel colour, stir in the nibbed hazelnuts. Pour the mixture over an oiled surface and allow to cool completely. (Other nuts can be used instead of hazelnuts, e.g. nibbed, flaked, split, and whole almonds.) The praline is produced simply by crushing the croquante into a fine powder. It can be stored in a sealed container and used as required.

Cornet biscuits:

Butter	50 g
Icing sugar	75 g
Egg whites	2
Flour	60 g

Cream the butter with the icing sugar, to a very light texture. Add the egg whites, and fold in the flour. Pipe onto a greased baking tray in rounds the size of a 10 pence piece, about 10 cm apart. Bake in the oven at 204 °C, to just colour the edges. Remove from the oven and immediately curl over a cone shape or a wooden-spoon handle. It is important to bake only one tray at a time, as these biscuits tend to dry very quickly. If this happens, return the tray to the oven, only for a few minutes, to soften them.

Butter two 20 cm savarin moulds generously, sprinkle with praline to completely cover the inside. Fill with the prepared egg custard, place in a bain-marie, half-filled with warm water. Place in the oven to poach, until set. When cooked remove from the tray and allow to cool completely. Turn out onto serving dishes. Fill with whipped cream flavoured with vanilla. Fill the cornets, one per portion with cream. Place a small crystallised violet in each. Arrange the cornets on top of the pie.

CRÈME ST CLAIRE
Proceed as for crème renversée, to serve surround the crèmes with syrup sauce flavoured with kirsch.

CRÈME RÉGENCE
Proceed as for crème renversée, to serve surround the crèmes with caramel sauce.

CRÈME FLORENTINE
Proceed as for crème renversée, mixing praline into the egg custard. Decorate with rosettes of crème and pieces of croquante.

CRÈME OPÉRA
Follow the same method as for crème caramel, using savarin moulds instead of dariole moulds. Fill the centre with whipped cream and pieces of meringue (crème caprice).

CRÈME VIENNOISE
Flavour the egg custard with cold soft caramel, proceed as for crème renversée.

CRÈME AU CHOCOLAT
Flavour the egg custard by adding 100 g of finely chopped or grated chocolate to the milk. Produce and complete as for crème renversée. Decorate with chocolate coupeaux.

CRÈME AU CAFÉ
Flavour the egg custard with coffee and add coffee colour. Continue as for crème renversée. Decorate top with a marzipan coffee bean, or roasted almonds.

Diplomat pudding, *Pouding diplomat*

Sponge cake	200 g
Currants	100 g
Sultanas	100 g
Glacé cherries (diced)	50 g
Mixed peel	50 g
Egg custard (as for crème renversée)	
Whipped cream	
Strawberry coulis	

Grease and sugar 10 dariole moulds, add a small amount of the mixed fruit, half-fill with diced sponge. Add the remaining fruit, fill with the prepared egg custard. Poach as for crème renversée. When cold turn onto serving dishes, decorate with whipped cream, and serve with strawberry coulis round the pudding and some separately.

CABINET PUDDING, *POUDING CABINET*
Proceed as for diplomat pudding, serve hot with sauce anglaise separately.

8 SWEET OMELETTES AND PANCAKES

There are four traditional omelettes:
1 Omelette confiture (jam);
2 Omelette au liqueur;
3 Omelette aux fruits;
4 Omelette soufflé.

When making omelettes remember that one of the secrets of success is to serve immediately. It is better for the customer to wait for an omelette, than to let the omelette wait for the customer. The eggs used must be perfectly fresh or pasteurised. If fresh hens' eggs have to be used, care must be taken to avoid contamination (see p. 16). Government recommendations advise the avoidance of eating raw eggs, which means that omelettes must be thoroughly cooked. The temperature must reach 70 °C and be maintained for at least one minute.

Beat the yolks and whites of the eggs separately if a light spongy omelette is to desired. Or beat together, and very slightly, if a firmer omelette is preferred.

Keep a small pan for preparing omelettes only. It should never be washed after using. Before use, rub the pan well with paper, remove any particles of egg with salt, then heat a small piece of lard, and again rub with paper.

If the omelette is to have a filling, have this prepared and ready before starting to cook the eggs.

Melt and clarify the butter in the omelette pan. When very hot, pour in the eggs. As it begins to set, loosen the edges away from the pan with a fork.

For a plain sweet omelette, beat eggs with a little sugar, a pinch of salt and milk or cream if desired. When cooked, fold over in the pan to form a half-circle. A few minutes cooking is sufficient. If other ingredients are to be added, such as fruit, jam or liqueur, add the filling just before folding.

Jam omelette, *Omelette à la confiture*

Eggs	2
Pinch of salt	
Castor sugar	10 g
Milk or cream	10 g
Jam of choice	20 g
Castor or icing sugar to dust	
(Serves 1)	

Method 1:
Break the eggs into a basin and beat lightly, adding the sugar, milk and salt. Melt some butter in the pan, pour in the mixture and cook gently until set, loosening the edges with a fork. To make, ensure the eggs are thoroughly cooked, lift the edge of the omelette to allow the uncooked egg to flow underneath. When cooked, spread jam in the centre, fold over, place on a lightly buttered serving dish. Dredge with castor or icing sugar, then using a red-hot iron singe a trellis pattern on top, or place under the salamander. Serve immediately.

Method 2:
Proceed as for plain sweet omelette, place on buttered, hot serving dish, make a long incision lengthways on top. Using a paper cornet,

pipe jam into the incision. Glaze as before, and if desired decorate with coulis or fruit.

Step-by-step jam omelette

Fruit omelette, *Omelette aux fruits*

Eggs	2
Castor sugar	10 g
Pinch of salt	
Grated lemon	½
Apricot jam	10 g
Castor sugar to dust	
Fruit of choice	

Proceed as for jam omelette, adding fruit before folding.

Rum omelette, *Omelette au rhum*

Eggs	2
Pinch of salt	
Castor sugar	10 g
Grated lemon	½
Rum	10 g

Proceed as for plain omelette. Hot rum can be poured round it and flamed when serving.

Omelette soufflé, *Soufflé omelette*

Egg yolks	4
Egg whites	6
Vanilla flavour or lemon zest	
Castor sugar	300 g
(Serves 4)	

Advanced preparation of utensils, ingredients and serving dish is very important.

Whisk egg yolks with the flavouring and half of the sugar over a bain-marie to ribbon stage. Whisk the egg white until it peaks, then whisk in the second half of sugar, to form a stiff meringue. Shape into an oval in the centre of a serving dish. Decorate the dish using the remaining mix, in a piping bag with a star tube. Dredge with castor sugar. Cook at 200 °C until golden in colour. Serve immediately.

■ PANCAKES, *CRÊPES*

Pancakes have been eaten since the Middle Ages. It is one of the most versatile dishes. The making of pancakes is traditionally associated with Shrove Tuesday. The Church prescribes Absolution following Confession and Penance, so that eggs and butter are used up in preparation for the Lenten Fast.

Pancake batter, *Pâte à crêpe*

Flour	150 g
Salt	2 g
Eggs	2
Castor sugar	20 g
Milk	4 dl
Butter (noisette)	50 g
(Makes 20 pancakes)	

Sieve the flour and salt into a bowl, make a bay. Pour in the milk, add the sugar and eggs, draw in the flour and mix to a smooth texture. Allow to stand for 10–15 minutes (for the flour to absorb all of the liquid). Add the noisette butter.

It may be necessary to adjust the consistency, with extra milk, according to the size of the eggs and the quality and grade of flour used. The batter should be of a flowing texture.

Heat a little oil in the pancake pan, then drain off. Pour in enough batter to thinly cover the bottom of the pan, pouring into the centre and turning the pan so that the batter forms a disk.

Repeat the process over two, three or four pans. When the last one is done, the first one should be ready for turning over, either using a palette knife or tossing the pancake over. Continue until all the batter is used up, oiling the pans each time. Serve three per portion.

In a busy establishment, pancakes are often on the 'á la carte' menu. They should always be part of the mise-en-place kept in the pastry refrigerator. Always store well covered, to prevent from drying.

LEMON PANCAKES, *CRÊPES AU CITRON*
Dredge the pancakes with castor sugar, sprinkle sparingly with lemon juice, fold into four, place on a serving dish and dredge with castor sugar again. Place under the salamander just prior to serving with one wedge of lemon per portion of three pancakes.

JAM PANCAKES, *CRÊPES A LA CONFITURE*
Roll hot jam into the pancakes, place on the serving dish. Dredge with icing sugar, singe the surface with a hot poker in a trellis pattern.

SUZETTE PANCAKES, *CRÊPES SUZETTE*
Á la carte service only.

Dredge with castor sugar, place on a round silver dish. This dish is flambéd with Grand Marnier or cognac by the waiting staff in front of the customer using the flambé method. Serve with butter, oranges and lemons.

NORMANDY PANCAKES, *CRÊPES NORMANDE*
Place two spoonfuls of apple marmalade in the centre of the pancake, fold over two sides, place on a serving dish. Dredge with castor sugar, place under the salamander to glaze. Serve very hot, two pancakes per portion.

CRÊPES DU COUVENT
Prepare as for Normandy pancakes, filling with crème pâtissiére flavoured with Poire Williams and diced pears. Serve very hot.

CRÊPES GEORGETTE
Prepare as for Normandy pancakes, filling with crème pâtissiére flavoured with kirsch and diced pineapples.

CRÊPES À LA RUSSE
Prepare as for Normandy pancakes, filling with crème pâtissiére flavoured with kummel.

ICE CREAM PANCAKES, *CRÊPES GLACÉS*
Roll a rock shape of ice cream or sorbet, of any flavour, in chilled pancakes, serve immediately with a coulis of the same flavour as the ice cream.

A selection of pancakes

SOUFFLÉ PANCAKES, *CRÊPES SOUFFLÉS*

Prepare the cooked pancakes on a baking tray lined with silicone paper, place on each, two spoonfuls of soufflé mix (p. 96) and flavour as desired. Fold over, place in the oven at 204 °C, for 12 minutes. Transfer to a hot serving dish, serve immediately with an appropriate hot sauce, separately.

CHOCOLATE PANCAKES, *CRÊPES AU CHOCOLAT*

Prepare the pancakes, using chocolate and rum flavoured crème pâtissiére, complete as for Normandy pancakes.

ALMOND FLAVOURED PANCAKES, *CRÊPES AUX AMANDES*

Prepare the pancakes and almond flavoured crème pâtissiére, complete as for Normandy pancakes.

BLACK FOREST PANCAKES, *CRÊPES FORET NOIRE*

Prepare the pancakes, blend a little boiled apricot jam with well-drained black cherries and kirsch. Place two spoonfuls on each pancake, fold over. Dredge with castor sugar, singe with a hot poker. Serve on a hot serving dish, with coulis and few black cherries as garnish.

BITTER CHERRY PANCAKES, *CRÊPES AUX GRIOTTES*

Proceed as for Black Forest pancakes, using morello cherries.

9 FRITTERS, *BEIGNETS*

■ **Frying batter,** *Pâte à frire*

Flour	500 g
Salt	10 g
Castor sugar	50 g
Yeast	20 g
Water	5 dl
Egg yolks	3
Egg whites	3

Sieve the flour and salt into a bowl, make a bay in the centre. Dissolve the yeast with the water, pour into the bay, then add the sugar to dissolve. Draw in the flour and mix to a smooth texture using a whisk. Leave to rise, covered with a cloth, for about 20 minutes.

Whisk the egg white using a clean and scalded bowl, adding a little extra sugar if desired, to form a light meringue. Avoid over whisking as it will cause the meringue to grain. Fold the meringue into the proved batter. It is not ready for use in fruit fritters – banana, pineapple, apple, etc.

Apple fritters, *Beignets de pommes*

Frying batter	1 mix
Apples (eating)	10
Cider	3 dl
Lemon (zest and juice)	1
Castor sugar	
(Serves 10)	

Prepare the frying batter, allow to stand for about 20 minutes, until doubled in size. Peel and core the apples and slice each into four

Making apple fritters

rings, lay the slices in a dish and cover with the cider, lemon juice and zest. For best results allow to marinade for about 20 minutes, then drain off. Dip apple rings into the batter and place in the hot friture, at 190–200 °C, cook until coloured then turn over to colour the other side. To test, insert the point of a small knife into the fried rings, when cooked the knife should enter with ease. Drain off well and place on absorbent paper. When all the fritters are cooked, roll them in cinnamon sugar or plain castor sugar.

Serve 4–5 rings per portion on a serving dish lined with dish paper, and with a separate syrup sauce made from the cider, syrup and lemon zest, thickened with cornflour.

Banana fritters, *Beignets de bananes*

Frying batter	I mix
Bananas	10
Rum	
Lemon (zest and juice)	I
Vanilla essence	
(Serves 10)	

Prepare the batter and allow to stand for about 20 minutes. Peel and cut the bananas in half, lay them in a dish and marinade with rum and lemon juice. Continue following the same method as for apple fritters. Serve with apricot sauce flavoured with kirsch.

Pineapple fritters, *Beignets à l'ananas*

Frying batter	I mix (p. 81)
Pineapple	I
Castor sugar	
Kirsch	
(Serves 10)	

Prepare the batter and allow to stand for about 20 minutes. Remove the pineapple peel and cut into rings 1 cm thick, then cut rings in half. Lay the rings in a dish and marinade with kirsch. Continue as for apple fritters. Serve three pieces per portion, with a separate apricot sauce flavoured with kirsch.

■ SOUFFLÉ FRITTERS *BEIGNETS SOUFFLÉS*

Butter	125 g
Water	300 ml
Castor sugar	10 g
Strong flour	250 g
Vol (optional), pinch	
Eggs	7–8
Orange or rose-flower water to taste (optional)	
(Serves 10)	

Make choux paste as described on page 42. If vol is used, add just a pinch after the eggs are completely mixed in. The paste should have a firmish texture. Orange or rose-flower water, if used, enhances the flavour of the finished product and gives the soufflé a very pleasant aroma.

Two methods can be used for deep-frying the beignets:

1 Using a piping bag and a large tube, pipe oval shapes onto oiled strips of grease-proof paper, 5–6 per strip. Holding the ends of the strip of paper, dip it into the hot friture, slide out the paper, which can be used again, allowing the fritters to disperse in the oil. Do not over-fill the friture as the choux paste will swell considerably. Cook until nicely browned. The fritters will turn themselves over as they cook. Remove from the friture and place on a paper-lined tray, or a clean cloth. When cold, roll the fritters into castor sugar or cinnamon sugar.

2 Using two tablespoons, form roche shapes and place on strips of oiled paper, cook as described above.

The beignets can be filled as desired, using jam, crème pâtissière, or mincemeat. If served cold, serve with ice cream, or fresh whipped cream and fresh fruit.

BEIGNETS SOUFFLÉ À LA FLEUR D'ORANGE
As for the basic recipe adding orange-flower water to the choux paste and crème pâtissière. Serve with apricot sauce flavoured with kirsch.

STRAWBERRY SOUFFLÉ FRITTERS, *BEIGNETS AUX FRAISES*
Using strawberry compound, flavour sufficient crème pâtissière to fill the fritters.

Serve hot or cold accompanied with strawberry coulis.

RASPBERRY SOUFFLÉ FRITTERS, *BEIGNETS AUX FRAMBOISES*

As for strawberry using raspberries.

CHESTNUT SOUFFLÉ FRITTERS, *BEIGNETS AUX MARRONS*

As for the basic recipe, blending in an equal quantity of chestnut purée with the crème pâtissiére.

CHOCOLATE SOUFFLÉ FRITTERS, *BEIGNETS AU CHOCOLAT*

As for the basic recipe, blending melted couverture into the crème pâtissiére until a suitable flavour is attained. Serve with hot chocolate sauce.

COFFEE SOUFFLÉ FRITTERS, *BEIGNETS AU CAFÉ*

Proceed as for chocolate fritters, using coffee flavour in place of chocolate.

BEIGNETS SOUFFLÉS HELENE

Slice the top off the fritter, brush its base with boiled apricot jam. Place a scoop of ice cream inside the fritter. Replace the top, dredge with icing sugar. Serve with hot chocolate sauce separately.

BEIGNETS SOUFFLÉS PRALINE

As for the basic recipe, blending an equal quantity of crushed praline into the crème pâtissiére. Serve with praline-flavoured sauce.

◼ SWEET RAVIOLI, *BEIGNET AUX RAVIOLI SUCRE*

Sweet ravioli are popular in Italy at Easter. They are eaten not only as an after-dinner sweet, but between meals and in some areas of Italy at Easter Sunday breakfast. They are made more compactly than unsweetened ravioli, and the edges are fringed with a fork or fancy cutter.

Sweet ravioli are made with the same paste as the savoury type, and filled with flavoured crème pâtissiére (jam, crushed macaroons, praline, and chestnuts). They are cooked by dipping in hot oil, and as they are very small, they tend to cook within two or three minutes. They are rolled in castor sugar when cooked.

HONEY CRUMPLED RIBBONS, *CROSTOLI AU MIEL*

Roll out ravioli paste as for ravioli (p. 33), about 15 cm in length, 3 cm wide and 5 mm thick. Allow to rest covered for 10 minutes. Cook in hot oil until light in colour. During cooking the ravioli will curl up irregularly. Drain off well and allow to cool. Coat with melted honey and roll in roasted nibbed almonds or roasted coconut.

10 FRUIT DISHES

■ BUYING AND STORING OF FRESH FRUITS

In bygone days the chef was forced to depend almost entirely upon local and seasonal produce. Now that delivery services, including refrigerated methods of transportation, are so efficient, foreign fruits, and those that were unobtainable at certain seasons, are now available all the year round.

The pastry chef can easily detect whether the fruit delivered daily to the pastry kitchen is in good condition or not. With a little experience ripeness and quality of fruit can be established, mustiness or blemishes noticed. The quality of fruit with thick rinds such as oranges or lemons can be gauged principally by the weight. Choose a fruit that feels heavy for its size, firm and not flabby when pressed. A light-weight fruit of this kind generally contains a great deal of pith and peel. All soft fruit such as raspberries, strawberries, red and blackcurrants, loganberries and blueberries, should be as freshly picked as possible. Mustiness can develop very easily, starting from the centre of the panets, especially if packed in damp or wet conditions.

The best flavoured bananas are usually from the Canary Islands. These are of a deeper yellow than others, and are rounded at the end. Jamaican bananas are cheaper but not considered as good in flavour. They are firm and make very good fritters. They are recognised by their pointed ends.

Apples are the best fruit for keeping. There are numerous kinds to choose from, but, as a rule, the rough-skinned apples are better for desserts and the smooth-skinned for cooking.

There are several varieties of pears, but the two commonly used are the dessert pear, which is juicy and sweet, and stewing pears, which are rather hard to the touch and sometimes tasteless, but very good for cooking. The Comice pear, when ripe, does not need any cooking, and is normally available in the autumn.

Apricots should be used as freshly gathered as possible.

Gooseberries with hairy skins have the best flavour. The green and yellow varieties are sweeter when ripe than the red.

Pineapple is tested for ripeness by pressing just below the leaves, where it should be soft to the touch. If it is turning brown it is over ripe.

Fresh fruit salad, *Salade de fruits frais*

For the syrup:	
Granulated sugar	*500 g*
Water	*5 dl*
Lemon	*l*
Cinnamon stick	*l*

Bring all the ingredients to the boil, reaching a density of about 20 Baumé. Remove the lemon as it will tend to produce slight bitterness in the syrup if left in. Allow to cool before using.

Preparing the fruit:

Apples (eating), 1: Wash, peel, cut into thin slices, removing the core.

Oranges, 2: Peel and cut in segments, remove pith and inner skin.

Pears, 1: Wash, peel, cut into thin slices, removing the core.

Peaches, 1: Blanch to remove the skin, slice.

Grapes, 50 g: Remove skin and pips, cut larger grapes in half.

Strawberries, 50 g: Wash and remove the calyx, slice neatly.

Bananas, ½: Peel and slice (this should be done just before serving).

Pineapple, 1 ring: Remove the skin and core, cut in wedges.

Raspberries, 50 g: Wash and serve.

Mango, ½: Peel and cut into small slices, until the stone is reached.

Kiwi, 1: Peel and slice into neat rings.

Lightly mix the fruit and syrup together, place into timbales with crushed ice, or in a glass bowl. Keep in the refrigerator until ready for serving.

The addition of liqueurs, just before serving (sherry, marsala or madeira), will enhance the flavour.

Summer pudding *Pouding d'été*

Bread	10–12 slices
Black cherries	300 g
Redcurrants	300 g
Blackcurrants	200 g
Raspberries	400 g
Blackberries	300 g
Castor sugar	250 g
(Serves 10)	

Other fruits can be used to make summer pudding, but dark or black fruit should predominate, to maintain the traditional flavour and appearance.

Method 1: Wash the fruit, place in a saucepan with the sugar and gently heat, until a syrup is formed. For cooking time the quality of the fruit has to be taken into consideration. Trim the crusts from the bread, cut slices in half and dip in the fruit syrup. Line the bottom and sides of individual moulds with the bread. Fill with the mixed fruit, avoiding excessive syrup, pack the fruit in tightly and cover with a ring of bread (or the crust can be used). Allow the puddings to stand in the refrigerator for at least 8 hours, preferably overnight. Turn out the puddings onto serving dishes and serve chilled, with half whipped cream served separately.

Method 2: Using individual wine or champagne glasses, cut rings of bread to the same diameter as the glass. Place a small amount of the mixed fruit at the base of each glass, then a soaked ring of bread. Continue in layers to about 1 cm from the top of the glass. Allow to set overnight. Add a layer of fruit, mixed with boiled apricot jam, to the top, serve chilled with a rosette of whipped cream.

A pyramid made from individual summer puddings

Stewed fruits, *La compote de fruit* **and** Cooked fruits, *Fruits cuits*

Fruits can be cooked or poached either on the stove (simmered gently), or in the oven at 204 °C, covered with paper or a lid. Use the same stock syrup as described for fresh fruit salad. For compotes the fruit can either be used whole, or cut into halves or quarters.

COMPOTE OF SUMMER FRUIT *COMPOTE AUX FRUITS D'ÉTÉ*

Marinade blackcurrants, seedless grapes, redcurrants, raspberries and black cherries in crème de cassis, brandy and lemon juice. Sprinkle with granulated sugar, serve chilled in glass bowls or glasses.

APPROXIMATE WEIGHT FOR 10 PORTIONS SERVED IN COMPOTIERS OR GLASS BOWLS			
Fruit	Season	Weight	Method
Pears	Late summer	2½ kg	Wash, peel, allow to boil gently.
Apples	Late summer	2½ kg	Wash, peel, bring to the boil then poach in the oven, until just soft.
Oranges	All year	4 kg	Peel, slice into rings or leave whole, simmer on the stove or poach in oven.
Rhubarb	Winter	4 kg	Remove the skin, wash, bring to the boil, poach in the oven.
Pineapple	All year	2	Remove the skins, cut into rings, or half rings, boil gently.
Plums	Late summer	1½ kg	Wash, cook whole, bring to the boil, simmer in the oven.
Apricot	Summer	1½ kg	Wash, cut and remove the stones, boil gently.
Gooseberries	Mid-summer	2 kg	Pick off the ends, wash, bring to the boil, poach in the oven.
Cherries	Mid-summer	3 kg	Remove the stalks, wash, bring to the boil, simmer in the oven.
Peaches	Mid-summer	4 kg	Blanch, refresh, remove skin, simmer.
Blackberries	Late summer	2½ kg	Clean, remove stalks, wash, poach gently.

Baked apple dumplings

Baked apple dumplings

(Pommes habille, Pommes de chambre, Pommes en cage, or Pommes en robe.)

Moulding paste (p. 29)	*1 kg*
Cooking apples (small)	*12*
Cinnamon sugar	*500 g*
(Serves 12)	

Peel and core the apples. Roll the paste into an oblong shape, about 100 cm by 50 cm, egg-wash all over and place the whole peeled apples on the paste in three rows, allowing plenty of space in between each one. Cut the paste into squares around each apple. Fill the apples with plain or cinnamon sugar, currants, sultanas, glacé cherries, mincemeat, marzipan, or praline. Fold the corners of paste to the top of each apple and seal. Water-wash or egg-wash all over and place on a greased baking tray. Decorate the tops with fluted pieces of trimmed paste. Bake at 204 °C to a light brown colour, testing the apples by inserting a small knife; if it penetrates with ease they are cooked. Serve hot with a separate custard sauce.

Apple meringue, *Pomme meringue*

Swiss roll (cut in 10 rounds)	
Kirsch	
Apple purée	
Poached eating apples (whole)	10
Egg whites	3 dl
Cube or granulated sugar	200 g
(Serves 10)	

Lay the rounds of swiss roll onto serving dishes, well spaced, saturate with kirsch and place a spoonful of apple purée on each, then place a poached apple on top of each round. Make an Italian meringue (p. 164). Using a piping bag, pipe the meringue in a spiral from the base to the top of each apple. Dredge all over with castor sugar and bake at 204 °C until the meringue is light brown in colour.

Baked apples, *Pomme bonne femme*

Apples (Bramleys)	10
Brown sugar	750 g
Cider	5 dl
Sultanas	150 g
Granulated sugar	200 g
Butter	50 g
Glacé cherries	10
(Serves 10)	

Choose 10 unblemished apples of equal size.

Wash, core and slit skins, place into a deep tray or dish. Half-fill cores with sultanas, fill each well over the top with brown sugar, place a little butter on top. Pour the cider into the dish and cook in the oven at 204 °C. The slight opening of the slits indicates the apples are cooked. Insert the point of a small knife to test, if it penetrates with ease, they are fully baked. Remove from the oven and pour the syrup into a saucepan, add the granulated sugar and boil to reduce to a slightly thick consistency. Pour over the apples, top each with a glacé cherry and serve hot custard sauce separately.

The apple should be slightly browned on top, if this is not achieved during baking, place them under the salamander to glaze.

Alternate fillings can be used, such as, currants, glacé cherries, cinnamon sugar, marzipan or mincemeat.

Apple charlotte, *Charlotte de pommes*

Apple charlotte

The name charlotte derives from an older dish called 'Charlets', the composition of which was originally entirely different. It was the French chef Careme who designed the charlotte russe, and the apple charlotte developed from that.

Apples (Bramleys)	2 kl
Castor sugar	150 g
Cinnamon powder	25 g
Lemon (zest and juice)	1
Sliced bread	18 slices
Butter	250 g
(Serves 10)	

Wash and peel the apples, cut into thick slices. Using some of the butter slightly fry the apples adding the zest and juice of the lemon, add the sugar, cook for a few moments to caramelise the syrup. Place aside. Remove the crust from the bread, cut six slices into triangles of four, and the rest in rectangular halves. Dip the slices in the melted butter, line the base of the mould with the triangles, and arrange the half slices around the sides, sealing them together. Fill with the apples ensuring the mould is well compacted. Place bread crust on top, just to prevent discoloration of the apples. Place the mould on a tray and bake in the oven at 204 °C, until the slices of bread on the side are slightly toasted. Remove from the oven allow to stand for five minutes, to settle the juices, then remove the crust and turn out the sweet onto a serving dish. Brush all over with boiled apricot jam, serve with apricot sauce flavoured with kirsch.

Apple strudel, *Apfel strudel*

(An Austrian speciality.)

For the paste:	
Flour	200 g
Salt	10 g
Egg yolks	2
Water	50 g
Olive oil	10 g
For the filling:	
Apples (eating)	2 kl
Breadcrumbs	100 g
Ground almonds	50 g
Castor sugar	150 g
Cinnamon	20 g
Sultanas	100 g
(Serves 10)	

Sieve the flour and salt onto a clean surface, make a bay and place in the centre the water, yolks and olive oil. Draw in the flour and mix to an elastic texture. Flatten the dough to a baton shape and rub oil over it, place into a polythene bag and allow to rest for about 30 minutes. Prepare the filling by washing, peeling and dicing the apples, mix in a bowl with the breadcrumbs, almonds, sugar and cinnamon. Partly roll out the paste, using a little dusting flour, then continue rolling the dough on a clean floured cloth, until the paste is fully stretched and is semi-transparent, maintaining a square shape. Evenly spread the apple mixture over the paste, sprinkle with sultanas. Holding the cloth with both hands, roll up, sealing in the filling. Place onto a lightly greased tray. Leave to rest for 10 minutes. Bake in the oven at 204 °C for about 30 minutes, occasionally brushing over with oil – this will improve the colour while baking. Serve hot or cold on a serving dish lined with a dish paper with a separate apricot sauce, flavoured with kirsch.

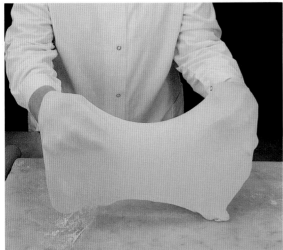

Step-by-step apple strudel

■ FRUIT PASTES, *PÂTES AUX FRUITS*

Apricots, peaches, cooking apples, quinces, pears are all suitable for fruit pastes. The fruit should be of good sound quality and ripe, picked over to remove any bruised areas. Wash the fruit thoroughly. Add to boiling water and cook gently until just soft, do not over cook. Allow to drain and cool over a wire sieve, pass the fruit pulp through the sieve and return it to the saucepan. Add an equal weight of sugar to fruit used, boil until it threads, about 107 °C. It is important not to over-beat the paste while reheating as it will quickly become cloudy. Pour the paste into another container, allow to cool. When cold it will set like a jelly, and will be very useful for all kinds of confectionery, especially those covered with fondant.

These pastes are a necessity for the pastry chef, and should be part of the routine mise-en-place, stored in the refrigerator covered with a lid. They can be used for glazing of gâteaux and pastries, and as filling for flans, gâteaux, tarts, turnovers, and pastries. Liqueurs can be added which complement the fruit used.

Pectin

Fruit pastes, pulp, purées or jellies, are made from reduction of the flesh of the fruit, mixed with sugar until a marmalade is formed. It is important to note that some fruits will achieve a finer gelatinised texture than others. The firmness of the jellying texture depends on the amount of both acids pectin present in the fruit.

Pectin is a water-soluble carbohydrate found in most fruits. It is a macromolecular substance which, when hydrolysed, yields galacturonic acid, galactose, arabinose and acetic acid. The fruits containing most pectin are apples, crab apples, brambles, blackcurrants, gooseberries, damsons, quinces, plums, grapes, oranges, cranberries, grapefruit and lemons. Fruit with a medium pectin content are blackberries, apricots, greengages, loganberries, and raspberries. Fruit with poor pectin content include cherries, pears, rhubarb, strawberries, peaches and pineapples. Fruits low in acid are sweet apples, quinces, bilberries, strawberries, raspberries, peaches and pears.

Fruits with poor pectin content can only be made into gels if they are mixed with some other fruits or fruit juices strong in pectin; alternatively a small amount of diluted cornflour or arrowroot boiled in the solution can stabilise the purée sufficiently for use as paste.

PECTIN TEST
Simmer the fruit pulp without sugar, then place a teaspoon of juice in a small container and allow to cool. Add a tablespoon of methylated spirit, shake well, stand for one minute, a transparent clot should form. If the clot is jelly-like then the pectin content is high. If there are a number of small clots or none at all then the pectin content is low – extra pectin is needed.

ADDING PECTIN
Commercial pectin can be available from suppliers, or obtained from the chemist. Always add according to the maker's instructions.

For strawberry, raspberry and pear pastes, adding one or two grated apples to the mix will supply sufficient pectin and will not impair the flavour.

AGAR-AGAR
Agar-agar is a dried, red seaweed, which grows along the shores of Japan and some American coast-lines. It can be purchased in powdered or flaky form. It is classified as a reinforcing agent, which can be added to natural jelly solution, giving it a piping consistency. It has similar properties to pectin.

Agar-agar has to be soaked in plenty of water for about ten hours, until most of the water is absorbed, before adding to other ingredients. Only dilute the amount required. It is mainly used for glazing or piping solutions.

Jelly

Granulated sugar	1 kg
Fruit syrup	1 kg
Pectin	4–5 g
Lemon juice	2–3 g

Thoroughly mix and sieve about 20 g of the sugar with the pectin. Very lightly warm the syrup then rain in the sugar mixture, whisking to dissolve, add the remaining sugar and bring to the boil. Reduce the heat, continue boiling until the mixture reaches 108–110 °C, check the temperature using a sugar thermometer. Allow to cool. Add the lemon juice. Store in sterile sealed containers. Use for glazing flans, tartlets, gâteaux, etc.

Fruits of high acidity will not require any lemon juice.

Compoting dried fruits, *Compotes de fruits secs*

Fruits such as prunes, apples, apricots, peaches, pears and figs can be used. 1½ kg of dried fruit will be required to produce 10 portions. Wash the fruit in cold water, place into a container adding three times the amount of water to fruit, cover with a lid. Allow to soak for about 24 hours, the fruit should then be fully swollen and soft. Drain off the water and place into a deep tray or saucepan, cover with syrup and cook, simmering gently until the fruit is soft. These compotes are served as a dessert for lunch or dinner, with cream or custard sauce, or often as an accompaniment to milk puddings, junkets and egg custard dishes. They are also served as breakfast, and even mixed with the cereal.

FRAISES ROMANOFF
Place washed strawberries in a timbale, sprinkle with sugar, pour curaçao over and cover with slightly whipped double cream. Sprinkle the top with crushed crystallised, rose petals or violets. Serve with shortbread biscuits.

PEARS IN RED WINE, *POIRES AU VIN ROUGE*
Use good quality, firm pears, preferably Williams. Wash and core, extracting the core from the base only. Peel the pear scraping the stalk clean, but leaving it attached to the pear. Bring to the boil equal quantities of stock syrup and full-bodied red wine, add a little cochineal, add the pears, bring back to the boil and allow to simmer. When nearly cooked add a small amount of diluted cornflour or fecule to just slightly thicken the syrup, continue cooking until the pears are just soft. Serve in a compotier or glass bowl, with the syrup reaching half-way up the pears.

POIRE À LA BOURDALOUE
Wash, peel, core, cut in half the pears and cook until soft. Drain and lay the pears in a deep serving dish, brush all over with boiled apricot jam, sprinkle the top heavily with crushed macaroon biscuits. Cover completely with crème pâtissiére. Allow to set, sprinkle with crushed praline, dredge with icing sugar and glaze under the salamanader, to just colour. Serve hot in the same dish.

LA CHÂTELAINE
Place a layer of chestnuts in the base of a deep serving dish. Coat with boiled apricot jam cooked in rum-flavoured syrup. Cover with crème pâtissiére, finish in the same manner as bourdaloue.

FRAISES À LA WALDORF
Pick out hulls and wash the strawberries, place in a serving dish. Completely cover with strawberry mousse, decorate with rosettes of cream and sprinkle with crushed, crystallised rose petals.

FRAISES À LA MONTE CARLO

Pick out the hulls and wash the strawberries. Place in a serving dish, sprinkle with brandy and cover with mousse flavoured with benedictine. Decorate with rosettes of cream and strawberries.

APRICOT ROMAINE

Make a semolina pudding (p. 64), flavoured with orange-flower water. Pour into a serving dish, arrange apricots (two halfs per portion), on top, brush with apricot glaze, decorate with rosettes of cream, glacé cherries and angelica.

POIRE D'AREMBERG

Poach the pears whole removing the stalk and the core at the base. Arrange the pears, filled with redcurrant jam, on tampions of swiss roll cut in 1 cm slices. Cover with aremberg sauce (p. 137). Pipe a spiral of redcurrant jelly from the base to the top. Place on serving dishes, decorate with rosettes of cream and roasted flaked almonds.

Poire d'aremberg

POIRE/POMME JEANNETTE

Arrange 6 cm rounds of sponge on a serving dish, spaced apart. Saturate with kirsch, place

a mound of cooked rice on top, then a poached apple or pear filled with raspberry jam. Pipe a spiral of Italian meringue around the base of each fruit to the top. Decorate the dish with more meringue, dredge with castor sugar, place in the oven to glaze. Serve hot or cold.

Pomme jeanette

FRUIT DIABOLO

Arrange the chosen fruit (pears, peaches, or apricots) on chocolate tampions, cover with chocolate ganache sauce, flavoured with rum. Place onto serving dishes and decorate with whipped cream and chocolate copeaux.

POIRES À LA PRINCESSE

Half-fill individual dishes with rice condé, place poached pears filled with praline crème pâtissiére on top. Cover with strawberry cream sauce, decorate with cream. Place a veil of spun sugar on top.

POIRES À LA MALTAISE

Half-fill individual serving dishes with rice condé, flavoured with orange zest and curaçao. Place a half poached pear on top of each, and two segments of orange. Cover with apricot sauce mixed with fine julienne of orange zest. Decorate with whipped cream.

SICILIAN PEACHES, *PÊCHES SICILIENNE*

Poach 10 firm peaches in syrup and maraschino until just soft. Remove skins and stones, replace the stone with crushed ratafia biscuits mixed with marzipan and place the peaches on tampions of sponge on a draining wire. Cover completely with double thick custard (p. 136), allow to set, brush all over with boiled apricot jam. Arrange the peaches onto serving dishes, sprinkle the tops with julienne of orange and a diamond of angelica. Serve hot or cold with syrup sauce made from the poaching syrup.

SICILIAN PEARS, *POIRES SICILIENNE*

Proceed as for peaches, removing the cores and stalks of the pears.

ANANAS FARCIS AUX FRUITS

Slice the top off a pineapple, remove the flesh by passing a small knife round the inside of the skin, discard the core. Dice pineapple and melon, add slices of peach and strawberry, marinade the fruit in a liqueur of choice, adding sugar to sweeten. Fill the pineapple shell with fruit, replace the lid, serve chilled on a dish surrounded with a serviette.

MELON FARCI AU PORTO/MARSALA

Use either a cantaloupe or gallia melon. Slice the melon in half, scoop out the pulp leaving an empty shell, discard the seeds. Dice the pulp and marinade in either port or marsala wine. Fill shells with the marinaded fruit and serve chilled, with plenty of granulated sugar on top. Place on a serving dish surrounded with a serviette.

ORANGE FARCI AU COINTREAU

Choose oranges with firmish skins, slice off the tops, scoop out the orange pulp from the shell. Dice the orange flesh removing the piths, marinade the diced fruit in cointreau, add sufficient sugar to sweeten, refill the orange shells with the marinaded fruit. Serve chilled on a serving dish with a serviette.

■ FRUIT FOOL

This is one of England's most elegant cold sweets, but it was also very popular throughout Europe in the Tudor times, especially when delicate fruits were available.

Fruit fools are made with combined quantities of fresh fruit purée, thick custard, and double cream. Colour, fruit compound and liqueurs can be added to improve the quality of the dish. Fresh fruit coulis and shortbread biscuits are served as an accompaniment.

Fruits suitable for use are: strawberries, raspberries, gooseberries, bananas, blackcurrants, fresh figs, persimmon, melon, apples, peaches, apricots, cherries, blackberries, rhubarb and kiwi.

11 SOUFFLÉS

■ HOT SOUFFLÉS, *SOUFFLÉS CHAUDS*

Soufflé pudding, *Pouding soufflé*

Soufflés are commonly served in hotels and restaurants for their special characteristic texture, flavour and the highly-skilled techniques needed in the production and service. The *pouding soufflé* is made by the buerré-manier method, which provides a cohesive texture in the mixture and therefore facilitates their production and service.

Vanilla Soufflé Pudding, *Pouding soufflé vanille*

Milk	1 ℓ
Vanilla flavour to taste	
Castor sugar	150 g
Butter	150 g
Flour	150 g
Eggs	15
(Serves 20)	

Grease 20 dariole moulds and dust the insides with sugar. Make the beurré manier by rubbing the butter into the flour (avoid making a paste). Boil the milk, remove from the heat and immediately add the flour mixture, stirring with a wooden spatula until well mixed and cohesive. Allow the mixture to cool. Separate the egg yolks from the whites. Whisk the yolks and half the sugar. In another bowl, scalded in hot water and not dried, whisk the whites until they peak, continue whisking adding the second amount of sugar to form a light but firm meringue. Fold the yolks into the cooked paste, then fold in the meringue, in two or three stages, maintaining as much volume as possible.

Using a piping bag, three-quarter fill the dariole moulds with the mixture. Place the moulds in a deep tray, half-filled with *hot* water (bain-marie). Place the tray over the stove and just bring to the boil. Cover with another tray, or greaseproof paper, and place in the stove at 204 °C. Allow to cook until well-risen and slightly coloured on top.

If not to be served immediately, return the tray to the stove on a very low heat, keep covered. Ensure the water level is maintained, so that the soufflés will not lose height before serving. Turn the soufflés out of the moulds onto the serving dishes and keep covered until they reach the customer. Serve with vanilla sauce or sauce anglaise separately.

LEMON SOUFFLÉ PUDDING, *POUDING SOUFFLÉ AU CITRON*
(also known as Pudding soufflé saxon)
Follow the same method as for vanilla pudding soufflé, adding finely grated zest of four lemons to the yolks when whisking with half the sugar. Serve with orange sauce or sauce anglaise.

ORANGE SOUFFLÉ PUDDING, *POUDING SOUFFLÉ A L'ORANGE*
As for lemon pudding soufflé using orange zest. Cointreau to taste.

CHESTNUT SOUFFLÉ PUDDING, *POUDING SOUFFLÉ AUX MARRONS*

Proceed as for vanilla pudding soufflé, whisking purée of chestnuts into the egg yolk mixture. Serve with sauce anglaise in a timbale of crystallised chestnuts sprinkled with kirsch.

POUDING SOUFFLÉ MALTAISE

As for orange pudding soufflé, adding 30 ml of curaçao to the egg yolk and sugar mix. Liqueur-saturated cubes of sponge can be folded into the completed mix. Compotes of oranges sprinkled with curaçao can be served with this, or serve with orange sauce.

POUDING SOUFFLÉ MONTMORENCY

Follow the same method as for soufflé pudding maltaise, mixing 100 g of diced glacé cherries with the yolks mix, and a timbale of poached cherries marinaded in kirsch. Serve with apricot sauce flavoured with kirsch.

CHOCOLAT PUDDING SOUFFLÉ, *POUDING SOUFFLÉ AU CHOCOLAT*

Proceed as for vanilla pudding, melting 100 g of chocolate couverture in the milk before the boiling stage is reached. Serve with hot chocolate sauce.

POUDING SOUFFLÉ À L'INDIENNE

Follow the same method as for vanilla pudding soufflé, adding 60 g of ginger powder to the flour and 60 g of finely chopped ginger to the egg yolk mix. Serve with ginger sauce or ginger syrup sauce.

POUDING SOUFFLÉ SANS-SOUCI

Proceed as for vanilla pudding soufflé, sieving 60 g of mixed spice with the flour and adding 100 g of currants. Serve with apricot sauce and a timbale of apple compote.

POUDING SOUFFLÉ VESUVIENNE

Cook the vanilla soufflé mix in a well greased savarin mould, when serving pour a chosen liqueur in the centre and set alight.

Pouding soufflé peruvienne

Semolina pudding	1 mix (p. 64)
Egg yolks	5
Egg whites	5
Crystallised fruit	150 g
(cherries, apricots, pears)	
Orange-flower water to taste (optional)	
Grand Marnier	50 g

Whisk the yolks with half the sugar, add the crystallised fruit. Whisk the egg whites to peaks, gradually add the rest of the sugar, continuing to whisk to a meringue. Add the orange-flower water and Grand Marnier. Fold the egg yolk mixture into the warm semolina pudding. Fold in the meringue, maintaining as much volume as possible. Spoon into the greased dariole moulds. Cook and serve as for vanilla pudding soufflé. Serve with vanilla sauce.

■ SOUFFLÉS

There are two basic soufflé recipes, one using a base of crème pâtissiére and the other of fruit purée. Unlike the pudding soufflés, these soufflés are cooked in a soufflé dish and must be served immediately. If delayed, the soufflé will collapse and will not be servable. In practice, the waiter should wait for the soufflé and not the soufflé wait for the waiter.

Timing in cooking soufflés is also very important; normally a customer ordering soufflé should inform the waiter at the early stage of the meal, so that adequate time is available for the cooking.

For two portions soufflé, allow 25–30 minutes; three or four portions, allow 30–40 minutes; five or six portions, allow 40–45 minutes. If eight portions are to be produced, then it is advisable to prepare and present the soufflé in two four portion dishes, and so on.

Vanilla soufflé, *Soufflé vanille*

Crème pâtissiére	4 tablespoons (p. 130)
Vanilla flavour to taste	
Egg yolks	4
Egg whites	6
Castor sugar	100 g
Butter	50 g
(Serves 4)	

Orange soufflé with Cointreau to taste

Grease and sugar a soufflé dish. Slightly warm the crème pâtissiére in a large sauteuse. With a wooden spoon stir in the yolks, butter and vanilla. Whisk the egg whites (in a scalded bowl), to stiff peaks, gradually add the sugar, forming a light but firm meringue. Avoid over-whisking the meringue, as it will become grainy in texture and unsuitable for folding.

Fold the meringue into the first mixture, maintaining as much volume as possible. Pour into the prepared soufflé dish. Place the dish on a tray, cook in the oven at 170–190 °C, until the soufflé is risen and has a light brown surface. There is no need to open the oven door for at least the first 15 minutes, do not leave the oven door open longer than necessary. Serve immediately.

ORANGE SOUFFLÉ, *SOUFFLÉ À L'ORANGE*
Proceed as for vanilla soufflé adding the zest of two oranges and spoonful of orange compound (if available) to the crème pâtissiére mix. Cook as vanilla soufflé.

LEMON SOUFFLÉ, *SOUFFLÉ AU CITRON*
As for orange soufflé using lemon zest instead of orange.

SOUFFLÉ AU LIQUEUR
Proceed as for vanilla soufflé adding 50 g of liqueur (Grand Marnier, curaçao, kirsch, grenadine, anisette, kummel, Cointreau, etc.) to the crème pâtissiére. Saturate either diced finger-biscuits or sponges, fold into the mix. Name the soufflé after the liqueur used.

CHOCOLATE SOUFFLÉ, *SOUFFLÉ AU CHOCOLAT*
Proceed as for vanilla soufflé, adding sufficient melted chocolate couverture to give adequate colour and flavour.

SOUFFLÉ À L'ARLEQUIN
Grease and sugar the soufflé dish, cut a card to fit vertically across the centre of the dish. Produce two soufflé mixtures, chocolate and vanilla. Pour both mixtures at the same time on either side of the card, remove the card from the dish. Cook as for vanilla soufflé.

SOUFFLÉ ELIZABETH

Using the basic vanilla soufflé mix, alternate with layers of crushed macaroons, saturated with kirsch. Cook as for vanilla soufflé and serve immediately with a veil of spun sugar, sprinkled with chopped, crystallized violets.

HAZELNUTS SOUFFLÉ, *AVELINES SOUFFLÉ*

Proceed as for vanilla soufflé adding 100 g of crushed praline to the crème pâtissiére. Cook as for vanilla soufflé.

Compote of fruit or fresh fruit salad can be served as an accompaniment with any of the above soufflés.

Rice soufflé, *Soufflé à la Francaise*

Rice condé half recipe (p. 68)	
Egg yolks	4
Egg whites	4
Castor sugar	120 g
(Serves 10)	

Prepare the rice condé, flavour with orange-flower water if desired. While still warm stir in the egg yolks. Whip the egg whites, add the sugar and whip a light meringue. Very gently fold the meringue into the rice mixture to maintain the volume as much as possible. Pour the prepared mixture into greased and sugared soufflé moulds, to about threequarters full. Place the dishes into a moderate oven, 185–200 °C. For a 15 cm soufflé dish the soufflé will be cooked in about 30–35 minutes. When cooked the soufflés should be well risen, about 1½ cm above the rim of the dish and still whitish on its sides. Serve immediately, with a separate kirsch-flavoured apricot sauce.

Fruit soufflé, *Soufflé aux fruits*

Crème pâtissiére	2 tablespoons	(p. 133)
Fruit purée 2 tablespoons		
Colour (optional)		
Egg yolks	4	
Egg whites	6	
Castor sugar	100 g	
Juice of one lemon juice		
(Serves 4)		

Grease and sugar the soufflé moulds. Warm the crème pâtissiére and the chosen fruit purée add the colour, if needed. Continue following the same preparation, cooking and serving methods as for vanilla soufflé.

FRUIT PURÉE

Strawberries, raspberries, peaches, mangoes, pomegranate, oranges, pineapple, bananas, coconut and pawpaw can all be used. Bring fruit to the boil, then liquidise the sieved fruit. Add 200 g of granulated sugar, add the juice of 1 lemon, allow to simmer for about 20 minutes until the purée is well reduced and most of the moisture is evaporated. Add colour if needed.

SOUFFLÉ LUCULLUS

Soak a 20 cm savarin, flavour with kirsch, place onto a serving dish, wrapped in silicone paper to prevent from drying. Fill the centre with the prepared chosen fruit soufflé. Place in the oven to cook, serve immediately with a timbale of sliced fresh fruit as used in the soufflé, marinaded in kirsch. Serve with hot fruit sauce flavoured with kirsch.

SOUFFLÉ ROTHSCHILD

Line the base of the soufflé dish with genoese soaked in curaçao, complete the soufflé by blending curaçao into the basic mix. Cook and serve as before.

■ COLD SOUFFLÉS, *SOUFFLÉS FROIDS*

Orange soufflé, *Soufflé à l'orange*

Egg yolks	6
Castor sugar	200 g
Oranges	5
Fresh cream	6 dl
Egg whites	6
Castor sugar	100 g
Gelatine	25 g
(Serves 10)	

Prepare the soufflé moulds by tying a strip of greaseproof paper on the outside with a string, 3 cm higher than the top of the mould. Place the gelatine to soak in cold water. Produce a sabayon (p. 73) using the yolks, first sugar and fruit juice and zest. Dilute the gelatine and gradually add to the hot sabayon mixture, colour and compound, if used, can also be added at this stage. Allow to cool, but not set. Make a firm meringue, using the egg whites and second sugar, avoid over-whisking, as this will result in a grainy texture. Whisk the cream and fold into the cold sabayon, then fold in the meringue in three stages, maintaining as much volume as possible.

Pour the mix into the prepared dishes, smooth the tops. When set and ready for service, remove the paper from the sides, cover the exposed soufflé sides with either roasted almonds, roasted coconut, or roasted cakecrumbs. Decorate the top with rosettes of whipped cream, segments of oranges and a timbale of compotes of oranges, cooked in Cointreau syrup, 22° Baumé.

Fresh fruit salad can be served as an accompaniment, sprinkled with kirsch. A finger biscuit will also enhance the presentation of cold soufflés.

LEMON SOUFFLÉ, *SOUFFLÉ MILANAISE*
Proceed as for orange soufflé, using lemons instead of oranges.

Lemon soufflé with individual portions

FRUIT SOUFFLÉ, *SOUFFLÉ AUX FRUIT FROID*
Prepare fruit purée as described for hot fruit soufflé, add 3 dl of purée, plus compound and liqueur to the sabayon mixture, continue as for orange soufflé.

CHOCOLATE SOUFFLÉ, *SOUFFLÉ AU CHOCOLAT FROID*
Add 200 g of chocolate couverture to melt with the sabayon mixture, 50 g of rum can also be added. Continue as for orange soufflé, decorate the top with 'grands copeaux de chocolat' (large chocolate scrapings). Serve with chocolate sauce separately.

12 BAVARIAN CREAMS, *BAVAROIS*

Bavarian creams were originally a frothy drink served to the Bavarian aristocracy. It then mainly consisted of a foundation of fresh seasonal fruit. The drink eventually found its way, through the nobility, across Europe, changes were made with the addition of egg yolks, milk, cream, and liqueurs. Whipped cream is of primary importance in the production of bavarois. Although various creams are available to the pastry chef, whipping cream contains 35% fat and its greater viscosity and density helps form a suitable emulsion and a stable foam when whisking. Creams containing less fat seldom reach the desired thickness. Whipping cream normally whips up to twice its original volume.

Cream must be whipped under the correct conditions; during whisking the fat increases in firmness as the temperature is lowered, 5 °C is usually the best temperature for maintaining the whipping properties. All utensils to be used must be clean and cool.

Over-whipping cream will cause the separation of the fat and water, and the cream will 'break'. If even slightly over-whisked the cream will become grainy in texture, which will create difficulties when mixing with other ingredients.

All fresh cream dishes must be used within the same day of production. Fresh cream items must not be kept out of the refrigerator for more than three hours, nor should they be returned to the refrigerator for further use.

Synthetic or mock cream consists of an emulsion of fat and milk powder, stabilised by the addition of emulsifying agents. It is often used in the production of bavarois, as it easily increases in volume, as well as being economically advantageous.

Bavarois are produced in two ways, either based on sauce anglaise, or on fruit and syrup.

■ SAUCE ANGLAISE-BASED BAVAROIS

Vanilla Bavarian cream, *Bavarois à la vanille*

Egg yolks	5
Castor sugar	75 g
Milk	3 dl
Leaf gelatine	25 g
Cream	4 dl
Vanilla flavour	
(Serves 10)	

Place the leaf gelatine in cold water to soak. Using a wooden spatula cream together the yolks, sugar and a little of the cold milk. Produce the sauce anglaise by bringing the remaining milk to the boil with the vanilla flavour, add to the egg yolk mixture, stir well and return to a low heat. Stirring continually, poach until the mixture slightly thickens and just coats the spoon. Whisk in the soft, drained gelatine, strain into a clean, large bowl, allow to cool completely.

Whisk the cream until it peaks, fold into the sauce anglaise mixture in three stages, avoid over mixing. Pour into charlotte or dariole moulds. Allow to set in the refrigerator for at least 45 minutes. Demould by immersing the mould into warm water for a few moments, turn out into serve dishes. Decorate by piping whipped cream on top and serve with, for example, sugar decorations, biscuits, fresh fruit. Keep in the refrigerator until the bavarois is required for service.

Alternatively, the mixture can be poured in glasses or torten rings and decorated in a similar way.

BAVARIAN CHOCOLATE CREAM, *BAVAROIS AU CHOCOLAT*

Proceed as for vanilla, adding 100 g of grated or finely chopped chocolate couverture to the sauce anglaise.

BAVARIAN COFFEE CREAM, *BAVAROIS AU CAFÉ*

Proceed as for vanilla adding sufficient coffee flavour until the correct colour and flavour is attained.

Bavarian chocolate cream

BAVARIAN RIBBONED CREAM, *BAVAROIS RUBANÉ*

Prepare three differently coloured and flavoured bavarois mixtures (e.g. vanilla, chocolate and strawberry). Layer in the moulds alternatively, allowing each one to set before adding the next.

BAVAROIS ARLEQUIN

Insert a piece of card in the prepared mould. Fill one side with a chocolate mixture and the other with vanilla, remove card to set.

BAVARIAN CHESTNUT CREAM, *BAVAROIS AUX MARRONS*

Add 100 g of chestnut purée to the sauce anglaise, when cooked. Decorate with whipped cream and pieces of marron glacé.

BAVAROIS AUX LIQUEURS

Proceed as for any of the bavarois mentioned above, adding 100 g of the chosen liqueur to the sauce anglaise when cooked.

■ FRUIT-BASED BAVAROIS

Raspberry Bavarian cream, *Bavarois aux framboises*

Raspberry purée	3 dl
Castor sugar	75 g
Red colouring (optional)	
Leaf gelatine	25 g
(Serves 10)	

Soak the gelatine in cold water. Boil the purée and sugar together, add colouring if necessary. Whisk in the soaked and drained gelatine, strain into a large bowl and allow to cool. Whisk the cream until it peaks, fold into the cold fruit mixture. Pour into the moulds, and continue as for vanilla bavarois. Decorate with whipped cream and slices of fruit. Serve with a coulis made from the same fruit used.

For other fruit bavarois follow the same recipe and method using the desired fruit purée.

Chartreuse aux fruits

Line (chemiser) charlotte moulds with lemon-flavoured jelly (p. 108). When the jelly is set, line the inside (base and sides) with the desired fruit, dipping it first into the jelly. Nearly fill the mould with layers of fruit bavarois mix and slices of dipped fruit. Allow to set, then turn out onto a dish lined with set lemon-flavoured jelly. Decorate with whipped cream and slices of the fruit used.

Chartreuse aux fraises	(strawberries)
Chartreuse d'abricots	(apricots)
Chartreuse aux pêches	(peaches)
Chartreuse aux bananes	(bananas)
Chartreuse a l'ananas	(pineapples)
Chartreuse aux raisins	(grapes)
Chartreuse aux cerises	(cherries)

When using tinned fruits for chartreuses, it is preferable to bring them just to the boil, then drain well before using. This will destroy the tinny taste and removes any acid the fruit contains.

13 MOUSSES

Mousse preparations follow the same principles as bavarois. Mousses differ only by being much lighter in texture, which is achieved by the addition of meringue. For the best results Italian meringue should be used, as this will give a lighter and firmer consistency.

As for bavarois, mousses are produced in two ways, based on sauce anglaise and based on fruit and syrups.

The richness in mousses can be enhanced with generous amounts of liqueur, compounds of fruit and flavours. Although mousses are designed to be served either chilled or frozen, it is advisable to use them on the same day of production.

Mousses can be prepared in torten rings, using sponge or japonaise bases and decorated with rosettes of cream and other garnishes. Alternatively the mixture can be poured into wine or champagne glasses, and again decorated accordingly. Serving shortbread, brandy snaps, palettes des dames or finger biscuits, with each portion nicely completes the dish.

Vanilla mousse, *Mousse à la vanille*

Egg yolks	4
Castor sugar	100 g
Milk	3 dl
Vanilla flavour to taste	
Leaf gelatine	25 g
Fresh cream	5 dl
Egg whites	3
Cube or granulated sugar	100 g
(Serves 10)	

Soak the leaf gelatine in cold water. Using a wooden spatula, cream together the yolks, sugar and a little of the cold milk. Produce the sauce anglaise by bringing the rest of the milk to the boil, add the vanilla flavour and yolk mixture, stir well and return to a low heat. Stirring continually, poach until the mixture slightly thickens and just coats the spoon. Whisk in the soft, drained gelatine, strain into a clean large bowl, allow to cool.

Whisk the cream until it just peaks, place in the refrigerator. Saturate and cook the cube sugar to 120 °C. Whisk the egg whites to peaks, making sure the sugar is ready at the same time. Very slowly but continuously pour in the boiled sugar while whisking. Continue until the meringue is firm. Fold the whipped cream into the cold sauce anglaise, then fold in the Italian meringue (p. 164) in three stages.

Pour the mixture into the prepared glasses or torten rings. Place in the refrigerator to set, approximately one hour. Demould when set. If torten rings are used, decorate the tops with rosettes of whipped cream, any chosen decorations and biscuits.

COFFEE MOUSSE, *MOUSSE AU CAFÉ*
Proceed as for vanilla mousse, replacing the vanilla with coffee flavour, until the correct flavour and colour is attained.

CINNAMON CHOCOLATE MOUSSE, *MOUSSE CHOCOLAT À LA CANELLE*
Proceed as for vanilla mousse, substituting chocolate and adding two cinnamon sticks to the milk, complete as for vanilla mousse.

Chocolate mousse, *Mousse au chocolat*

Egg yolks	4
Castor sugar	75 g
Milk	3 dl
Couverture	100 g
Leaf gelatine	25 g
Fresh cream	5 dl
Egg whites	3
Cube or granulated sugar	100 g
(Serves 10)	

Proceed as for vanilla mousse, adding the finely chopped or grated chocolate to the milk, boil together. Decorate with rosettes of whipped cream and chocolate copeaux.

Fruits mousse, *Mousse aux fruits*

Fruit purée	350 g
Castor sugar	100 g
Colour	
Leaf gelatine	25 g
Fresh cream	5 dl
Egg whites	4
Cube or granulated sugar	100 g
(Serves 10)	

Bring the fruit purée and sugar to the boil, add the soaked gelatine, strain and allow to cool. Add the colour, then proceed as for vanilla mousse. Decorate with rosettes of whipped cream and with sections of the fruits used.

Some fruits contain a higher percentage of acid than others, which does affect the setting of the gelatine and therefore the stability of the mousse. If purée is made from fruits such as kiwi, oranges, pineapples, plums, red and blackcurrants, it is advisable to increase the amount of gelatine to 35–40 g.

Opposite and over page: step-by-step strawberry mousse

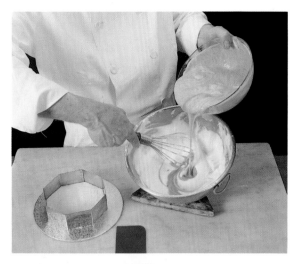

Almond mousse, *Mousse aux amandes*

Egg yolks	4
Castor sugar	100 g
Milk	3 dl
Ground almonds	50 g
Leaf gelatine	25 g
Fresh cream	5 dl
Egg whites	3
Cube or granulated sugar	100 g
Roasted, nibbled or flaked almonds	75 g
(Serves 10)	

Prepare the sauce anglaise as for vanilla mousse, adding the ground almonds to the milk, add the gelatine, strain. Continue as for vanilla mousse folding in the roasted almonds just before the meringue. Decorate with rosettes of whipped cream and glazed almonds.

MOUSSE CHOCOLAT CRÉOLE

Marinade 200 g of grapes in rum, preferably a couple of days in advance. Continue as for chocolate mousse, folding in the grapes just before the meringue. Decorate the top with rosettes of cream, chocolate copeaux and grapes.

MOUSSE À L'ORANGE MIROIR

Line the base of torten rings with a ring of plain genoise, about ½ cm thick, moistened with Cointreau-flavoured stock syrup. Cover the surface with segments of oranges, add a layer of orange mousse, 1 cm thick. Repeat the process once more, filling the ring to about ½ cm from the top. Place the mousse in the refrigerator to set, about 20 minutes. Cover the top with orange flavoured jelly and few juliennes of crystallised oranges. Serve with orange coulis round the base and half-whipped cream separately.

14 TRIFLES

Sherry trifle including an individual portion

Trifle, also known as Tipsy cake, is a sweet made of sponge sandwiched with jam and soaked with sherry or jelly or both. It is covered with boiled custard and decorated with ratafia biscuits and almonds. Today's trifle is a slight deviation from the original composition, which dates back to the late 17th century. Originally it was a frivolous confection made with dried sponges and biscuits soaked in either white wine or French brandy.

Sherry trifle

For the filling:
Sponge cake or swiss roll
Raspberry jam
Sherry

For the custard:	
Milk	1 ℓ
Castor sugar	150 g
Custard powder	75 g
Liquid cream	1 dl
Vanilla flavour	
(Serves 10)	

Sandwich the sponge or swiss roll with jam and compact into glass bowls or wine glasses, to half fill. Dilute part of the milk with the custard powder and sugar. Bring the rest of the milk to the boil with the vanilla flavour, whisk in the diluted custard and reboil for a few minutes to cook. Saturate the sponges with the sherry and immediately pour in the custard, filling almost to the top. Allow to cool, decorate with rosettes of fresh cream, diced glacé cherries, angelica and roasted almonds. Place a macaroon or ratafia biscuit on each portion.

JELLY TRIFLE
Proceed as for sherry trifle using hot jelly (flavour as desired) instead of the sherry.

FRUIT TRIFLE
Follow the same method as sherry trifle, placing a layer of fresh fruit (raspberries, strawberries, peaches, etc.) on top of the soaked sponge, continue as before. Decorate the top with slices of fruit, rosettes of fresh cream and macaroon biscuits.

English original trifle

For the filling:
Sponge cake or swiss roll
Strawberry jam
Macaroon biscuits
Brandy
White wine

For the custard:	
Single cream	1 ℓ
Egg yolks	12
Castor sugar	100 g
(Serves 10)	

Sandwich the sponge with jam and macaroons, arrange in the base of the serving glasses, lightly moisten with brandy then liberally moisten with wine. Prepare the yolks and sugar in a bowl, boil the cream and add to the yolks, stirring with a wooden spatula. Return to the heat and, stirring continually over low heat, cook until it thickens (a bain-marie may be used). Pour over the prepared dishes, to three-quarters full. Allow to set, preferably overnight. Fill the glasses with a syllabub mixture. Chill to set, for 2–3 hours. Sprinkle with roasted almonds.

15 JELLIES

Gelatine

Gelatine is made from a protein obtained from animal tissues, bones, skin and tendons. It dissolves in hot water to give a viscous solution and cools to form a jelly. It is available in powder and leaf form. *Isinglass* is a very pure gelatine, obtained from the dried swimming-bladder of the sturgeon. It dissolves easily in warm water.

For the pastry chef the principal use of gelatine is in the preparation of custards, creams and jellies. 150 g of gelatine to one litre of liquid will set as jelly.

Jellies

Originally calves feet were used for the preparation of jellies. The other ingredients were water, lemons, oranges, wines, spirits, bay leaves, lump sugar, cloves, coriander seeds, cinnamon sticks, egg whites (including the shells) and isinglass if necessary. It was sold in jars and retailed at high prices. Consumers had great faith in its nutritive value, and so were prepared to pay much more for 'calves foot jelly' made by confectioners, and sold in most grocers' shops.

Jelly (using gelatine)

Leaf gelatine	150 g
Water	2½ ℓ
Lump sugar	300 g
Bay leaves	3
Cloves	6
Brandy	2 dl
Sherry	1 dl
Coriander seeds	15 g
Egg whites	5
Lemon juice	3
Lemon rind	1
Cinnamon stick	½

(Makes approximately 3 litres)

Soak the gelatine in some of the cold water. Grate the lemons, extract the juice, slightly whisk the egg whites. Place all the ingredients into a saucepan, except for the wine, spirit and gelatine. Heat thoroughly, but do not boil. Stir in the gelatine, using a whisk continue stirring and bring to the boil, remove from the heat, cover and allow to stand for about 20 minutes (clarification stage). Add the wine and spirit, and filter through a jelly bag or a filter. Pour into appropriate moulds and allow to set in the refrigerator. When set, demould by immersing in warm water for a few moments, this is sufficient to release the jelly onto the serving dishes. Decorate as desired.

When making jellies, always remember the following.
1 Always add the gelatine solution to the liquid.

2 Heat gently, over-heating or boiling will cause it to loose its viscosity and impair its gelling ability.

3 If acid fruits or fruit juices are used in the jellies, the gelatine may not set. This applies to such fruits as pineapple, kiwi and pawpaw.

4 Jellies and derivatives do not freeze, prolonged exposure to very cold temperatures will impair the gel structure, caused by the enlargement of ice crystals.

5 Jellies and derivatives should be used within 24 hours of production, and kept refrigerated until ready for serving.

6 Jelly moulds should be washed just before using and left wet, this will help to release the jelly when turning out.

LEMON JELLY, *GELÉE AU CITRON*

Proceed as for the basic recipe, adding three lemons, zest and juice. Remove the fruit when boiled, if left in it will produce a bitter flavour. Colour can also be added to match the flavour.

ORANGE JELLY, *GELÉE À L'ORANGE*

Proceed as for basic recipe, using five oranges and one lemon, zest and juice. Remove the fruit when boiled. A little orange colour can also be used.

Fruit jelly, *Gelée aux fruits*

> Jelly (any flavour)
> Maraschino to taste
> Macédoine of fruit

Pour some of the prepared jelly into moulds and allow to set in the refrigerator. Arrange a little of the maraschino-flavoured macédoine on top, add more jelly and set. Continue the process until the mould is nearly full. Decorate and present as desired.

SPRING JELLY, *GELÉE PRINTANIERE*

Proceed as for fruit jelly, using mixed grapes, walnuts, hazelnuts and cherries, with maraschino flavour.

AUTUMN JELLY, *GELÉE D'AUTOMNE*

Proceed as for fruit jelly, flavouring the jelly with curaçoa, and adding a small amount of red colour. Decorated with seasonal fruits and chocolate leaves.

RIBBONED JELLY, *GELÉE RUBANÉ*

Prepare at least three different coloured and flavoured jellies. Set in alternate layers allowing each layer to set, until the top of the mould is reached. Decorate as desired.

Champagne jelly, *Gelée au champagne*

Water	2 dl
Gelatine	60 g
Castor sugar	50 g
Champagne	2 75 cl bottles
Grapes (seedless)	500 g
(Serves 10)	

Soak and dilute the gelatine in hot water, letting the mixture get very warm. Add the champagne and sugar. Pour most of the liquid into 10 champagne glasses (it will have a cloudy appearance). Place in the refrigerator to set. Dip the grapes into egg white and roll them in yellow-coloured castor sugar. Arrange on top of filled glasses. Whisk the remaining jelly into a froth and pour around the grapes, to represent the froth of champagne. Serve chilled.

N.B. To ascertain the consistency of the jelly, while still in production, put a small amount in a dariole mould in the refrigerator. After a short time check to see whether the jelly requires more gelatine or more water.

Piping jelly (using agar)

Granulated sugar	1 kg
Liquid glucose	1 kg
Citric acid	3–4 g
Water	1 ℓ
Agar-agar (powder form)	75 g

Soak the agar-agar in the water for about one hour. Place over a bain-marie, add the acid, bring to the boil. Add the sugar and boil to 104 °C, checking the temperature with a thermometer. Allow to cool, add colour and flavours as desired. Store in sterile sealed containers.

16 COLD CHARLOTTES, *CHARLOTTES FROIDS*

From the top: Charlotte russe, charlotte royale (below) and charlotte colinette

Charlotte Royale

Jelly (lemon flavoured)	6 dl
Swiss roll	3 eggs mix (p. 144)
Bavarois (vanilla flavour)	1 mix (p. 99)

Thorougly chill two charlottes, bombe moulds or pudding basins and line with cold, liquid, lemon-flavoured jelly. Allow to set. Slice the swiss roll, no more than 5 cm thick, dip into liquid jelly, use to line the inside of the moulds from the base to the top. Fill with the prepared vanilla bavarois, place in the refrigerator to set.

To demould, immerse the moulds in warm water for just a few moments, shake out gently allowing it to drop onto the serving dish. The serving dish can be previously lined with the same jelly.

Charlotte russe

| Finger biscuits | 1 mix (p. 157) |
| Vanilla bavarois | 1 mix (p. 99) |

Line the bases of two 12 cm charlotte moulds with finger biscuits, trim neatly to avoid gaps in between them. Fill with the bavarois mixture, place in the refrigerator to set. Demould by turning onto the serving dishes and decorate as desired with whipped cream, glacé cherries and angelica.

Fresh fruit can be used with either of the charlottes mentioned above; name the dish by adding the name of the fruit used (e.g. Charlotte de fraises à la royal). Coulis, with or without liqueurs, can enhance the flavour and presentation of the sweet by pouring around it, and serving separately.

CHARLOTTE ANDALOUSE
Proceed as for charlotte russe, mixing crystallised julienne of orange zest with the bavarois and incorporating segments of fresh oranges in alternate layers. Turn out onto serving dishes with orange coulis and decorated with segments of oranges.

CHARLOTTE POMPADOUR
Line the charlotte mould with rolled brandy snaps, fill with praline flavoured bavarois. Decorate the top with small brandy snap cornets with rosettes of cream.

CHARLOTTE COLINETTE
Proceed as for charlotte russe, using meringue finger biscuits instead of sponge biscuits.

CHARLOTTE ARLEQUIN
Prepare half mix of vanilla and half mix of chocolate bavarois. Line the moulds with the biscuits half-dipped in white and half-dipped in chocolate fondant. Fill the moulds with half of each flavour bavarois. Demould and decorate with rosettes of whipped cream and chocolate copeaux.

CHARLOTTE D'AUTOMNE
Line the moulds with chocolate finger biscuits, fill with rum-flavoured chocolate bavarois, mixed with diced marrons glacé. Demould onto the serving dishes and decorate with rosettes of cream and marrons glacé.

CHARLOTTE RELIGIEUSE
Line the moulds with finger eclairs. Fill with alternate layers of chocolate and vanilla bavarois. Demould, and decorate the top with ring-shaped choux paste, or small choux buns, alternatively flavoured chocolate and vanilla.

CHARLOTTE MONTREUIL
Line the mould with finger biscuits, fill with kirsch-flavoured bavarois and segments of peach.

CHARLOTTE MOSCOVITE

Line the bottom of a charlotte mould with red jelly. Arrange finger biscuits on the sides, as for charlotte russe. Fill with vanilla bavarois.

CHARLOTTES MIGNONS

As above, but prepared in dariole moulds (individual portions).

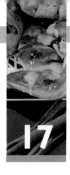

17 YEAST GOODS, *LEVURE*

Yeast is a microscopic, single-celled fungi, used in making fermented goods such as bread and in alcohol production. Fresh yeast consists of hundreds of thousands of yeast cells compressed into crumbly, putty-like blocks of greyish colour, and has a fresh fruity smell. It can be bought from most bakers, and should be stored in a cool place for 2–3 days.

Yeast was discovered by accident, through leaving moist flour paste in a warm place for several hours where it collected 'wild' yeasts (present in the husks of grain) which multiplied and caused fermentation. This type of yeast was used for many thousands of years. A piece of moist dough would be kept from one batch of breadmaking to be added to the next batch of fresh dough. Wild yeast used for other purposes, such as fermenting beer, would produce surplus yeast and this could also be used for breadmaking.

Today the yeast used for breadmaking is cultivated from molasses or from malted grain. It is usually a by-product of distilling. It is called *compressed yeast*.

Dried yeast can be stored indefinitely if kept dry and sealed. It is more concentrated than compressed yeast, therefore should be used approximately in half the quantity required, and soaked in tepid water, half an hour before use.

Structure of the yeast cell

Each cell is slightly oval in shape, and contains a clearly defined nucleus, the vital part of the cell. Within the cell is a watery solution of proteins, fat, and mineral matter. Some of the proteins are enzymes which, under suitable conditions, enable the yeast to become active, expand and bud (i.e. reproduce).

Reproduction of the yeast cell

Placed in a suitable medium containing the food yeast needs for growth, the cell will begin to increase and reproduce itself; this process is known as germination or budding. When a bud on the parent cell is sufficiently large, part of the nucleus divides into the young bud. The daughter cell separates from the parent and reproduces in the same manner.

Fermentation

This is the name given to the process by which a mixture of flour and water, made into a dough, is changed from a solid, tough elastic substance to a light tender material suitable for bread making. Briefly, this change occurs through the activity of the enzymes contained in the yeast cells and flour. As the yeast cells become active, the enzymes prepare and process sugars to provide food for the yeast. This produces carbon-dioxide and alcohol, which aerate the dough and give flavour. Other enzymes soften the tough gluten, making it more elastic and thus better able to rise by the gas production.

Dough production temperatures

It is important to observe the temperatures of ingredients and of the dough itself during any dough-making techniques. 25–30 °C is the optimum range of temperature to control the speed of fermentation.

1 The yeast cells are inactivated at 42 °C.
2 Yeast cells begin to die at 55 °C.
3 Coagulation of the glutens begin at 74 °C.
4 Oven baking temperatures should be from 220 °C to 260 °C.
5 Temperature of liquids used must not exceed 43 °C.

Yeast foods

Yeast is fed by sugar, but as strong flour naturally contains 2–3% sugar, along with the gluten which is soluble during fermentation, it has sufficient material for feeding the yeast without needing additional sugar. Excessive sugar used in the yeast solution can kill the yeast cells, and will give the bread an unpalatable yeasty taste.

Use of salt

Breads baked without salt will have a very insipid colour and poor crumb texture. Salt helps stabilise the gluten, and thus controls the rate of fermentation. If too much salt is used in a dough, yeast activity is greatly retarded, the gluten is tightened, resulting in smaller, heavy and rubbery loaves of bread.

Dough manipulation

Mechanical mixers now reduce much of the physically hard work needed for producing a bulk of dough for breadmaking. However, attention must be paid to ingredients and temperature, as well as the kneading, to produce a dough sufficiently elastic to stretch the gluten and preserve the gases.

The well-kneaded dough should have a springy texture, and must be allowed to stand to give time for the yeast to work. The dough is then allowed to relax, kept covered, preferably on a warm surface. It must be left until doubled in size, but not over-proved; if this happens the dough will deflate and the gases will escape.

It is also necessary to 'knock back' the dough to restore the even texture, to help the gas expulsion, and to maintain an even temperature throughout the dough. During the proving process the dough must be kept well covered, to prevent it from crusting.

The action of yeast in bread making

The action of producing CO_2 (carbon dioxide) from yeast and flour is complicated. Flour contains approximately 2% sugar, and an enzyme called *diastase*, which change some of the flour starch to a sugar called *maltose*.

Yeast contains three enzymes:
(a) *Maltase* which changes *maltose* to *glucose*.
(b) *Invertase* which changes *gucrose* to *glucose* and *fructose*.
(c) *Zymase* which changes *glucose* to CO_2 and *alcohol*.

The CO_2 is needed to raise the dough and the alcohol is allowed to evaporate during cooking.

Steps in the process of bread making

Creaming: of the yeast and sugar provides the initial supply of food.

Sponging: liquid is added to yeast and sugar and rapid fermentation occurs under the right condition.

Mixing: the yeast is distributed thoroughly throughout the dough in order for it to obtain the maximum amount of food. The protein in the flour absorbs water to form an elastic gluten.

Kneading: will develop the gluten and help spread the yeast throughout the dough.

Rising: the process of fermentation continues; warm conditions during rising are ideal for multiplication of yeast cells and enzyme action. The structure resembles honeycomb but it will collapse and become soiled if over risen.

Kneading: breaks down large bubbles of CO_2 into small ones of even size.

Shaping: the dough is cut and shaped.

Proving: fermentation proceeds and more CO_2 is produced. The volume of the dough expands again, but is more uniform in texture. The gluten recovers from the strain of shaping.

Baking: At first the dough rises rapidly, the gluten is pressed up by the gases, the yeast is killed by the gases and heat, so generating further CO_2. The oven temperature should be at least 220 °C, this will caramelise the crust, eventually attaining a brown colour, known by bakers as the 'bloom' of the loaf.

FLOURS

A wide variety of flours are available for the particular production of bread. Strong flour has the highest gluten content, and is the best for expansion and texture of the dough.

FATS

Butter, margarine, lard or shortening, can be used in yeast doughs, except in brioche dough. They are added by rubbing into the flour. Fat gives the bread a softer crumb and helps to preserve its freshness.

EGGS

These should be used only in enriched doughs. They improve the colour and flavour, and increase food value. Eggs can also make the dough lighter in texture.

Potatoes can also be used to produce yeast, as this recipe from *Gunters modern confectioner*, by William Jeanes, proves.

POTATO YEAST

> 4 quarts of cold water or milk
> 6 large potatoes
> 8 oz of moist sugar

Grate the potatoes into water or milk let it stand for 12 hours, then pour off the water, strain through a sieve. Pour the boiling water or milk over the sugar, allow to cool, add half a pint of the sieved fermented potatoes, whisk together. The next day it will be ready for use. Keep in a stone jar. From this you may make yeast as often as you please, and no other is as good for bread.

POTATO YEAST BREAD

> 2 quarts of milk and water
> 7 lb of flour
> ½ pt prepared yeast

Put the flour in a pan, make a hole in the middle, and put in a handful of salt with the prepared yeast, the milk and water. Mix to a batter, and leave to rise for half an hour, then knead well for quarter of an hour. Make the loaves as you please, put them in tins before the fire to rise, when risen, bake for about two hours.

Such recipes had been developed purely by empirical methods; it is only within the past few centuries that scientists have been able to explain the processes of fermentation. It was a

Dutchman, Anthony van Leeuwenhoek, who first discovered yeast to be a living organism, he died in 1723. It wasn't until 1862 that the French biochemist Louis Pasteur established the vital theory of fermentation.

■ BREAD DOUGH, *PÂTE À PAIN*

Bread rolls, *Petits pains*

Strong flour	*I kg*
Salt	*15 g*
Butter or shortening	*10 g*
Sugar	*10 g*
Yeast	*30 g*
Water	*6 dl*
(Makes 30 rolls)	

Sift the flour and salt onto a clean surface and rub in the fat finely. Make a large bay. Dilute the yeast with the water (35–40 °C), pour into the bay. Gradually draw the flour mix into the water, mix to form a smooth, very pliable dough. Continue kneading the dough until it releases itself from the surface. Ball up, place aside in a warm place (30 °C), well-covered with a damp cloth, prove until it has doubled in size, approximately one hour. Place the dough onto a clean surface and deflate it by pushing down from the centre to the outside (knocking back), *do not* work the dough any more, just ball up and again allow to relax for about ten minutes.

Divide the dough into two halves, roll into long even shapes and cut each one into 15 equal pieces (approx. 50 g each). Ball up each of the rolls and place under a clean cloth, leave to rest for about ten minutes. Place onto slightly greased trays, 10 cm apart for plain rolls, or shape as required. (If desired, at this stage the rolls can be egg-washed and sprinkled with sesame or poppy seeds.) Place the trays to prove in a warm place, 30 °C (or in a prover if available), until they have doubled

in size, transfer immediately to a hot oven, 230–250 °C. Bake until pleasantly browned, remove from the oven and place rolls onto cooling trays.

Various roll shapes

Plain rolls: Ball up each piece and place onto the greased baking trays. Complete as desired.

Knots: Roll each piece into 20 cm lengths, tie into knots.

Double knots: Same as for knots, roll into two longer pieces and knot together.

Marcus: Roll each piece into 20 cm lengths, and make a knot at each end.

Winkles: Roll each piece to a long shape, thicker at one end, roll up starting at the thicker end.

C roll: Roll to a long shape, thicker at the ends, roll towards the centre from both ends.

S shape: Roll to a long shape, thicker at the ends, roll up each end the opposite way.

The twin: Using a rolling pin, roll each piece to about 20 cm in length, fold the ends towards the centre, slightly stretching at the same time.

The cannon: Proceed as for 'the twin', folding one end across the other.

Single plait: Roll each piece to a 30 cm length, loop over itself using alternate ends.

Double plait: Divide each piece in half and roll to 20 cm lengths, hold the two pieces close together and twist either end.

A variety of bread roll shapes

Treble plait: Divide the piece into three and roll each one to 20 cm in length. Place them next to each other, plait together starting from the right.

■ WHOLEMEAL BREAD

In Roman times brown bread was only fed to the poor. These days consumers tend to prefer wholemeal bread, for its pleasant wheaty flavour, and as a healthier food. Wholemeal flour is coimpletely natural, with nothing added or taken away. It contains the germ of the wheat which is of high nutrient value and gives its sweet, characteristic taste. Wholemeal flours absorb a great deal of water; the dough is normally softer, and the proving process noticeably slower, than doughs made from white flours.

Wholemeal flour	1 kg
Salt	20 g
Yeast	50 g
Water (25 °C)	½ ℓ

Sieve the flour and salt onto a working surface, make a large bay, dilute the yeast in the water, pour into the bay. Draw in the dry ingredients and mix to form a pliable dough. Work the dough until it releases itself from the table. Leave in a warm place to prove, approximately 30 minutes. Divide the dough into five equal batches, ball up, place the rolls in greased bread tins. Allow to prove again until the dough reaches the tops of the tins. Bake at 220° C, when cooked turn out onto cooling trays.

Milk bread, *Pain au lait*

Strong flour	*1.5 kg*
Salt	*30 g*
Butter	*30 g*
Milk	*500 g*

Proceed as for bread roll dough. When proved, scale the dough into five 400 g batches, ball up, allow to relax for 10 minutes covered with a cloth. Grease the tins, mould dough into oval shapes and place in the tins. Using a sharp knife or blade make three or four slits in the tops. Place to prove until double in size, then bake at 240 °C. Remove from tins when cooked.

■ FERMENTED BUNS

Basic dough

Strong flour	*I kg*
Salt	*10 g*
Butter	*150 g*
Castor sugar	*150 g*
Yeast	*75 g*
Milk	*½ ℓ*
Flavour	
Eggs	*2*
(Makes 30 buns)	

A variety of fermented buns – from the top: Swiss buns, Chelsea buns, Danish buns and currant buns

This dough has to be proved in a bowl; if possible a large bowl should be placed in a warm place, maybe on top of the oven, well in advance.

Sift the flour and salt onto a clean surface and rub in the butter finely. Make a large bay, in the centre place the diluted yeast and milk, eggs, sugar and flavouring (depending on the use of cooked product). Gradually draw in the flour and mix to a smooth pliable dough, work well until it releases itself from the table. Dust the surface very lightly with flour and place the prepared dough into the warm bowl. Cover with a cloth, place aside to prove until doubled in size. Proceed producing buns according to individual method.

Rich penny buns

Basic bun dough	*I mix*
Mixed peel	*50 g*
Currants	*30 g*
Lemon flavour	
Castor sugar	

Add the mixed peel and currants to the flour at the rubbing-in stage. When proved divide into two halves, roll into long shapes and cut each roll into 15 equal pieces.

Ball up, place buns onto a lightly greased tray, egg-wash, dust generously with castor sugar, allow to prove until twice original size, bake at 230–240 °C. Place onto a cooling tray when cooked.

Danish buns

Basic bun dough	I mix
Lemon flavour	
Fondant (p. 190)	

Divide the dough into half, roll into long shapes and cut each into 15 equal pieces. Roll into finger shapes and place onto a lightly greased tray to prove until doubled in size. Bake at 230–240 °C. Place on a cooling tray when cooked. When cold coat the tops with lemon flavoured fondant.

Bath buns

Basic bun dough	I mix
Sultanas	75 g
Mixed peel	75 g
Lemon zest	I
Lemon flavour	
Egg wash	
Nibbed sugar	

Flavour the dough with the lemon flavour and add the sultanas, mixed peel, lemon peel and lemon zest to the mix at the rubbing in stage. Divide by tearing (not cutting) into 30 rough pieces. Place onto greased baking trays and brush over with egg-wash. Sprinkle with crushed cube sugar, or nibbed sugar. Bake at 230–240 °C. Place onto cooling trays when cooked.

Hot cross buns

This bun is traditionally eaten on Good Friday. In medieval times the cross was placed on all yeast products, to prevent evil spirits from interfering with the dough. The cross has since developed a more specific religious meaning.

Basic bun dough	I mix
Currants	50 g
Sultanas	50 g
Mixed peel	30 g
Lemon zest	I
Mixed spice	30 g
Liquid bun spice	
Egg-wash	
For the cross:	
Flour	100 g
Olive oil	20 g
Water	100 g

Make the bun dough, adding the fruit, mixed spice and zest at the rubbing in stage, and adding the bun spice to the milk. Divide the dough into two, form into long shapes and divide each equally into 15 pieces, 30 in all. Ball up and place in rows on the greased baking trays. Egg-wash all over. Prepare the cross mixture by beating together the measured ingredients. Pipe a cross on each using a piping bag or paper cornet. Prove until doubled in size, then bake at 230–240 °C. Place on cooling trays when cooked.

Devonshire splits

Traditionally these were produced in the west country, cut through the centre and filled with local cream and home made strawberry jam. It was known by the locals as 'lightning and thunder'.

Basic bun dough	1 mix
Egg-wash	
Fresh double cream	
Strawberry jam	
Icing sugar	

Divide the dough in two pieces, form into long shapes and divide each into 15 equal pieces, 30 in all. Ball up, and place on a greased tray. Egg-wash well, place to prove until doubled in size.

Bake at 130–140 °C, to a light brown colour. Place onto a cooling tray when cooked. When cold split the tops with a sharp knife, pipe in whipped cream and decorate with strawberry jam.

Chelsea buns

A popular bun in English tea and confectionery shops, dating back to the early 18th century. It originates from a bakery shop in Chelsea, London, owned by a man known as 'Captain Bun'. He was occasionally visited by royalty for the indulgence of bun eating, to the delight of the fashionable London crowds. The spicy recipe eventually found its way out of London to other bakeries and for the enjoyment of everyone.

Basic bun dough	1 mix
Lemon zest	1
Sultanas	100 g
Butter	100 g
Cinnamon sugar	50 g
Bun glaze	
Fondant	

Roll the proved dough into a large rectangle, about 50 cm by 30 cm. Brush with the melted butter, sprinkle all over with sultanas and cinnamon sugar.

Roll up starting with the longest edge, not too tightly. Brush again with melted butter and cut evenly into 30 pieces. Place the pieces in Chelsea buns tins, or flan rings, not too closely together. Prove until doubled in size, then bake at 230–240 °C. When cooked transfer onto cooling trays, brush with bun glaze, when set shake a little sugar over them.

Currant buns

Basic bun dough	1 mix
Currants	100 g
Egg-wash	

Make the bun dough adding the currants at the rubbing in stage. Ball up and egg-wash the tops, place onto greased baking trays. Prove to twice their size and bake at 130–140 °C. When baked remove from the oven and transfer to cooling trays.

Jam buns

Basic bun dough	1 mix
Egg-wash	
Castor sugar	
Jam	

These buns are square in shape. Roll out the dough to about 50 cm by 50 cm. Cut into even squares, place onto a greased baking tray. With the palm of the hand flatten them down slightly, egg-wash the tops and sprinkle with castor sugar.

Allow to half prove, insert corks dipped in grease into each bun and continue proving. When baked remove the corks (they can be reserved for further use). Fill the centres with jam of any flavour.

Doughnuts

The original idea travelled to America in the early 17th century from the Isle of Wight (then called dough-nuts). It returned to England and is now traditionally eaten on Shrove Tuesday, particularly in the Bedfordshire area.

```
Basic bun dough        I mix
Egg-wash
Jam
Cooking oil for frying
```

Roll out the proved dough, large enough to cut 60 8 cm rounds, using a plain cutter.

Place half of the cut rounds on paper lined tray, egg-wash, using a paper cornet, pipe a little red jam in the centre of each round. Place the other rounds on top of each, pressing down to seal with the back of a smaller cutter. Cover with a clean cloth, allow to prove (not in a prover, as the steam will make them sticky). When doubled in size, place them top side down into hot oil, 210 °C, cook until pleasantly browned. Remove from the oil, place onto trays lined with absorbant paper. When cold roll in castor sugar or cinnamon sugar.

FINGER DOUGHNUTS

Ball up the proved dough, roll into a long shape and cut into 30 equal pieces. Ball up each piece and allow to rest for 10 minutes, covered with a cloth. Roll into finger shapes and place onto a paper-lined tray. Cook in the hot oil, top side down, complete as for jam doughnuts.

RING DOUGHNUTS

Roll out the proved dough to a square large enough to cut out 30 8 cm rings, using a plain cutter. Place the rings onto paper lined trays and cut out the centres with a 3 cm cutter. Allow to prove covered with a clean cloth. When doubled in size, place into the hot oil top side down. Cook and complete as for jam doughnuts. The dough trimmings can be used for making finger doughnuts.

CREAM DOUGHNUTS

Using cooked round, finger or ring doughnuts, slit the tops or ends using a sharp knife, pipe a small amount of jam in the middle and fill with fresh whipped cream.

Swiss buns

```
Basic bun dough        I mix
Egg-wash
Apricot jam
Fondant
```

Make the basic bun dough. Ball up, shape into fingers. Place onto a greased baking tray, egg-wash, allow to prove until double in size. Bake at 130–140 °C. When cold brush with boiled apricot jam, coat with white lemon-flavoured fondant.

Lardy cakes

These were originally produced to celebrate harvest time in the West Country. They are made of bread dough prepared in layers like puff paste. The dough uses lard blended with sugar and fruit if desired.

```
Bread dough      I mix (p. 116)
Lard             250 g
Brown sugar      250 g
Mixed spice      50 g
Sultanas         100 g
Currants         100 g
```

Roll the proven bread dough into a rectangle shape, about 50 cm by 30 cm. Mix the lard with sugar and fruit (if used), spread over the rolled dough, fold into three, then cut in half, place into well-greased tins, egg-wash the tops, allow to prove to twice original size and bake in the oven at 230–250 °C. When well baked transfer to cooling trays.

■ DANISH PASTRIES, *PÂTISSERIES DANOIS*

Danish paste, *Pâte Danoise*

Strong flour	*1 kg*
Salt	*10 g*
Butter	*50 g*
Castor sugar	*50 g*
Eggs	*2*
Skimmed milk powder	*40 g*
Water	*6 dl*
Lemon flavour	
Butter or tough margarine	*500 g*
(Makes 50)	

A selection of Danish pastries

Prepare the paste as for croissant paste (p. 126). Rest the dough, well-wrapped, in the refrigerator for at least 30 minutes before using. Do not use a prover.

TURNOVERS, *CHAUSSONS*
Roll the dough to a 6 mm thickness, maintaining a tidy square. Cut into 12 cm squares, egg-wash. In the centre of each square, place a small amount of jam, apple purée or lemon curd. Fold one corner over to the opposite side, seal in the filling, egg-wash again. Place onto a greased baking tray to prove, until doubled in size. Bake in the oven at 230–240 °C. When cooked brush over with boiled apricot jam and thinned lemon-flavoured fondant. Transfer to cooling trays.

WINDMILLS
Roll the dough to a 6 mm thickness, cut into 12 cm squares. Cut each square diagonally across from each corner to half-way towards the centre. Egg-wash and fold each right-hand corner to the centre. Place onto greased baking trays, fill centres with any desired filling, such as jam, curd, mincemeat, or crème pâtissiére. A half glacé cherry can be placed in the centre of each. Prove to twice

the size, bake at 230–240 °C. Complete as turnovers.

CUSHIONS
Roll the dough to a 6 mm thick square, cut into 12 cm squares, egg-wash. Place a small amount of crème pâtissiére in the centres, fold the four corners toward the centre and seal. Place onto greased baking trays. Prove to twice the size and bake at 230–240 °C. Complete as turnovers.

FRUIT ROLL
Roll the paste to a 6 mm thick square. Spread with frangipane, sprinkle all over with sultanas, currants, mixed peel and diced glacé cherries. Roll up like a swiss roll, cut the roll into 50 pieces, place onto greased baking trays. Egg wash and prove to twice the size. Bake at 230–240 °C. Complete as for turnovers.

ALMOND SNAILS, *ESCARGOTS AUX AMANDES*
Roll the paste to a 6 mm in thick square. Spread with frangipane, sprinkle all over with

flaked almonds. Roll up from both ends towards the centre, cut into 1 cm pieces, place onto greased baking trays. Prove to twice the size and bake at 230–240 °C. Complete as for turnovers.

■ BRIOCHE

Originally known as *fougasse* in French, and *fogaccia* in Italian, brioche is a very light, rich and full-flavoured dough. It is normally eaten hot at breakfast with coffee, toasted for tea, or served as a sweet with fresh fruit.

The paste is also very suitable for covering pies, fillet and fish dishes en croute, and for making large and small loaves.

Brioche paste, *Pâte à brioche*

Strong flour	1 kg
Salt	10 g
Yeast	100 g
Sugar	100 g
Eggs	8
Milk (27 °C)	100 g
Butter	250 g

Sift the flour and salt onto a clean surface, make a large bay. Dilute the yeast into the milk, pour into the bay, add the eggs and sugar. Mix together gradually drawing in the flour, to form a smooth pliable dough with a very elastic texture. Place in the warm to prove to twice the size, gradually beat in the softened butter in stages, continue beating until all the butter is blended in well and the dough has a silky appearance. Place the dough in a sealed container or polythene bag and refrigerate for about one hour, to set to a firm texture. Scale the dough to the size required, ball up, place into well-greased putty loaf tins as desired and described in the following recipes. Place to prove again to

double in size. Bake in the oven, from 220 °C for larger items and at 250 °C for the smaller ones. When baked remove from the tins and transfer to cooling trays.

Cottage brioche, *Brioche à tête*

Brioche paste	1 mix
Egg-wash	
(50 portions)	

Knock back the proved dough, but do not over work at this stage. Roll out to a long shape, divide into 50 equal pieces. Ball up and place aside covered with a cloth. Taking one or two at a time, roll dough balls, squeezing on the table to form a head, twist the head round to the top and place rolls in greased tins. Using a small wooden stick dipped in flour, push through the middle to form a hole. Egg-wash, place to prove until well risen. Bake in the oven at 240–250 °C, remove from the tins when cooked.

The têtes can be emptied by removing the heads, scooped out and filled with cream, fruits and liqueurs. If the sugar is omitted from the dough they can be filled with savoury fillings or left plain and used as bread rolls.

Apple brioche, *Fougasse au pomme*

Brioche paste	1 mix
Apple purée	500 g
Eating apples	500 g
Lemon juice	1
Lemon zest	1

Roll out the brioche to about 1 cm thick, cut out four 30 cm circles. Place the circles aside to rest for 10 minutes. Mix the lemon zest and juice into the purée, add the thinly sliced apples. Mould two of the circles into greased flan rings, overlapping the edges. Fill with the apples mixture. Wet the edges, cut a pattern on the other two circles, and place on top, seal edges and cut off the surplus. Egg-wash well, place to prove. When risen egg-wash a second time and bake at 220 °C. When baked, remove from the oven and place on cooling trays. Serve as a sweet or for afternoon tea, hot or cold.

Other fruits can be used instead of apples, and the dish named after the fruits used: for example, fougasse au brioche d'abricot (apricot), fougasse au brioche à la pêche (peach), or fougasse au brioche d'ananas (pineapple).

Crown brioche, *Brioche couronne*

Brioche paste	1 mix
Mixed peel	100 g
Lemon zest	1
Icing sugar	
(10 portions)	

Divide the dough into two equal pieces, ball up, make a hole through the middle of each. Widen the holes, by rotating the dough, to about 8 cm. Place the rings on greased baking trays. Prove until well risen and bake at 220 °C. When baked lightly dredge the tops with icing sugar. Serve at tea time or at breakfast with the coffee.

The couronne can also be sliced and used for croûtes.

BRIOCHE DE NANTE

Produce the brioche dough (p. 00), divide into five equal batches and ball up, place aside to rest for 10 minutes. Divide again into five, ball up each piece and egg-wash. Arrange the rolls side by side in five 15 cm savarin moulds, just touching each other. Prove to double in size, egg-wash a second time, bake at 220 °C. Turn out onto cooling trays.

Twelfth Night cake, *Galette des Rois*

Brioche dough	1 mix
Orange-flower water to taste	
Egg-wash	
Roasted flaked almonds	
Icing sugar	

Prepare the ring brioche as for couronne, using a small amount of orange-flower water added to the milk and omitting the fruit. When baked brush the top with boiled apricot jam. Sprinkle with roasted flaked almonds, dredge with icing sugar.

■ FRUIT BREADS

Stollen

Traditionally eaten at Christmas and very popular in Germany, Austria and Scandinavian countries. Stollen has a religious significance; the shape is meant to represent the holy crib.

Flour	1.5 kg
Salt	15 g
Yeast	150 g
Butter	220 g
Castor sugar	200 g
Mixed spice	25 g
Sultanas	500 g
Mixed peel	150 g
Milk (25 °C)	6 dl
Marzipan	500 g
Fondant	

Sieve the flour, salt and mixed spice onto a clean surface, rub in the butter, add the sultanas and mixed peel. Make a large bay. Dilute the yeast into the milk, pour the milk into the bay, gradually draw in the dry ingredients and mix to form a smooth and very elastic dough. Prove to double the size. When proved scale down to 500 g batches, ball up, rest for 10 minutes well covered. Taking one batch at a time, with a rolling pin roll into a baton shape forming an indentation in the centre, place in a strip of marzipan and enclose the batch to seal. Prove again to twice the size, bake at 220 °C to a firm loaf texture. When baked brush with thinned fondant and shake roasted flaked almonds on top.

Other fillings or fruit can be used, such as currants, walnuts, pralines, cherries.

Currant bread

Strong flour	1 kg
Salt	15 g
Mixed spice	10 g
Yeast	50 g
Castor sugar	50 g
Butter	120 g
Milk	6 dl
Currants	350 g

Sift the flour, salt and mixed spice onto a clean surface, rub in the butter, add the currants, make a large bay. Dilute the yeast and milk together, pour into the bay with the sugar, mix drawing in the dry ingredients, forming a smooth dough. (Avoid damaging the currants while mixing, as this will discolour the dough.) Prove the dough to double the size, divide into five batches, ball up and place into greased 15 cm cake tins. Place to prove again, then bake in the oven at 230 °C. When baked turn out of the tins onto cooling trays.

WALNUT AND RAISIN BREAD
Proceed as for currant bread, using raisins and walnuts.

Croûtes aux fruits

Using savarin or brioche dough, mould the dough into loaves of 200 g each, place into well-greased and floured charlotte moulds. Prove and bake. Allow to stand overnight in the refrigerator, well wrapped. Cut into 1 cm slices. Dredge with icing sugar then fry in a plat sauter to a brownish colour. Remove crust, if necessary, using a round cutter, arrange fresh fruit on top and glaze with apricot glaze. Decorate with whipped cream or serve hot with sauce anglaise.

CROÛTE ROYALE
Decorate with apricots, glaze, serve hot with sauce anglaise.

CROÛTE LYONNAISE
Decorate with marron glacé and whipped cream.

CROÛTE À L'ANANAS
Decorate with slices of pineapple, glaze. Complete with whipped cream, glacé cherries.

CROÛTE AUX POMMES MERINGUES
Decorated with slices of poached apples, glaze with apricot glaze. Pipe a pattern using meringue on top, dredge with icing sugar and glaze under the salamander.

■ CROISSANTS

These are crescent-shaped rolls made in a laminated structure using bread dough. Aeration is created by the combination of fermentation and lamination.

Croissants date back to the late 17th century when Turkey invaded Austria. As the Turks raided the city during the night the Viennese bakers raised the alarm, and the city was saved. To commemorate the occasion all the bakers in Vienna baked a special bread in the shape of the crescent (*croissant*) emblem of the Turkish flag.

Over the years croissants have become the most popular breakfast item throughout Europe.

Croissant paste, *Pâte à croissant*

Strong flour	1 kg
Yeast	30 g
Salt	10 g
Butter	50 g
Skimmed milk powder	50 g
Water	8 dl
Lemon flavour	
Butter	350 g
(Makes approximately 50)	

Sift the flour, milk powder and salt onto a clean surface, rub in the first butter and make a large bay. Dilute the water, milk powder, yeast and lemon flavour then pour into the bay. Gradually draw in the flour and mix to form a smooth pliable dough, work well until it releases itself from the table. Cover with a cloth and allow to relax for 10 mintues. Roll out to a rectangle shape, place the butter covering half the top as for puff paste. Fold over the other half of the paste and give the paste two turns (see p. 36). Wrap the paste well in a damp cloth, rest in the refrigerator for at least one hour, give the paste another two turns, wrap well again and it is ready for use.

1 The water used in the dough must be kept chilled, 25 °C, to avoid the dough reacting during mixing.
2 The butter also must be kept in the refrigerator until ready for use.
3 Always keep the dough well wrapped to prevent it skinning.

4 The dough can be left until the following day between turns.

CROISSANTS
Allow the dough to relax and roll out to a square, about 4–5 mm thick. Divide into 18–20 cm lengths, then cut into triangles 12 cm wide. Egg-wash the tip of the triangles, roll up from the base towards the tip. Turn each roll to form a crescent. Place onto a greased baking tray to prove to twice the size. Bake in the oven at 230–240 °C. Serve hot or cold.

Tough margarine can be used for producing croissants. When butter is used, avoid placing in the prover, a warm corner of the pastry room should be sufficient.

■ SAVARINS

Savarin is a very light fermented dough, rich in butter and eggs, named after Brillat Savarin, a famous writer of gastronomy. It is also used for making babas and pomponettes. It is considered one of the best quality and most versatile doughs.

Savarin paste, *Pâte à savarin*

Strong flour	250 g
Salt	10 g
Yeast	15 g
Castor sugar	30 g
Milk	30 g
Eggs	3
Butter (melted)	100 g
(10 portions)	

Warm a bowl on top of the oven for best results. Sieve the flour and salt into the bowl, pour into the centre the diluted milk and yeast, add the eggs and beat the mixture to a very elastic and silky texture. Place the bowl in a warm place for the dough to prove until doubled in size, with the melted butter poured over the top. This helps to prevent a skin forming and to keep the dough warm. When proved, knock back and mix in the butter until well blended. The dough is ready for use.

Savarin chantilly

Savarin paste	1 mix
Savarin syrup (p. 186)	
Maraschino	2 dl
Fresh cream	½ ℓ
Apricot glaze	
(Serves 10)	

Well grease and flour savarin moulds (one 30 cm, or two 18 cm). One third fill the moulds with paste, using a piping bag. Prove until the dough has reached the top of the mould, place in the oven at 230 °C until well baked and the dough has released itself from the moulds. Turn out onto a cooling tray.

Prepare the syrup. At the boiling stage and at 20° Baumé, immerse the savarin in the syrup. Using a ladle pour more syrup on top until the savarin has absorbed as much as possible, and is completely immersed. Drain off well, using a large spider or a draining wire tray. Pour a small amount of maraschino, glaze with boiled apricot glaze, place on serving dishes. When cool fill the centres with fresh whipped cream flavoured with vanilla, decorate with rosettes of cream and crystallised violets and roses. Serve on the same day of production.

INDIVIDUAL SAVARIN
Produce the savarin dough following the basic recipe. Pipe into small savarin moulds, proceed and decorate as above.

ORIENTAL STYLE SAVARIN, *SAVARIN À L'ORIENTALE*
Soak and glaze the savarin as for chantilly, allow to drain, sprinkle with the desired amount of maraschino or curaçao. Brush boiled apricot jam all over (with the soaked savarin on a cooling wire), pour warm fondant over to cover completely. When set, place onto a serving dish. Decorate the tops with thin marzipan shapes, glacé cherries and angelica. Present with a veil of spun sugar on top.

Oriental-style savarin (top) and fruit savarin (bottom)

FRUIT AND RUM SAVARIN, *SAVARIN AU RHUM ET AUX FRUITS*
Soak the savarin as for chantilly, allow to drain well, sprinkle with the rum. Brush over with boiled apricot jam flavoured with rum. Place on serving dishes, fill the centre with drained fresh fruit salad, sprinkle with rum. Serve chilled, decorated with more fresh fruit and, if desired, rosettes of fresh cream.

SAVARIN WHITE LADY *SAVARIN DAME BLANCHE*

Soak the savarin as for chantilly, allow to drain well, sprinkle with Cointreau. Brush all over with boiled apricot glaze, flavoured with Cointreau. Pour to cover completely with mousseline sauce (p. 137). Sprinkle roasted flaked almonds over the top.

Babas au rhum

Savarin paste	*I mix*
Currants	*100 g*
Rum	
Apricot glaze	

Produce the paste incoporating the currants in the dough at the rubbing-in stage. Pipe the mixture to one third fill 10 greased dariole moulds, place to prove in a warm place, until the mixture has risen to the top. Bake at 230 °C. When cooked place on cooling trays. Soak the cold babas in the same manner as savarin, when well swollen stand to drain. Sprinkle with rum and glaze with apricot glaze. Decorate the tops with rosettes of fresh cream, diced glacé cherries and angelica.

Rum babas (bottom) and marignans (top)

MARIGNANS

Pipe the savarin paste into barquette-shaped moulds. Continue as for rum babas. When soaked and cold they can be slit across the middle and filled with a rope of whipped cream. Decorate with pistachio or almond.

POMPONETTES AUX FRUITS

Pipe the savarin paste into well-greased round or fluted putty tins. Continue as for rum babas. When soaked and cold they can be completed as for rum babas or the tops can be cut off, hollowed out, and filled with fresh fruits with kirsch and whipped cream.

POMPONETTES AU CAFÉ

Proceed as for pomponettes aux fruits, fill with coffee-flavoured crème chiboust (p. 134). Decorate with whipped cream and a marzipan coffee bean.

POMPONETTES AU CHOCOLAT

Proceed as for pomponettes aux fruits, filling with chocolate flavoured crème chiboust (p. 134).

■ KOUGLOF

This rich light cake, originating from Russia, is now greatly favoured in Germany. Many bakers use a basic savarin dough to produce kouglof.

Strong flour	*I kg*
Salt	*10 g*
Butter	*300 g*
Castor sugar	*200 g*
Yeast	*30 g*
Eggs	*8*
Milk	*3 dl*
Raisins	*150 g*
Currants	*150 g*
Mixed peel	*50 g*
Lemon zest	*I*
Filleted almonds	*100 g*

Produce the dough following the method for savarin, incorporating half of the filleted almonds and the fruit. Half fill five 15 cm savarin or fluted moulds sprinkle in the remaining almonds, continue filling with dough. Prove until the dough reaches the top of the rim, bake at 230 °C, turn out onto cooling wires, when cool dredge with icing sugar.

■ CRUMPETS

Originally crumpets were known as 'curled up cakes', as they probably curled during cooking, when pancakes or 'crumps' were first made towards the end of the 16th century. Modifications in the recipe and production of crumpets have eradicated the propensity to curl.

Flour (medium or soft grade)	1 kg
Butter	15 g
Yeast	50 g
Water	1 ℓ, 5 dl
Salt	15 g
Sugar	10 g
Bicarbonate of soda	10 g

Dilute the bicarbonate of soda in water and allow to stand for about 15 minutes. Dissolve the yeast in the liquid, add to the rubbed flour, salt and butter and mix to softish dough. The mixture may have to be adjusted with more liquid – add extra water if necessary.

Place greased crumpet rings onto the hotplate, ladle batter into each ring. Allow to cook and hole before turning over to brown the other side. It is very important to avoid over cooking, cook just long enough to take away the appearance of rawness.

Place the cooked crumpets on a clean cloth and repeat with remaining dough.

■ MUFFINS

It was during the last century and the early years of this century that 'The Muffin Man' was seen walking the streets of the big cities, selling hot muffins in a basket and announcing his wares by ringing a bell. Muffins are now on full display in bakeries and supermarket shelves.

Flour (strong)	1.75 kg
Butter	20 g
Sugar	15 g
Yeast	75 g
Salt	25 g
Water	1 ℓ, 3 dl

Make up the dough, which must be slack: a good beating is necessary to toughen the texture. When ready, scale and mould. Because of their softness muffins are proved on cards heavily dusted with ground rice. When ready lift gently and place into the greased muffin rings on the hot plate. Turn them over when the bases begin to colour. Remove to a cooling tray, use as required.

■ ITALIAN CHRISTMAS CAKE
PANETTONE

Strong flavour	750 g
Salt	3 g
Yeast	50 g
Water	2 dl
Butter	250 g
Castor sugar	200 g
Egg yolks	7–8
Mixed peel	150 g
Raisins	200 g
Almonds (whole)	100 g
Nutmeg	5 g
Orange zest	2

(Sufficient for 2 × 15 cm cake tins)

Sieve the flour and salt onto a clean surface. Make a large bay, place in the centre the lightly warmed water, egg yolks, and sugar. Mix to a smooth dough, allow to prove to double in size. Work in the fruit, the roughly chopped almonds, orange zest, and nutmeg. Finally chop in the butter (using a large knife).

Divide the dough in half, ball up, place into well-greased cake tins or in a pirottino (a large paper case, 10–20 cm high, especially available for baking 'Panettonis'). Allow to prove again until well risen. Brush over with beaten egg yolks mixed with a little milk. Place in the oven at 220 °C for at least 40 minutes, until well baked. It is important to lower the heat to 185 °C, 15 minutes after placing the panettone in the oven.

Mix one tablespoon of flour in a bowl with the yeast melted in the warm milk, and allow the mixture to rise to double in volume. Add the flour, sugar, butter, egg yolks, grated lemon and orange, mixed peel, and rum. Work the dough until it is soft and supple. (This will take a long time, but the success of the dough depends mainly on this phase.) Roll out the dough onto a well-floured cloth in a rectangular shape, about 2 cm thick. Spread with stiffly beaten egg whites, sprinkle on the filling (walnuts, sugar, cocoa and grated zest). Add the raisins (soaked in milk) and pine kernels. Finally dot the whole with small pieces of butter.

Roll up and arrange in a spiral on a baking tin. Allow to prove for two hours. Bake at 220 °C, reducing the temperature after 15 minutes.

■ CHRISTMAS ROLL (Italian style)

For the dough:	
Strong flour	500 g
Yeast	100 g
Milk	1 dl
Castor sugar	100 g
Butter	100 g
Eggs	2
Lemon zest	1
Orange zest	1
Rum	100 g
For the filling:	
Walnuts	250 g
Castor sugar	120 g
Cocoa	20 g
Orange zest	1
Lemon zest	1
Raisins (soaked in milk)	250 g
Pine kernels	100 g
Butter	100 g

BUTTER CREAMS, *CRÈMES AU BEURRE*

18

These creams can be produced from a base of various fats: shortening, margarine or butter. The latter is considered the most advantageous for the production of high quality, richly flavoured butter creams. Cheap and stale butter should on no account be used for this purpose. Sweetening agents such as icing sugar, syrups, fondants, granulated and cube sugars, can be used in boiled goods (Italian meringue).

Butter cream, as a water-and-oil emulsion, is susceptible to the multiplication of harmful bacteria; the pastry chef has to take care with the utensils used, particularly avoiding the creaming or whisking of dairy products in copper vessels. The reaction of fatty acids with metallic containers may produce soaps which have oxidising properties.

Butter creams can be flavoured to suit the requirement with the addition of liqueurs, syrups, honey, melted chocolate, coffee, pralines and flavoured compounds, with the appropriate colour, if required. Orange and rose-flower water are commonly used. Liqueurs should be added to a cold cream mixture, as heat may dissipate the flavour of the liqueur.

Butter creams are used for filling gâteaux, pastries, petits fours, yule logs, etc.

Butter cream 1

Butter	500 g
Icing sugar	400 g
Cornflour	100 g
Stock syrup or liqueur as required	

Cream the butter until soft and light, add the icing sugar and cornflour, continue creaming gradually pouring in the syrup mixture or liqueur (or both). The cream should have a light but firm texture, suitable for spreading and piping. Flavour and colour as desired.

Butter cream 2 (Syrup method)

Lump sugar	300 g
Water	1 dl
Egg yolks	10
Butter	500 g
Liqueur if required	

Saturate the sugar with the water, boil to 150 °C, using a thermometer. Slightly whisk the egg yolks in a bowl, gradually add the hot syrup. Continue whisking until completely cold, then add the softened butter, a little at a time, while beating. Add flavour, colour and liqueur as required.

Butter cream 3 (Italian meringue method)

Lump sugar	250 g
Water	1 dl
Egg whites	2 dl
Butter	500 g
Flavour as required	

Saturate the sugar with the water, boil to 150 °C, using a thermometer. At the same time, whisk the egg whites to a point, gradually pour in the boiled syrup, continue whisking until cold. Add the softened butter in stages, continue beating to a smooth texture. Add colour, flavour and liqueur as required.

Butter cream 4 (sabayon method)

Egg yolks	8
Castor sugar	300 g
Water	I dl
Butter	600 g
Flavour as required	

Whisk the egg yolks, water and half the sugar over a pan of very hot water, until of a light and foamy texture. Beat the butter with the other half of sugar, gradually add the egg yolk mixture. Add flavour and colour as required. Avoid over mixing.

This method is ideal if wines are to be used, such as sherry, marsala, port and particularly fruit wines. The wine can replace the water.

Butter cream 5 (custard method)

Egg yolks	8
Castor sugar	250 g
Milk	2 dl
Butter	500 g
Flavour as required	

Boil the milk and the flavour. Whisk the yolks with the sugar, gradually add the boiled milk. Return to the saucepan, cover with a lid, allow to stand for five minutes to thicken. Strain into a bowl through a fine strainer and allow to cool. Cream the butter well, to a very light texture, gradually pour in and mix the prepared custard. Add colour, extra flavour or liqueur as required.

19 PASTRY CREAMS, *CRÈME PÂTISSIÉRE*

■ PASTRY CREAM,
CRÈME PÂTISSIÉRE

Egg yolks	10
Castor sugar	250 g
Flour	200 g
Milk	1 ℓ
Vanilla flavour	

Boil the milk and the flavour, allow to cool slightly. Mix the egg yolks with the sugar, then add the flour, beating well. Add the hot milk, strain back in the saucepan. Return to the heat, stirring continually with a wooden spatula until it has boiled well and the flour is cooked. Pour into a bowl, sprinkle with castor sugar to prevent a skin forming, cover with a lid. Use as required.

Crème pâtissiére is one of the most versatile and widely used creams by the pâtissiére. When cold it should be stored in the refrigerator as part of the pastry mise-en-place. It is best if used on the same day of production.

CHOCOLATE PASTRY CREAM, *CRÈME PÂTISSIÉRE AU CHOCOLAT*

Proceed as for crème pâtissiére, adding 50 g of melted couverture to the mixture while still warm, or sufficient to obtain the required colour.

Chocolate couverture acts as a thickening agent, it may be necessary to adjust the crème consistency with a little cream.

ALMOND PASTRY CREAM, *CRÈME PÂTISSIÉRE D'AMANDÉ*

Add 50 g of ground almonds to the milk and boil together, proceed as for crème pâtissiére.

Almond flavour or compound can be added at the cooking stage in place of the ground almonds.

COFFEE PASTRY CREAM, *CRÈME PÂTISSIÉRE AU CAFÉ*

Proceed as for crème pâtissiére, using sufficient coffee flavour to obtain the desired coffee colour and taste.

FRUIT PASTRY CREAM, *CRÈME PÂTISSIÉRE AUX FRUITS*

Add approximately 100 g of fruit paste (strawberries, raspberries, apricots, apples, etc., p. 89) to the basic recipe and colour to taste.

Crème Saint Honoré

Crème pâtissiére	½ mix
Gelatine	10 g
Egg whites	5
Italian meringue (p. 164)	
Granulated or cube sugar	150 g
Flavour as required	

Add the soaked gelatine and flavour to the crème while still hot, at the same time prepare Italian meringue. Fold the meringue into the crème while it is boiling, this will help to stabilise the consistency of the crème. It is now ready for use in Gâteaux Saint Honoré, polkas or pastries.

Crème chiboust I

Crème pâtissiére	½ mix
Butter	250 g
Flavour as required	

Mix half the butter into the crème pâtissiére as soon as it is made, allow to cool. Place in a mixer, add the required flavour, liqueur or colour as required, whisk at a medium speed, adding the remaining butter. At top speed continue whisking to a firm emulsion and doubled in volume. It is now ready for use.

CRÈME CHIBOUST 2

Mix an equal quantity of fresh whipped cream to crème pâtissiére and flavour as required.

CRÈME CAPRICE

Fold approximately half the quantity of broken meringues into one quantity of fresh whipped cream, add sugar and flavour to taste.

This cream can be moulded to form a sweet portion, then decorated as desired. It can also be used in savarins and for crème opéra.

Almond cream, Crème frangipane

This cream is of French origin. It usually consists of a cake mix with the main ingredient, ground almonds or cake crumbs, or both. The recipe dates back to the 17th century, devised by the chef of Count Frangipani. It is used for gâteaux Pithiviers, jalousie d'amande, tarte Belge, fruit flans, tartlets and barquettes, Bakewell tart.

Frangipane is a very versatile cream and commonly used by the pâtissier. It should be part of the pastry mise-en-place, kept stored in the refrigerator for up to five days.

Butter	500 g
Castor sugar	500 g
Eggs	4
Ground almonds	500 g
Flour	100 g
Flavour to taste	

Cream the butter and sugar to a light creamy texture, using a large bowl. Add the eggs gradually, fold in the sieved ground almonds and flour.

Flavours such as almond, compounds, lemon zest, praline and chocolate can be added as desired. A small amount of rum enhances the flavour.

For economical advantage the ground almonds can be replaced or partly replaced with cake crumbs.

20 SWEET SAUCES, *SAUCE DOUCE*

Egg custard sauce, *Sauce Anglaise*

Egg yolks	10
Castor sugar	250 g
Milk	1 ℓ
Vanilla flavour to taste	
(Serves 10)	

Bring the milk and flavour to the boil, with half of the sugar. Allow it to cool slightly. Place the freshly separated egg yolks in a clean bowl. Add the remainder of the sugar and the slightly cooled milk, stirring thoroughly with wooden spatula. Using a bain-marie poach the mixture, continually stirring with the spatula until the mixture thickens slightly, just coating the spatula. Pass through a fine strainer (chinois). The sauce is now ready for serving in a sauce boat.

This sauce will contine cooking and eventually scramble (brouiller) if kept over strong heat for a long period. For service keep in the bain-marie, over very gentle heat. Sauce anglaise should be used on the same day of production, as an egg custard sauce would be difficult to reheat maintaining the correct consistency. The yolk coagulates at 65 °C, which is not sufficient to kill any harmful bacteria. Even if the sauce is intended for use cold, it is still very susceptible to bacterial activity.

Sauce anglaise is used for ice cream dishes, mousses, fruit dishes, steamed puddings, fruit pies and tarts, soufflés.

Apricot sauce, *Sauce abricot*

Apricot jam	1 kg
Stock syrup	1 ℓ
Cornflour	50 g
Kirsch	30 ml
(Serves 10)	

Bring the jam and stock syrup to the boil, thicken to the required consistency with diluted cornflour. Pass through a strainer. Yellow colour can be added to improve the appearance. Serve separately as required with strudel, apple charlottes, fritters, jam puddings.

Almond sauce, *Sauce amande*

Castor sugar	100 g
Cornflour	50 g
Milk	1 ℓ
Ground almonds	30 g
Almond flavour to taste	
(Serves 10)	

Blend the sugar and cornflour with a little of the milk. Bring the rest of the milk and ground almonds to the boil, then whisk the cornflour solution into the boiling milk. Pass the sauce through a fine strainer, discarding the ground almonds. Correct the consistency with a little liquid cream, if necessary. A little green colour can be added to enhance the appearance of the sauce. Serve with steamed puddings, ice creams, fruit dishes, fritters.

Custard sauce

Castor sugar	100 g
Custard powder	50 g
Milk	1 ℓ
Vanilla flavour to taste	
Cream	150 ml
(Serves 10)	

Using a small whisk, mix the castor sugar and custard powder together, add a small amount of cold milk, to dilute to a liquid. Boil the remaining milk and vanilla flavour, whisk in the diluted mixture and reboil. Pass through a fine strainer, add the liquid cream. Serve separately as required with steamed puddings, fruit tarts, fruit pies, fritters.

WHITE VANILLA SAUCE
As for custard sauce, using cornflour instead of custard powder. Serve with puddings, egg custard dishes, Christmas pudding.

Chocolate sauce, *Sauce au chocolat*

Castor sugar	250 g
Cocoa powder	50 g
Cornflour	50 g
Milk	1 ℓ
Cream	150 ml
Couverture	100 g
(Serves 10)	

Using a whisk, mix the sugar, cocoa powder and cornflour together, add a small amount of cold milk, to dilute to a liquid. Boil the remainder of the milk, whisk in the diluted cornflour mixture, reboil. Add the chopped chocolate couverture, stir to dissolve, add the liquid cream. Serve as required.

Strawberry sauce, *Sauce aux fraises*

Strawberries	750 g
Castor sugar	500 g
Lemon juice	1
Red colour	
(Serves 10)	

Remove the calyces from the strawberries, wash the fruit. Pass through a fine sieve. Place the fruit, sugar, lemon juice and a little red colour into a saucepan, bring to the boil, allow to simmer until the required density is attained. A small amount of diluted cornflour can be added to improve the consistency. A small amount of compound can also improve the flavour of the sauce.

Serve with fruit dishes, fruit flans, fruit tarts, fruit fools, mousses, cream dishes.

RASPBERRY SAUCE, *SAUCE AUX FRAMBOISES*
As for strawberry sauce using raspberries.

Hot chocolate sauce, *Sauce Hélène*

Chocolate couverture	500 g
Stock syrup	
(Serves 10)	

Melt the chocolate in a bain-marie, stir in enough stock syrup to attain the required consistency. Bring to the boil and it is ready to use. Serve with ice cream dishes, soufflés, mousses, steamed puddings.

Ganache sauce, *Sauce ganache*

Chocolate couverture	500 g
Castor sugar	100 g
Cream	1 ℓ
Rum (optional)	100 ml
(Serves 10)	

Melt the chocolate couverture in a bain-marie, bring to the boil the cream and castor sugar, add gradually to the melted chocolate, stirring thoroughly. Add the rum, if desired. Serve as required with ice cream dishes, soufflés, mousses, sweet omelettes.

Jam sauce, *Sauce à la confiture*

Cornflour	50 g
Castor sugar	100 g
Stock syrup	1 ℓ
Jam	250 g
Kirsch (optional)	100 ml
Colour, if required	
(Serves 10)	

Blend the cornflour and castor sugar with a little of the cold stock syrup, to thin down to a liquid. Bring the remainder of the syrup to the boil, whisk in the diluted solution, reboil, pass through a strainer. Add colour and kirsch, as desired. Serve separately with fruit puddings, fritters, soufflés, jam rolls, strudel.

Melba sauce, *Sauce melba*

Original recipe: Equal proportions of raspberry jam, strawberry jam and redcurrant jelly are boiled together.
Updated recipe: Boil strained raspberry purée with sufficient syrup to obtain the correct consistency. Add a little red colour and fruit compound if required. Serve with peach melba, mousses, fruit dishes, cream dishes.

Sauce mousseline

Stock syrup	500 g
Vanilla flavour to taste	
Egg yolks	15
Cream	1 ℓ
Liqueur of choice (optional)	100 g

Boil the stock syrup and flavour, gradually add to the egg yolks, stirring well with a spatula. Cook in a bain-marie, until it slightly thickens. Using a large mixing bowl, whisk until the mixture increases in volume and reaches the ribbon stage, add the liqueur, if used. Stir in the cream. Serve separately as required.

ARENBERG SAUCE *SAUCE D'ARENBERG*

1 As for sauce mousseline.
2 Equal quantities of crème pâtissiére and whipped half cream, mixed together to the correct consistency.
   Liqueurs can be added as required. Serve with poire d'arenberg, mousses, Christmas puddings, fritters, profiteroles.

SAUCE MOUSSELINE AUX FRUITS

Follow the same method as sauce mousseline, mixing passed fruit pulps and little lemon juice instead of the stock syrup.

Sabayon sauce, *Sauce sabayon*

Egg yolks	5
Marsala wine	100 g
Castor sugar	100 g
Cream	5 dl
Lemon juice	
(Serves 10)	

Place the egg yolks, marsala wine, castor sugar and a squeeze of lemon juice in a scalded bowl, whisk over a bain-marie until it ribbons and the mix is very warm. Half whip the cream and fold in the sabayon. Keep warm over a bain-marie, serve separately as required with Christmas puddings, mousses, fritters.

BRANDY OR RUM SAUCE

Add brandy or rum to sabayon sauce or vanilla sauce to taste. Serve separately as required.

Cream sauce, *Sauce chantilly*

Fresh cream	1 ℓ
Castor sugar	250 g
Vanilla flavour to taste	
(Serves 10)	

Whisk the cream and sugar over ice, until it reaches just a ribbon consistency.

WHITE (LADY) CREAM SAUCE, *SAUCE DAME BLANCHE*

As for sauce mousseline, served with white lady savarin.

PISTACHIO CREAM SAUCE, *SAUCE PISTACHE*

As sauce mousseline, using pounded pistachio nuts or compound in the whisking with a tinge of green colour. Add 100 g of maraschino if desired.

SAUCE SARAH BERNHARDT

As for sauce mousseline, flavouring with orange juice, or orange compound, adding 100 g of curaçao.

REDCURRANT SAUCE, *SAUCE BAR-LE-DUC*

As for jam sauce, using pounded redcurrants, passed through a fine strainer. Add a few redcurrants before serving.

CARDINAL SAUCE, *SAUCE CARDINALE*

As for jam sauce using raspberry jam, passed through a fine strainer. Add little red colouring.

Caramel sauce, *Sauce caramel*

Cube sugar	1 kg
Water	3 dl

Saturate the sugar in a clean copper saucepan, boil until a light caramel colour is reached (230 °C), place aside for the colour to strengthen. Gradually add the remaining water (hot), bring back to the boil. More water can be added to adjust the consistency if necessary.

21 SPONGE GOODS

Sugar

Fine castor sugar produces the best sponges; coarse grades, such as granulated sugar, should be avoided. Suitable sugar mixes readily with eggs, helping to break and cream the yolks. Coarse sugar tends to remain crystalline in the sponge batter; the baked sponges will be speckled on top. This is even more noticeable in sponges which are made by beating the yolks and whites separately.

Flour

Fairly soft flour is best for the texture and flavour of sponge cakes. For slab or any fruit cakes, a medium grade flour provides a crumbly texture and is better for holding the fruit. Strong flour will result in a close, heavy texture and a round instead of flat top. On all occasions flour should be sifted before using, to facilitate light mixing without toughening the batter.

Method of work

For cake mixtures the fat and sugar should always be well creamed until light and fluffy before the flour is added. All ingredients used should be of average room temperature. Butter or margarine to be used for creaming must be taken out of the refrigerator well in advance.

For genoise mixtures it is important to scald the mixing bowl and utensils before adding the ingredients – the smallest amount of grease present will prevent the eggs from rising to a foamy texture. When whisking the eggs and sugar together it is better to warm the ingredients. This may be done by standing the mixing bowl on a bain-marie, or by adding warm sugar to the eggs. Warm mixtures lighten more readily as the heat quickly expands the tiny cells made by the egg albumen during whisking. In this way the whole mixture becomes light and full of air cells.

Decorating the sponge cake

A wide variety of materials are available to decorate gâteaux and pastries; these are attractive both in appearance and to the taste.

Decorative materials include: marzipans, sugar pastes, jams, jellies, butter creams, fresh cream, chocolate, meringues, nougat, praline, biscuits, boiled sugar items (ribbons, flowers and leaves), fresh and tinned fruits, and fondant.

Preparation of bases

As soon as the sponges are removed from the oven, it is best to turn them out onto a cooling rack. This will prevent sweat forming while the cakes are cooling.

Bases made from cake mixtures are best used as soon as they have cooled. Genoise bases improve in flavour and are more easily cut if left for a day after baking. When masking sponge bases with fondant, it is important to coat the top and sides with boiled apricot jam. This will provide a little sharpness to the overall flavour. It also prevents crumbs or moisture from the cake getting into the fondant while coating.

Fresh cream gâteaux and pastries

Fresh cream used (as a filling) in gâteaux and pastries, spread or piped, adds richness and delicacy to the product. Care should be taken to ensure that the flavours of the base and fresh cream complement each other. Additional ingredients complete the cream gâteaux or pastries:

1 Fruit such as strawberries, raspberries, kiwi, banana.
2 Tinned fruits suitable for the purpose required.
3 Chocolate work, such as piped items, shaped pieces, scraping.
4 Decorations, such as roasted almonds, nuts, angelica, glacé cherries, confits. (Coconut absorbs moisture, it should therefore be added at the last moment.)

All fresh cream items should be kept refrigerated. They should be removed from the refrigerator only for as long as is necessary to complete them. Only sufficient cream for the job in hand should be kept on the preparation surface while working.

Aeration in sponges

Aeration occurs by two means: (a) *mechanical*, important in obtaining complete emulsion in the mix, and (b) *chemical*, to assist the expansion of air cells. A good sponge mix should show an even distribution of small air cells, a good colour and sheen. If the aeration consists of unevenly sized holes, then the sponge would have a coarse, unattractive appearance.

Air and carbon dioxide, together with water vapour pressure, are the factors produced. The process is then terminated by the swelling of the starch and the coagulation of the egg and flour proteins.

Faults in sponge mixes

Thick crust on top: Oven too hot. A crust forms on top before the centre of the cake is cooked.

The creaming mixture curdles: Eggs added too quickly; eggs and butter at different temperatures; butter contains too much water; weak and watery eggs.

Cakes sinking: Too much baking powder; insufficiently baked; unbalanced ingredients; oven door left open.

Heavy textures: Insufficient creaming; eggs added too quickly; overmixed; loss of aeration.

Fruit sinking: Fruit used wet or with syrup; too much baking powder; too much butter.

Discoloration: Unbalanced baking powder.

Spots on the cake: Sugar not creamed sufficiently; excess sugar.

Uneven aeration: Uneven blending of ingredients.

Crumbly texture: Wrong flour used; too much sugar; too much baking powder.

Cauliflower top: Oven too hot; tin overfilled.

Note: All cakes should be turned out of the tin onto a cooling rack and covered with greaseproof paper immediately on removal from the oven. Allow to cool completely before storing.

CAKE MIXTURES

Basic recipe

Castor sugar	200 g
Butter	200 g
Eggs (3)	200 g
Flour	200 g
Baking powder	10 g

Basic techniques

The butter intended for cake mixing should have plenty of body and be free from salt and water. For creaming purposes, the butter must be used at room temperature (21 °C); in cold weather it may be necessary to warm the butter slightly. The sugar should be beaten into creamed butter, until light and fluffy, before adding the eggs. The eggs are broken into a separate container. Make sure that the eggs are in good condition and that no bits of shell are accidentally dropped into the creamed mixture. Pour one or two eggs at a time into the creamed sugar and butter while mixing, allowing about 2–3 minutes between each addition. This prevents curdling. Flour should be added at the very last stage. Baking powder or cocoa powder must be previously sieved with the flour. Although it may be easier to use a mixing machine to cream the basic mixture, for best results the flour should be folded in by hand. This maintains the aeration and avoids toughness in the baked sponge.

Victoria sponge

This is a light sponge made from cake mixture, baked in paper-lined, greased and floured, crimped or plain pans, usually 13–14 cm in diameter and 2½ cm deep. Combine the ingredients as described in basic techniques; creaming butter and sugar, add eggs gradually, fold in sifted flour and baking powder. Bake in two prepared tins at 180–190° C. When pressed lightly with the fingertips the surface should feel springy. The appearance should be of an even colour and have a slightly convex shape. When cold, they are sliced, if necessary, sandwiched together with jam and/or a layer of cream. Tops are usually dusted with icing sugar.

CHOCOLATE SANDWICH

Sieve 60 g of unsweetened cocoa powder with the flour. A little vanilla will enhance the flavour. If a cream filling is used, it may also be flavoured with chocolate, piped on top then sprinkled with pistachio nuts.

ORANGE SANDWICH

Flavoured with orange zest at the creaming stage. Fill with cream and segments of fresh oranges. Spread top with orange flavoured fondant, decorate with orange confits.

COFFEE SANDWICH

Flavoured with coffee at the creaming stage. A strong concentrate is advisable. The cream for the filling can be flavoured with coffee brandy. Sprinkle roasted almonds on top.

The sandwiches can be presented whole or semi-sliced on a serving dish and doily. Cut into triangular sections they can be used for afternoon pastries.

The following recipes are prepared and baked in the same way as the Victoria sponge. Follow stages up to and including the baking stage.

Madeira slab cake 1×20 cm size tin or hoop (40 to 50 slices)

Castor sugar	250 g
Butter	250 g
Eggs (4)	250 g
Lemon zest	3
Flour	250 g
Baking powder	10 g

Produce the basic recipe as described in Basic techniques, adding the lemon zest whilst creaming. Fold in the flour and baking powder. Place the mixture in a paper-lined and greased baking tin, or hoop, smooth the top.

Bake at 180–190 °C, for approximately 40 to 45 minutes. Test by pressing the surface with the tips of the fingers, if it results with a springy action, the sponge is baked.

Genoa slab cake 1 × 25 cm size tin or hoop

Castor sugar	200 g
Butter	200 g
Eggs	3
Flour	220 g
Baking powder	10 g
Mixed peel	30 g
Sultanas	50 g
Currants	50 g
Mixed spice	15 g

Proceed as for Madeira slab cake, fold in the washed and dried fruit, after the flour and baking powder.

Cherry slab cake 1 × 20 cm size tin or hoop

Castor sugar	250 g
Butter	250 g
Eggs	4
Flour	250 g
Glacé cherries	100 g
Lemon zest	1
Baking powder	10 g

Proceed as for Madeira slab cake. Add the cherries, after the flour and baking powder. The cherries are not washed and they can be diced, if desired.

Christmas cake 1 × 25 cm size tin

Castor sugar	200 g
Butter	200 g
Flour	220 g
Eggs	3
Currants	130 g
Sultanas	150 g
Mixed peel	30 g
Mixed spice	15 g
Brandy or rum	1 glass
Marzipan	500 g
Royal icing	

Proceed as for Madeira slab cake. Add the washed and dried fruit after the flour. Store the cake, moistened with the brandy or rum, well wrapped in greaseproofed paper, for at least 7 days, to allow the cake to mature and the crumb to settle. Marzipan and ice as described in the wedding cake method (pp. 219 and 221).

GENOESE SPONGE

Genoise sponges have a very wide variety of uses. They should always be available as part of mise-en-place in the pastry. The baked sponge can be stored, well wrapped in polythene bags, in the refrigerator or freezer. For best results use genoise sponges baked at least a few hours in advance. The sponge will be well rested and will not disintegrate while cutting.

Basic recipe

Castor sugar	125 g		625 g
Eggs	4	for	20
Flour	125 g	five	625 g
Butter (melted)	25 g	cakes	250 g
(One cake serves 10)			

Grease and line a 20 cm cake tin with grease-proof paper, sieve the flour onto greaseproof paper and melt the butter. Whisk the eggs and sugar in a scalded bowl over a bain-marie, until very warm. Continue whisking over the heat, either by hand or mechanically. The mixture is ready when it has trebled in volume and is of a firm foamy texture, known as 'ribbon stage'. Using a large metal spoon, fold in the flour in various stages, simultaneously adding the melted butter, again in stages. It is very important to finish fold quickly, otherwise it will suffer a loss of volume, resulting in a heavy sponge.

Bake in the oven at 180–190 °C, until well risen and of a springy texture. Do not use a knife for testing, as if it is not cooked, the mix will deflate and will not rise again. When baked, remove from the tins onto cooling trays, allow to cool.

Step-by-step genoese sponge

Chocolate genoese, *Génoise au chocolat*

Castor sugar	125 g		
Eggs	4		625 g
Flour	100 g	for	20
Cocoa powder	20 g	five	500 g
Butter (melted)	25 g	cakes	100 g
			250 g

(One cake serves 10)

Prepare as for plain genoese, sieving the cocoa powder with the flour.

COFFEE GENOESE, *GÉNOISE AU CAFÉ*

As for plain genoese adding sufficient coffee concentrate to the mixture while whisking to obtain a pleasant coffee colour.

Swiss roll, *Biscuit roulade*

Eggs	3
Castor sugar	100 g
Flour	100 g
Hot water	1 tablespoon
Butter cream or jam	

Rolling a Swiss roll

Place the eggs and sugar into a basin or whisking bowl. Whisk together over a pan of very hot water to ribbon stage. Fold in the previously sieved flour, avoid over mixing. Spread out the mixture thinly on a greased and papered baking tray 11 by 14 inches. Bake at 210–215 °C. Turn out onto a sugared cloth or paper, and allow to cool. Spread thinly with jam or butter cream and roll up tightly. Store as for genoese sponges.

Swiss rolls are kept in the oven for a very short period only; this helps maintain a soft crust which will not crack when rolled. The addition of water also serves the same purpose, the extra moisture forms an elastic texture, preventing it from cracking while rolling.

Yule log, *Bûche de Noël*

Swiss roll (chocolate flavour)	3 egg mix
Stock syrup	
Rum	
Apricot jam	
Fresh cream	
Chocolate butter cream	

Prepare a chocolate-flavoured swiss roll sieving 25 g of cocoa into 75 g of flour. Allow to cool. Moisten with a solution of syrup and rum. Spread lightly with apricot jam. Spread evenly with fresh cream, roll up, place in the refrigerator to set. Cut off one end at an angle, spread over with chocolate butter cream. Place the sliced end on top, cover with butter cream, mould with a fork to resemble a log. Decorate as desired with chocolate coupeaux, leaves and berries or other Christmas decorations. Keep refrigerated. Yule log can be served as a sweet or afternoon pastry.

Coffee and hazelnut roll, *Roulade d'aveline*

Swiss roll (coffee flavour)	3 eggs mix
Stock syrup	
Tia Maria (to taste)	
Apricot jam	
Fresh cream	3 dl
Hazelnut flour	20 g
Hazelnuts	
Fondant	

Prepare a coffee-flavoured swiss roll adding coffee concentrate while mixing, allow to cool. Moisten with a solution of syrup and Tia Maria. Lightly spread with apricot jam. Mix the hazelnut flour with the whipped cream and spread over the sponge evenly. Sprinkle with chopped hazelnuts, roll up. Place on a draining wire, brush all over with boiled apricot jam. Coat with warm coffee-flavour fondant, allow to set. Trim the ends, decorate as desired with cream, melted chocolate, crystallised flowers, glazed fruit etc.

Chocolate and hazelnut roll, *Roulade au chocolat*

Swiss roll (chocolate flavour)	3 eggs mix
Stock syrup	
Rum	
Apricot jam	
Fresh cream	
Chocolate butter cream	
Chocolate fondant	

Proceed as for coffee and hazelnut roll, using chocolate flavour instead of coffee.

Chocolate and hazelnut roll

Gâteau Monte Carlo (top) gâteau aux fruits (right) and chocolate gâteau

Chocolate gâteau, *Gâteau au chocolat*

Chocolate genoese	1 × 20 cm
Butter cream (chocolate flavoured)	500 g
Apricot jam	50 g
Rum	50 g
Stock syrup	50 g
Cake card (1 × 20 cm)	

Flavour the butter cream with half the rum. Mix the syrup and remaining rum together.

Divide the genoise in three or four evenly cut rings. Place the base on a cake card, moisten all the sponges with syrup and rum. Spread with a thin layer of jam then a layer of butter cream about 1 cm thick. Proceed with all the layers until the gâteau is assembled. Using a turntable, if available, spread the remaining butter cream on the sides then on top, giving smooth sides and a flat top. Cover the sides with roasted almonds, coconut or chocolate vermicelli.

Gâteau aux fruits

Genoese	1 × 20 cm
Butter cream (plain)	500 g
Apricot jam	100 g
Kirsch, Cointreau, etc.	50 g
Stock syrup	50 g
Cake card	

Choose the desired fruit, e.g. strawberries, raspberries, kiwis, peaches, apricots, mandarins, mangoes, and prepare fruit, first by washing then slicing into fine rings or segments. Proceed as for chocolate gâteau, placing slices of fruit in every layer. Decorate the top with butter cream and slices of the fruit previously glazed with some of the jam.

Gâteau dauphinois

Genoese	1 × 20 cm
Coffee ganache (p. 193)	250 g
Walnuts	150 g
Chocolate butter cream	250 g
Rum	50 g
Stock syrup	50 g
Cake card (1 × 20 cm)	

Proceed as for chocolate gâteau, using the coffee ganache mixed with the walnuts for the filling. Decorate the top with chocolate copeaux and walnuts.

GÂTEAU PRALINE

As for chocolate gâteau, incorporating finely crushed praline in the butter cream. Decorate the top with croquante shapes.

GÂTEAU POMPADOUR

Slice the plain sponge into three rounds. Sandwich together with butter cream of any flavour. Mask the sides and top with the same butter cream. Arrange on top cornets filled with the butter cream, and rosettes of cream.

The cornets can be made of biscuit or ginger snap mixture.

GÂTEAU CYRANO

Slice the plain sponge into three. Sprinkle with kirsch, sandwich together with apricot jam or with diced fruit flavoured with kirsch and bound with boiled apricot jam. Brush all over with boiled apricot jam and place onto a serving dish. Mask the side and top with Italian meringue. Glaze in a hot oven.

GÂTEAU MONTE CARLO

Slice the plain sponge into three. Sprinkle with a liqueur, sandwich with apricot jam. Brush all over with boiled apricot jam. Place onto a draining wire. Pour white fondant over the top, allow to set. Using two wet palette knives, transfer from the wire onto a serving dish, decorate the side with pieces of bent croquante (praline). Decorate with rosettes of cream, glacé cherries and angelica.

GÂTEAU DANIER

Slice a *square* shaped plain sponge into three. Sprinkle with rum, sandwich together with apricot jam. Brush all over with boiled and passed apricot jam. Using royal icing, pipe even lines across the top to form 64 squares. Using paper cornets, fill the squares alternately with chocolate and white fondant.

GÂTEAU CIGARETTES

Slice a plain sponge into three. Sandwich together with fresh whipped cream. Mask the sides and top with the same cream. Mask the sides with chocolate flakes. Arrange chocolate cigarettes on top and decorate with rosettes of whipped cream.

GÂTEAU SARAH BERNHARDT

Slice a plain sponge into three. Sprinkle with curaçao or Cointreau. Sandwich together with fresh whipped cream and fresh strawberries. Mask the sides and top with whipped cream. Place roasted almonds on the side. Make an arrangement of strawberries on top. Glaze with flan glaze, finish with rosettes of whipped cream.

GÂTEAU PITHIVIERS

Roll out 1 kg of puff paste to 5 mm thick, about 52 cm in length and 28 cm wide. Cut two rounds 25 cm in diameter. Place one round onto a greased baking tray. Prick the centre, pipe frangipane, starting from the centre to within 15 mm to the edge. Egg-wash the edge and cover with the other paste round ring. Make sure the frangipane is sealed in. Egg-wash the surface. Make a hole in the centre. With a small, pointed knife, cut a series of semi-circular incisions in the top to form a cartwheel pattern. Allow to rest in the refrigerator for 30 minutes. Bake at 210 °C, until the frangipane is cooked inside. When nearly cooked remove from the oven, dust with icing sugar and return to the oven to glaze.

GÂTEAU MILLE-FEUILLES

Roll out puff paste trimmings to about 3 mm thick and sufficiently wide to cut out three 25 cm rounds, place the rounds onto a greased baking tray, prick all over. Allow to rest for 30 minutes. Bake at 215 °C, until well dry. When cold, sandwich together with crème pâtissiére, and spread on the sides. Brush the top with boiled apricot jam. Spread the surface thinly with chocolate flavoured and coloured fondant. Immediately pipe a spiral of fondant, starting from the centre out to the edge. Pull a small knife across the surface eight times, starting from the centre to the outside and eight from the outside to the centre. The result should resemble a spider's web effect. Place crushed cake crumbs on the sides.

Gâteau Pithiviers (top) and mille feuilles (bottom)

GÂTEAU ST HONORÉ

Roll out one 25 cm disc of puff paste trimmings or sweetpaste, prick the centre. Using a 10 mm tube, pipe choux paste around the edge to form a ring. On a separate tray pipe about twenty 20 mm balls using the remaining choux paste. Bake both trays at 204 °C, until well dry. When cold dip the choux balls in light caramel sugar and place them on the ring of choux paste. Fill the centre with rochées of crème St Honoré (p. 133), the filling must retain the spoon shape. Serve with spun sugar on top.

GÂTEAU RELIGIEUSE

Roll out a round of sweet paste about 10 cm in diameter, bake at 204 °C. Pipe and bake 16–18 eclairs (slightly spatulated in shape), a choux ring of 10 cm, another of 8 cm, and one small bun. Glaze the éclairs, half with white fondant and half with chocolate fondant, allow to set. Line the inside of a charlotte mould with oiled greaseproof paper, arrange the eclairs, in alternate colours, inside the mould. Fill the inside with a bavarois mixture (p. 99), allow to set. Turn out onto the sweet paste base, previously brushed with apricot jam. Dip the rings and bun in chocolate and white fondant, arrange them on top of the bavarois, decorate with whipped cream.

GÂTEAU TOM POUCE

Roll out two rounds from puff pastry trimmings and bake. Trim the rounds to fit a 20 cm torten ring. Place one in the base. Fill with a bavarois mixture to reach nearly the top of the ring. Place the other disc on top. Place in the refrigerator to set. When ready, demould, cover the surface with fondant, complete as for gâteau mille-feuilles.

▦ TORTEN

There may not seem much difference between gâteaux and torten, in fact the main distinction is their countries of origin – gâteau is French and torten is German.

Torten tends to be decorated for serving in set portions. In the continental confiseries, large wedges of torten can be purchased individually. The classical names are very strictly maintained, such as torten forêt noir, kirsch torten, dobos and sacher tortens. The use of flavours and liqueurs is very important; lack of moisture in the basic sponge will result into a dry and unpalatable cake. On the other hand, too much liquid will spoil the cutting, serving and eating quality of the product. A carefully blended mixture of stock syrup, with the addition of liqueurs and spirits, will guarantee good results.

I disc of shortbread or japonaise for the base	25 cm
I genoese base	25 cm
Fresh fruit	
Stock syrup and liqueur	
Butter cream	750 g
Cake crumbs or roasted almonds to coat the sides	

Assemble the cake by first placing the base on a cake card. Spread with a little apricot jam, place the genoise layer on top. Moisten by using a brush dipped into the syrup and liqueur mixture. Pipe in a spiral of flavoured butter cream, and arrange on top any fresh fruit (if used). Place another layer of sponge on top. (Another layer of filling sponge can be added, but the total height should not exceed 8–9 cm.) Evenly spread butter cream on the top and sides, coat sides with crumbs or almonds, decorate the top. Mark the portions by piping tidy lines on the top. The portions can be cut in advance and reassembled on the serving dish. Fresh cream can be used in place of butter cream.

The following combinations of fruit and liqueurs can be used.

Peach – Peach brandy
Cherry – Kirsch, maraschino, cherry brandy
Pineapple – Kirsch, rum
Orange – Grand Marnier, curaçao
Chocolate – Rum
Coffee – Tia Maria, rum, brandy

If tinned fruit is used, the juice should be used for soaking the sponge with the addition of liqueur or spirit.

Dobos torten

Egg yolks	5
Egg whites	6
Castor sugar	150 g
Butter	120 g
Flour	150 g
(Serves 10)	

Cream the butter with half of the sugar, add egg yolks. Whisk the whites until they peak, whisk in the remaining sugar. Blend the meringue into the creamed mixture, alternating with the sieved flour. Spread into four greased 20 cm flan rings. Bake at 210 °C to a gold brown, place onto cooling wires. Coat one layer with caramel. Sandwich the other three with caramel-flavoured fresh cream. Mask the sides and top with the same cream. Cut the caramel layer into segments and arrange the triangles fanwise on the remaining torte. Decorate the side with roasted cake crumbs.

Sacher torten

Butter	180 g
Castor sugar	150 g
Chocolate couverture	180 g
Egg yolks	200 g
Egg whites	250 g
Flour	150 g
Stock syrup with rum	
(Serves 10)	

Cream the butter with half the sugar, add the melted chocolate and vanilla. Beat in the yolks gradually. Whip the egg whites until they peak, fold in the rest of the sugar. Fold the flour into the yolk mixture, alternating with the whipped egg whites. Place into two 20 cm flan rings or cake tins, bake at 175 °C. When cold, moisten with rum syrup, sandwich with apricot jam. Brush all over with boiled apricot jam, allow to set. Cover all over with chocolate ganache, allow to set. Decorate with the same ganache, and crystallised violets.

Sacher torten

La torta Torino (Italian speciality)

Produce the chocolate sponge bases as in sacher torten. Marinade 500 g of chopped chestnuts in sambuca for at least 3–4 hours. Carefully mix the marinaded chestnuts with some ganache, sandwich the chocolate bases with the mix. Complete as for sacher torten. Decorate the top with pieces of crystallised chestnuts rolled in castor sugar.

CHOCOLATE PROFITEROLES, PROFITEROLES AU CHOCOLATE

Choux paste	3 dl
Crème chiboust (chocolate flavour)	
Chocolate sauce or ganache	
Chocolate shavings	
Whipped cream	
(Serves 10)	

Chocolate profiteroles with gâteau St. Honoré (above)

Using 2 cm piping tube, pipe small ball shapes at 4 cm intervals on a lightly greased baking tray. Bake at 204°C, until well dry. Using a 5 cm tube fill with the flavoured 'crème chiboust' and mound in a glass or silver bowl. Cover with chocolate sauce, place an arrangement of chocolate shavings or cigarettes on top. Decorate with rosettes of cream.

Strawberry/Raspberry profiteroles,
Profiteroles aux fraises/framboises

Proceed as for chocolate profiteroles, filling

the small choux buns with crème chiboust flavoured with either strawberry or raspberry purée. Coat with sauce mousseline flavoured accordingly, decorate with whipped cream and crystallised rose petals.

Coffee Profiteroles, *Profiteroles au café*

Proceed as for strawberry profiteroles flavouring the filling and sauce with coffee flavour.

CROQUENBOUCHE

Choux paste	3 dl
Crème chiboust (vanilla flavoured)	
Cube sugar	500 g
Glace cherries	
Angelica	
Whipped cream	
(Serves 10)	

Using a 2 cm piping tube, pipe small ball shapes on lightly greased baking trays, starting at 3 cm in diameter down to 1½ cm resulting with large and small profiteroles. Bake at 204°C until well dry. Using a 5 cm piping tube fill with crème chiboust. Saturate and boil the sugar to a very light caramel colour. Using a dipping folk and a small knife dip half the profiteroles in the boiled sugar. With the aid of an oiled turned-over bowl, build a pyramid shape round the bowl with the dipped profiteroles. Fill the pyramid with the remaining filled profiteroles. Decorate with whipped cream, sliced glaced cherries and angelica. Using the remaining cooked sugar, produce sufficient spun sugar to encircle the pyramid.

Croquenbouche

FRENCH PASTRIES, *PÂTISSERIES FRANÇAISE*

22

Dartois

Roll out fresh puff paste 5 mm thick and about 20 cm wide. Spread a small amount of apricot jam across the middle, then pipe frangipane over the top, egg-wash. Fold over so that the frangipane is sealed in. Egg-wash the top and mark the portions. Make a pattern on top with the point of a small knife. Allow to rest for 30 minutes, bake at 218 °C, making sure the frangipane is well cooked. When cold divide into portions.

Othellos

Prepare biscuits à la cuiller mix (p. 157). Pipe out tall dome shapes, about 3 cm in diameter. When baked and cold form a cavity in the flat sides. Sandwich two together with crème pâtissiére, brush all over with boiled apricot jam, place onto a draining wire. Cover with chocolate fondant, then pipe a spiral on top using the same fondant. Place a crystallised violet on top.

Friand

Ground almonds	250 g
Castor sugar	250 g
Melted butter	120 g
Flour	15 g
Egg whites	3

Mix the almonds, sugar and flour, add the eggs, add the melted butter last. Half fill well-greased barquettes moulds and bake at 204 °C. Remove from the moulds immediately and allow to cool. Brush over with boiled apricot jam and place a half glacé cherry on each.

Madeleines

Castor sugar	560 g
Eggs	12
Melted butter	200 g
Baking powder	2 g

Whisk the eggs and sugar as for genoise, fold in the flour then fold in the melted butter. Half fill madeleine moulds and bake at 190 °C. When cold dip in boiled apricot jam and roll in desiccated coconut (roasted). Decorate them with whipped cream and glacé cherries.

Pain de genes

Butter	250 g
Castor sugar	500 g
Eggs	10
Ground almonds	250 g
Flour	250 g
Rum or curaçao	100 g

Cream the butter and sugar. Add the eggs gradually and continue beating until the mixture is light and fluffy. Add the liqueur, mix well. Fill buttered and floured moulds and bake at 204 °C. Allow to cool and serve dusted with icing sugar.

Fondant dips

Use either victoria sponge mix, pain de genes mix, or German paste.

Various fondant dips

Bake the sponges in flat tins (preferably swiss roll tins). When cold sandwich together with jam or jam and butter cream. Brush over with boiled apricot jam and cover with a thinly-rolled layer of marzipan. Using a sharp wet knife, cut into the desired shape. Using a small knife dip each one into boiled apricot jam and place on a draining wire, well spaced. When the jam has set, cover with the desired flavoured and coloured fondant. Allow the fondant to set then decorate by piping fondant on top. Add crystallised decorations. Serve in paper cases.

Battenburg

Bake square victoria sponge bases (p. 141) of two or more colours and matching flavours. Sandwich two colours together using boiled apricot jam and cut into strips of 2 cm. Reverse one strip. Brush again with boiled jam. Join two strips together so the colours alternate. Roll out sufficient marzipan to cover the rectangle. Brush the marzipan with boiled apricot jam and wrap round the sponges to seal. Cut into slices 12–15 mm thick and lay flat in paper cases for serving.

Brandy snaps

Golden syrup	200 g
Brown sugar	80 g
Butter	150 g
Flour	100 g
Ginger powder	4 g
(Makes 38–40)	

Bring the sugar, butter and syrup to the boil, stir in the flour and ginger powder, mix to a smooth paste. Allow to become cool. Roll into a long sausage shape and cut into even pieces, ball up. Place onto well-greased baking trays, well spaced, flatten down and bake at 204 °C. When removed from the oven, allow to stand for a moment, then roll round cream-horn moulds or wooden handles. They can be filled with cream or served plain.

Florentines

Butter	100 g
Castor sugar	110 g
Glacé cherries (diced)	30 g
Mixed peel	30 g
Sultanas	50 g
Almonds	150 g
Cream	30 g
(Makes 24)	

Bring to the boil the butter and sugar. Remove from the heat. Add the fruit and almonds, stir well. Mix in the cream. Neatly arrange the mixture in heaps on well-greased baking trays, well spaced. Bake at 204 °C. As soon as removed from the oven, tidy the edges using a plain round cutter. When set, place on cooling wires and when cold dip or partly dip in melted chocolate.

Japonais

Egg whites	200 g
Castor sugar	300 g
Ground almonds	200 g
Cornflour	40 g

Make a meringue using the egg whites and sugar. Sieve the ground almonds and cornflour together. Fold into the meringue gradually. Pipe the mix onto paper-lined trays in disc shapes 3 cm round. Bake in a low oven, 160–180 °C. When cold sandwich together with butter cream or ganache. Mask the pastries with the same cream and decorate as desired.

Pyramide au café

Pipe round biscuits à la cuillier 3 cm in diameter. When baked and cool use a palette knife to form a pyramid of coffee butter cream on each. Place onto a draining wire and set in the refrigerator. Cover with coffee flavoured fondant and pipe a spiral on top.

Gaufrettes Viennoises

Castor sugar	250 g
Butter	500 g
Flour	500 g
Ground almonds	500 g
Royal icing (see p. 221)	50 g

Cream well the butter and the sugar to a very light texture. Sieve the flour and ground almonds and fold into the creamed mixture, set in the refrigerator. Divide into two. Roll out each half to fit two swiss roll tins. Mark one into 5 cm squares and pipe royal icing criss-cross over it. Allow to dry slightly. Using a wet knife, cut through the icing and paste. Bake both trays at 204 °C. When baked immediately sandwich together with raspberry jam, placing the previously cut pieces on top, cut through the pattern to the bottom. Serve individual pieces in paper cases.

Éclairs au chocolat et café

Prepare the choux paste (p. 42). Using a 10 mm piping tube, pipe finger shapes 80 cm long onto lightly-greased baking trays. Egg-wash, and pass a fork over the top. Bake at 204 °C, until well dry. When cold, slit the tops with a small knife and fill with crème chiboust or dip the fingers in chocolate or coffee fondant. Serve in paper cases.

Coating éclairs

Choux à la crème fondant

Prepare the choux paste. Using a 10 mm piping tube, pipe balls 3 cm in diameter onto lightly-greased baking trays. bake at 204 °C, until well dry. When cold slit the tops and fill with crème chiboust or whipped cream. Dip into a prepared fondant, which can be of any colour and flavour. Serve in paper cases.

CHOUX À LA CRÈME

Proceed as for choux à la crème fondant, sprinkling the balls with almonds before baking. Fill with whipped cream. Just dust with icing sugar instead of fondant.

SALAMBÔ

Prepare the choux paste. Pipe and bake plain choux buns as for choux à la crème. When cold fill from the base with crème chiboust. Dip the buns into a light caramel. Place a pistachio nut on top.

Montes Carlo

Prepare the choux paste. Using a 10 mm piping tube, pipe triangular shapes, each of three 10 mm balls nearly touching, on lightly-greased baking trays. Bake at 204 °C, until well dry. When cold, fill each one with whipped cream, using a small piping tube inserted in the base. Dip the buns into white fondant. Pipe a spiral on each one using chocolate fondant.

Cygnet chantilly

Prepare the choux paste. Using a star tube, pipe out spatula-shaped bodies onto greased baking trays. Using a 3 mm piping tube, pipe neck shapes on greased trays. Bake both trays at 204 °C, until well dry. (N.B. The necks will bake much more quickly.) Cut off the tops of the bodies, and cut lids in half, to be used for the wings. Brush the inside of the cases with boiled apricot jam. Fill with whipped cream. Arrange the wings and insert the necks to resemble swans. Serve in paper cases.

The cygnets can be used as sweet. For this, arrange them on a dish lined with green jelly. For cygnets glacé, use a ball of ice cream in the choux case. Decorate with cream.

Rognons

Prepare the choux paste. Using a 10 mm piping tube, pipe crescent shapes onto greased baking trays. Bake at 204 °C, when cold, slit the sides and fill with crème chiboust. Dip in fondant of desired colour and flavour. Piped a pattern on top using the same fondant. Serve in paper cases.

Almond tiles, *Tuiles d'amande*

Flaked almonds	500 g
Castor sugar	300 g
Flour	100 g
Egg whites	8
(Makes 23–25)	

Beat the egg whites and sugar to a firm meringue. Fold in the flour and almonds. Using two teaspoons, place heaps of the mixture on lightly-greased baking trays, tap the trays lightly to even the surfaces. Bake in a hot oven, at 230–240 °C, until the edges have browned. Immediately remove from the tray and place in a savarin mould, to form a curved shape. One side of the biscuit can be brushed or partly dipped in melted couverture.

Finger biscuits, *Biscuits savoie, Biscuit de Savoie cuiller*

Castor sugar	200 g
Eggs	8
Flour	200 g
(Makes approximately 100)	

Separate the yolks of the eggs from the whites. Using a scalded bowl whisk the yolks with half of the sugar, over a bain-marie to just warm. Simultaneously whisk the egg whites to firm peaks, adding the remaining sugar, to form a meringue. Having the two mixtures prepared and the flour sieved, fold about a quarter of the meringue in the yolks mixture, add a little of the flour, then more meringue, folding continually add more flour and meringue until all blended, maintaining as much volume as possible. Immediately pipe the mixture on baking trays lined with silicone paper, well spaced out, using a 1 cm piping tube, either finger shapes, 5–6 cm in length, or round, as desired. Bake at 180–190 °C, to a light brown colour. These biscuits can be stored on the paper on which they are baked.

CHOCOLATE FINGER BISCUITS, *BISCUITS SAVOIE AU CHOCOLAT, BISCUITS Á LA CUILLER AU CHOCOLAT*

Proceed as for previous recipe replacing 100 g of flour with 100 g of cocoa powder.

Piped shortbreads, *Sablés à la poche*

Castor sugar	250 g
Butter	400 g
Eggs	2
Flour	500 g
Vanilla flavour	
Yellow colour (optional)	
(Makes approximately 50)	

Thoroughly cream the butter and sugar to a light emulsion, add the eggs a little at a time. Fold in the flour, flavour and colour as desired. Pipe various shapes on greased baking trays, using a large star tube. Decorate the tops with bits of glacé cherries, angelica or nuts. Bake at 180–200 °C, to a light brown colour. Remove from the tray immediately. The ends can be dipped in melted chocolate if desired. Sandwich with flavoured butter creams as desired.

Scottish shortbreads

Castor sugar	150 g
Butter	250 g
Flour	400 g
(Makes approximately 50)	

Thoroughly cream the butter and sugar to a light emulsion (on a clean working surface). Add the flour and mix to a smooth paste, avoid over mixing. Wrap the paste well and place in the refrigerator to set. Roll out using a little dusting flour to 5 mm thick, cut various shapes, using a knife or fancy cutters. Place the cut pieces on clean baking trays, bake at 180–190 °C, to a light brown colour. Remove from the oven immediately. Dust with castor sugar.

BLOCKED SHORTBREADS
Using wooden block moulds, lightly dusted with ground rice or semolina, mould sufficient shortbread mixture to fill the cavity, scrape off the surplus, tip the moulded shape onto a clean baking tray, bake at 190 °C to a light brown colour.

CHOCOLATE SHORTBREADS
Either the piped or rolled shortbread can be flavoured chocolate, by sieving 50 g of cocoa powder with the flour, and adding chocolate colouring if desired.

CHERRY SHORTBREADS
Proceed as for scottish shortbreads, adding 100 g of diced glacé cherries with the flour.

SULTANA SHORTBREADS
Proceed as for scottish shortbreads, adding 100 g of sultanas to the flour.

Mirliton

Puff paste trimming	1 kg
Eggs	5
Castor sugar	200 g
Ground almonds	200 g
Raspberry jam	
(Makes approximately 50)	

Line tartlet moulds with the trimmings, quite thinly. Place a small amount of raspberry jam in the centres. Separate the egg whites from the yolks. Whisk the yolks and half the sugar over a bain-marie, to a ribbon stage. Whisk the egg whites to peaks, gradually whisk in the remaining sugar, forming a light meringue. Fold the meringue, in two or three stages, into the yolk mixture. Fold in the sieved ground almonds. Nearly fill the prepared tartlet moulds, dredge heavily with icing sugar, allow to stand for 15–20 minutes, dredge again with icing sugar. Bake in the oven at 180–190 °C, until light brown in colour with a pearl effect.

Chinese lanterns, Lampions

Sweetpaste	1 kg
Frangipane	1 kg
Raspberry jam	
Icing sugar	
Vanilla butter cream	
(Makes approximately 50)	

Roll out the sweetpaste 3–4 mm thick, cut out rounds using a 7–8 cm fluted cutter. Place in tartlet moulds, allow to rest for 10 minutes. Thumb up, raising the sides to just above the rims. Place a small amount of raspberry jam in the centres, three-quarters fill with frangipane and bake at 200 °C, to a light brown colour. Immediately remove from the moulds and turn over onto a cooling wire. When cold remove the middle using 1½ cm plain cutter, place aside. Dredge the surface with icing sugar. Pipe a tall spiral of butter cream in the cavity of the tartlets. Spread some raspberry jam on the removed piece and place on top of the cream.

Chocolate scraping barquettes,
Barquettes copeaux

Line barquette moulds close together, on the working surface. Roll out sufficient sweetpaste to cover all the barquettes, using a rolling pin place the rolled paste on the tartlets. Using a lump of puff paste trimming, press on top pushing the paste into the moulds. Using two rolling pins, roll over the tops, cutting off and removing the surplus paste. Place a small amount of raspberry jam in each, fill with frangipane using a palette knife, flattening to the rim. Bake at 200 °C, to a light brown colour, turn over onto a cooling wire when baked. When cold, brush with boiled apricot jam, coat the top with chocolate butter cream. Decorate with chocolate shavings, sprinkle lightly with icing sugar.

BARQUETTES ARLEQUIN
Prepare and bake barquettes as described above. When baked and cold, brush the tops with boiled apricot jam. Dip one side of the tops in chocolate fondant and the other side in vanilla fondant. Place a diamond of angelica in the centres.

CONVERSATIONS
Line tartlets moulds as described for Chinese latnerns, using puff paste trimming instead of sweetpaste. Three-quarters fill with frangipane, cover with another thin layer of the same paste. Allow to rest for 10 minutes. With a palette knife, spread a layer of royal icing on top. Arrange a pattern with very fine strips of paste on top. Bake in the oven at 204 °C, to a light brown colour.

CONVERSATION BARQUETTES
Proceed lining and filling the barquette moulds as for copeaux, then complete and bake as for conversation tartlets.

Congress tartlets

Sweetpaste	1 kg
Castor sugar	1 kg
Ground almonds	600 g
Ground rice	50 g
Egg whites	400 g
(Makes approximately 50)	

Line the tartlet moulds as described for Chinese lanterns. Prepare the filling, beating the sieved ground almonds and ground rice into the egg whites, add the sugar, beat well. Three-quarters fill the prepared moulds, place a few flaked almonds on top, bake at 204 °C to a light brown colour.

Allumettes

Puff paste (fresh)	1 kg
Royal icing	
(Makes 50)	

Roll the puff paste to 50 cm by 80 cm, spread the royal icing evenly on top. Allow to rest for 10 minutes. Using a wet large knife, cut five strips 8 cm wide, then cut each strip into 5 cm portions, making 50 pastries. Lay the cut pieces slightly apart on a greased baking tray. Bake in the oven at 210 °C. When cold the allumettes can be filled with fresh cream.

Cornets à la crème

Puff paste (fresh)	1 kg
Raspberry jam	
Fresh cream	
Castor sugar	
(Makes 30)	

Roll the puff paste to 60 cm by 30 cm. Fold the paste over and cut 30 strips 2 cm wide. Unfold the strips, water-wash all over. Twist the strips over a cornet mould, dip the top in castor sugar, place on a greased baking tray. Allow to rest for about 15 minutes. Bake in the oven at 220 °C. Remove from the mould immediately. Place a small amount of raspberry jam in each of the baked cornets, fill with a rosette of whipped cream.

Vanilla slices, *Mille feuilles*

Puff paste (fresh)	*2 kg*
Mincemeat (p. 242)	*1.5 kg*
Castor sugar	
(Makes 50)	

Roll the puff paste to thinly cover three baking trays 80 cm by 60 cm, dock all over, allow to rest at least 20 minutes. When baked, set aside the best one, to be used for the top, brush boiled apricot jam over the other two. Spread the smooth crème pâtissiére over one of the layers, place another layer on top, spread the second layer with crème pâtissiére, place the third layer on top, using the back of a tray press down lightly to even out. Brush the top with boiled apricot jam. Prepare the warm fondant, in a small basin flavour a little fondant with chocolate, pour into a paper cornet, keep warm. Pour the remaining fondant on top and spread evenly, immediately pipe lines over using the prepared cornet, with a small knife score all over forming a feathering pattern. Allow the fondant to set, cut into 5 by 8 cm strips, using a wet large knife, then divide each strip into 5 cm pieces, totalling 50.

Apple turnovers, *Chaussons aux pommes*

Puff paste (fresh)	*I kg*
Apple purée	
Castor sugar	
(Makes 50)	

Roll out the puff paste large enough to cut 10 × 5, 10 cm squares, water-wash all over, place a good tablespoon of apple purée on top, fold over into triangles, press to seal. Water-wash the tops, dip in castor sugar, place on greased baking trays, allow to rest for at least 20 minutes. Bake in the oven at 220 °C. The paste can be cut using a 10 cm round cutter, if desired.

Apple turnovers

JAM TURNOVERS, *CHAUSSONS AUX CONFITURES*
Proceed as for apple turnovers, using a spoonful of jam instead of the apple purée.

VANILLA TURNOVERS, *CHAUSSONS BRUXELLOIS*
Proceed as for apple turnovers, using a

spoonful of vanilla flavoured crème pâtissiére instead of the apple purée.

CHOCOLATE TURNOVERS, *CHAUSSONS AU CHOCOLAT*

Proceed as for apple turnovers, using chocolate flavoured crème pâtissiére instead of the apple purée.

Well of Love, *Puits d'amour*

Puff paste	1 kg
Crème pâtissiére	6 dl
Egg-wash	
Apricot jam	
Rose-flower water	
Curaçao	

Produce small vol-au-vents, using a 6 cm cutter. When cold, pipe a small amount of apricot jam into each, fill with whipped crème pâtissiére flavoured with rose-flower water and curaçao. Pipe a small rosette of fresh cream on top. Dip the puff paste lid in pink fondant, place on the cream. Decorate with glacé cherry quarters and angelica.

Mince pies (1)

Mince pies made from puff paste, are the most suitable for a busy service, they keep well in the hot plate, especially if the puff paste is made with butter.

Puff paste (fresh)	2 kg
Mincemeat (p. 242)	1.5 kg
Castor sugar	
(Makes 50)	

Roll (slightly) less than half the puff paste, sufficient to cut 50 rounds using 6 cm cutter. Place the cut pieces on a greased baking tray, water-wash all over, pipe the mincemeat on top, 30 g per portion. Roll the other half of the paste, cut the rounds slightly larger, place over the mincemeat, seal well using the back of a smaller cutter. Water-wash all over, sprinkle well with castor sugar. Allow to rest for at least 30 minutes. Bake in the oven at 220 °C.

Mince pies (2)

Sweetpaste	2 kg
Mincemeat	1.5 kg
Castor sugar	
(Makes 50)	

Line the tartlet moulds with the sweetpaste as described for Chinese lanterns (p. 158), three-quarters fill with mincemeat. Roll out thinly the remaining paste with the trimmings, cut rounds using a 5 cm cutter. Water-wash, turn over, place on the prepared tartlets, press to seal. Water-wash the tops, dredge with castor sugar. Allow to rest for at least 20 minutes. Bake in the oven at 200 °C, to a light brown colour.

Apple slices, *Tranche aux pommes*

Sweetpaste	1 kg
Cooking apples	1 kg
Cinnamon sugar	
Sultanas	
Kirsch	
(Makes 50)	

Line an 80 cm by 50 cm baking tray with half the sweetpaste, allow to rest for 10 minutes. Bake in a medium oven for 10 minutes to partly cook. Remove from the oven, fill with sliced apples, sprinkle with sultanas and cinnamon sugar. Roll out the remaining paste, place over the fruit, seal the edges. Dock all over, egg-wash. Allow to rest for 10 minutes, bake in the oven to a light brown colour. Allow to stand until cold and well set. Cut into five strips, then cut each strip into 5 cm slices.

Pigs ears, *Palmiers*

> Puff paste   1 kg
> Castor sugar
>   (Makes 50)

Roll out the puff paste to 30 cm by 50 cm, 5 mm thick, using castor sugar instead of flour for dusting. Fold both ends of the longer edges twice towards the centre. Press down flat and cut into 5 cm wide pieces. Place cut sides down on well-buttered baking tray, spacing well apart. Allow to rest and spread for 20 minutes. Bake in the oven at 220 °C, until nicely browned. Transfer immediately to cooling trays. The biscuits can be partly dipped in melted couverture, and can be sandwiched with fresh or butter cream as desired.

BUTTERFLIES, *PAPILLONS* (Also known as bow ties, or cravats.)
Proceed as for pigs ears, rolling the paste to 2.5 mm thickness. Cut into 5 or 6 8 cm strips and place on top of each other. Using a rolling pin, press across the middle to thin slightly. Cut lengthwise into 5 mm wide strips and twist both ends in opposite directions, making a half-turn in the centre. Place on a well-buttered baking tray and complete as above.

Lemon meringue tartlets, *Tartelettes au citron meringué*

> Sweetpaste   200 g
> Lemon curd (p. 46)
> Meringue (p. 164)

Roll the sweetpaste to about 2 mm thick, cut out ten rounds using an 8 cm fluted cutter, place into the dip tartlet moulds, allow to rest for 10 minutes. Thumb up the edges. Place tartlet cases in each and fill with flan beans, bake at 204 °C to a light brown colour. Remove the beans and cases, fill the tartlets with lemon curd, allow to cool. Pipe meringue on top of each. Return to the oven to colour the meringue. Serve as sweet or with afternoon tea.

ORANGE MERINGUE TARTLETS, *TARTELETTES À L'ORANGE MERINGUE*
Prepare the curd filling as described on page 46, using oranges instead of lemons, eliminating the water and using just half the orange juice for dilution. Continue as above.

ALMOND MERINGUE TARTLETS, *TARTELETTES D'AMANDE MERINGUE*
Prepare and bake frangipane tartlets as for Chinese lanterns. Brush the tops with boiled apricot jam. Pipe the prepared meringue on top, sprinkle with flaked or nibbed almonds, place in the oven to glaze the meringue. Serve with lemon sauce or coulis.

FRUIT TARTLETS, *TARTELETTES AUX FRUITS*
Line the tartlet moulds with sweetpaste as described for Chinese lanterns, blind bake, as for lemon tartlets. When cold, half fill with crème pâtissiére flavoured with orange-flower water or with any desired liqueur. Make an arrangement of fresh fruit on top, glaze with apricot glaze. Pipe a small rosette of fresh cream on top.

FRUIT BARQUETTES, *BARQUETTES AUX FRUITS*
Proceed as for fruit tartlets, using barquette moulds instead of tartlet moulds.

Banbury cakes

Puff paste (trimmings)	500 g
Cooking apples	1 kg
Brown sugar	250 g
Raisins	50 g
Cake crumbs	100 g
Apple purée	100 g
Currants	50 g
Lemon zest	2
Mixed peel	50 g
Mixed spice	20 g

Finely dice the apples, place in a bowl, add the rest of the ingredients and mix together. Roll out the puff paste trimmings, to the thickness of a 10 pence piece. Using a 10 cm by 6 cm oval plain cutter, cut out 25 pieces and lay side by side on the working surface. Water wash all over, place a good tablespoonful of filling on each. Draw over the sides to cover the filling. Close up the paste so that each cake is pointed at the ends, slightly flatten with the hand. Turn over, brush with egg white, dip the tops in castor sugar, place on a greased baking tray. Allow to rest for 20 minutes. With a sharp knife make three incisions on top. Bake in the oven at 220 °C, to a light brown colour.

ECCLES CAKES
Proceed as for Banbury cakes, forming a round shape instead of oval.

Imperial star

Puff paste (fresh)
Castor sugar
Apricot jam
Crème pâtissiére
Glacé cherries

Roll the paste out to a square shape, using a hot wet knife cut 10 cm squares. Cut the paste squares from each corner to within 15 mm of the centre. Brush over with water. Fold every other half corner over to the centre (see diagram). Dip in castor sugar, place on a greased baking tray, rest for 20 minutes. In each centre place a small amount of crème pâtissiére and a half glacé cherry. Bake in the oven at 220 °C.

Vanilla fancies

Puff paste
Egg-wash
Greengage jelly

Roll the puff paste out to a square shape, cut 10 cm-squares. Using a hot wet knife, cut the two opposite corners and fold one over, as shown in the diagram. Fold the other corner over the top. Allow to rest, egg-wash, bake in the oven at 220 °C. When cold fill the cavity with greengage jelly.

Queen cakes

Flour	250 g
Salt	pinch
Baking powder	10 g
Butter	125 g
Castor sugar	125 g
Eggs	2
Sultanas	60 g
Currants	60 g
Lemon zest	1
Milk	50 g

Cream the butter and sugar until light and creamy. Add the eggs gradually, stir in the sieved flour, baking powder and salt, mix well. Finally add the fruit zest and milk. Using a piping bag with a 1 cm plain tube, three-quarters fill pastry paper cases. Bake in the oven at 200 °C.

23 MERINGUE GOODS

It is strongly recommended that all the equipment used for whisking should be scalded in hot water. *Do not dry.* The smallest amount of grease will prevent the egg whites from rising. Meringues should always be baked, or dried, at a very low heat, 110–120 °C. Twenty-five egg whites makes about one litre.

Swiss meringue *Meringue Suisse*

Egg whites	½ ℓ
Castor sugar	I kg

Whisk the egg whites and sugar in a bowl over a bain-marie. Continue whisking until very warm, 50 °C. Remove from the heat and continue whisking until cold and of the required volume.

Italian meringue *Meringue italienne*

Egg whites	½ ℓ
Cube sugar	400 g to 1.5 kg
Water to saturation	

The amount of sugar varies depending on the use. Boil the saturated sugar to the required temperature:
  118 °C (soft ball) marzipan and fondant
  221 °C (hard ball) soufflé surprise
  138 °C (small crack) nougat montelimar
Whisk the egg whites until firm, making sure that the sugar is ready at the same time. Very slowly but continuously pour in the boiled sugar while whisking. Continue until the meringue has a firm texture. Avoid over whisking as this will cause the meringue to grain and will later be difficult to use.

Basic meringue

Egg whites	3 dl	½ ℓ
Castor sugar	600 g to 1 kg	250 g
Vanilla flavour		

Whisk the egg whites to a firm texture. Gradually add half the castor sugar while whisking. Fold in the remaining sugar; make sure it is well blended. Using a 10 mm piping tube, pipe the required shapes onto paper-lined baking trays. Dry the meringues into a cool oven, 110 °C, or leave overnight on a hot plate. The meringues should be well dry and not coloured.

Piping different meringue shapes

FRESH CREAM MERINGUES, *MERINGUES CHANTILLY*
Produce the meringue mix, pipe various shaped shells, dry in a warm oven. When cold

Vacherin aux fruits

sandwich two together to form a ball. Decorate the tops with glacé cherries, angelica, almonds, pralines.

VACHERIN
Pipe meringue onto paper-lined trays, in the shape of discs, sizes as required. Bake as for meringues.

VACHERIN CHANTILLY
Prepare three meringue discs, trim to make sure they are of equal sizes. Sandwich together with whipped cream. Mask the sides and top with the same cream. Place cake crumbs or almonds on the sides. Decorate the top as desired with rosettes of cream and crystallised decorations.

VACHERIN AUX FRUITS
Proceed as for vacherin chantilly, using well-drained fruit inside and for decoration on top.

VACHERIN AU CHOCOLAT
Proceed as for vacherin chantilly, using chocolate-flavoured fresh cream, and chocolate copeaux decoration.

VACHERIN MONT JURA
Prepare vacherin bases in shape of a well, dry as described. Place on a layer of sponge moistened with stock syrup and brandy. Fill with cream cheese, decorate the top with fruit, chocolate copeaux and whipped cream.

WELLS OF LOVE, PUIT D'AMOUR AUX FRUITS
Pipe the meringue mixture in the shape of little wells (individual portions), dry as described. Fill the wells with fruit of choice, preferably glazed and marinaded in liqueur. Decorate the top with rosettes of cream and almonds.

24 ICE CREAMS

Food and Drugs Act 1962

In the British Isles, as well as in most European countries, there are very strict regulations governing the preparation and sale of ice cream. The legislation is designed to guarantee the quality of the finished product, and ensure that the preparations are carried out under hygienic conditions.

Anyone wishing to manufacture, sell or use ice cream in food for sale must apply for a special licence. Premises where ice cream is manufactured or sold have to be inspected and regularly visited by the local Department of Environmental Health. Licence registration can be refused or cancelled.

The occurrence of certain diseases among any staff working where ice cream is made or used, must be reported to the Public Health Officer of the local authority. These are enteric fever (including typhoid and paratyphoid fevers), scarlet fever, dysentery, diphtheria, acute inflammation of the throat, gastro-enteritis, undulant fever.

Food Standard Regulations 1970

Ice cream must contain not less than 5% fat and 7% milk solids other than fat. If ice cream contains fruit, fruit pulp or fruit purée, its production is still subject to the ice cream regulations. Dairy ice cream must contain not less than 5% milk fat and no other type of fat, and not less than 7% milk solids other than fat.

Pasteurisation

The ice cream mixture is raised to and kept at a temperature of not less than 140 °C for at least two seconds. After the mixture has been pasteurised or sterilised it must be reduced to a temperature of not more than 7 °C. Immediately after the mixture has been sterilised, it is placed in sterile, air-tight containers under sterilised conditions and the container remains unopened. Ice cream must not be sold if at any time its temperature rises above 28 °C.

In the pâtisserie, ice cream should be stored in a regular freezer at 18 °C. The consistency of ice cream or sorbet should be checked about an hour before serving. If it is too hard, transfer it to the refrigerator.

■ ICE CREAM

Although it is known that the Romans ate a form of frozen dessert consisting of fruit pulp mixed with snow, it is the Chinese who are generally credited with the invention of ice cream. Originally a bowl filled with a suitable mix was placed into a bath of liquid consisting of saltpetre and cold water. The bowl was then rotated until the mixture was frozen. This method was introduced in Europe (which was still using the Roman method) by Marco Polo, and was perfected by his Italian countrymen, who used sauce anglaise as the base ingredient.

Vanilla ice cream, *Glacé vanille*

Milk	2 ℓ
Vanilla pod	I
Castor sugar	750 g
Egg yolks	10
Fresh cream	I ℓ
(Serves 40–50)	

Bring the milk and vanilla to the boil. Mix the eggs with the sugar in a separate bowl. Add the hot milk gradually, using a small whisk. Place back into the saucepan, using a *wooden spatula*, stir continually to just coat the back of the spatula. Strain through a conical strainer and allow to cool. Add the liquid cream. Pour into an ice cream machine and allow to rotate until it has doubled in volume and is firm in texture. Place into a storage compartment for service.

COFFEE ICE CREAM, *GLACE AU CAFÉ*

Proceed as for vanilla ice cream, adding coffee flavour and colour.

Chocolate ice cream, *Glacé au chocolat*

Egg yolks	8
Castor sugar	450 g
Milk	12 dl
Cream	12 dl
Chocolate couverture	350 g

Proceed as for vanilla ice cream, adding the melted couverture to the yolk mixture, or grated couverture to the milk. Extra chocolate colour may be required.

Fruit ice creams, *Glacé aux fruits*

Milk	12 dl
Fruit pulp	6 dl
Cream	12 dl
Castor sugar	840 g
Lemon (juice)	I

Bring the milk, purée, castor sugar and juice to a heat just sufficient to dissolve the sugar. Stir in the cream. Pass through a strainer and pour into an ice cream machine. Allow to rotate until it doubles in volume. Store in the freezer.

■ SORBETS

In the vast array of culinary terms, there are few of wider application or more uncertain meaning than the word 'sherbet'. At first it was a simple beverage, originating from Persia, consisting of fruit juice, sugar and a handful of mountain snow. It developed with first a sprinkle of liqueur, then the addition of champagne. The Italians adopted the method and called it 'sorbetti'. The refreshment soon became familiar all over Europe, with modifications for the snow.

For producing sorbets, the fruits or syrups used *must be pasteurised*; similar legal requirements to ice cream making have to be observed. *Syrup* is simmered for one minute and then rapidly cooled. *Pulp* is heated for 30 minutes, at 60 °C, and immediately cooled. Check the density using a saccharometer, 14–17 degrees Baumé.

Lemon water ice, *Sorbet au citron*

Water	12 dl
Castor sugar	200 g
Sliced lemons	2
Egg whites	2
Cube sugar	150 g
Egg white	I
(Italian meringue – p. 164)	

1 Follow the pasteurisation procedure, mentioned above.
2 Produce an Italian meringue using the second sugar. Place the pasteurised solu-

tion into an ice cream machine and allow to rotate until the mixture has increased in volume. Add the Italian meringue. Store in the freezer.

Fruit water ice, *Sorbets aux fruits*

SWEET FRUITS
As for lemon water ice using the appropriate syrup, and pulp. Any fruit can be used to produce sorbets: peaches, pears, apricots, plums, lychees, bananas, etc. Particularly acidic fruits are cranberries, blackberries, grapefruits, pineapples, kiwis, mangoes, etc.

SORBETS BASED ON ALCOHOLIC BEVERAGES
Any wines such as muscat, sherry, port, madeira, champagne, etc. These can replace or partly replace the water, resulting with an overall density of not more than 18° Baumé before freezing. Liqueurs: any naturally flavoured liqueurs. Add just enough to flavour the syrup.

AROMATIC PLANTS
Mint, lavender, thyme, lemon, fennel, etc. Make an infusion of the herb into the syrup.

■ BOMBES, *APPAREILS À BOMBES*

Once the basic bombe mixture is produced, it can be flavoured in a wide variety of ways, using liqueurs, fresh fruits, and any natural flavouring. The pâte à bombe appareil is also the base for other frozen desserts, such as parfaits, frozen soufflés, biscuits glacés. For the production of bombes *all ingredients must be pasteurised*, and similar regulations to those for ice cream must be observed.

There are three basic methods of production:
1 cooking yolks, sugar and milk (sauce anglaise method).

2 adding cooked sugar (120 °C) to the egg yolk mixture;
3 gentle cooking of the yolks and sugar (bain-marie);

The cooking procedure of the yolk mixture requires much attention. If the yolk is undercooked the mixture will loose its richness and cream-like texture, if over-cooked, the end product could become grainy, which would completely spoil the appearance and flavour of this highly praised dessert.

A selection of ice creams: plombière glace on ice soccle (top right), napolitaine (below), coupe Antigny (p. 174) and bombe with spun sugar (top left)

Pâte à bombe (Sauce anglaise method)

Castor sugar	150 g
Milk	120 g
Egg yolks	6
Vanilla pod	1
Cream	6 dl

Boil the water, sugar and flavour. Allow to cool (slightly), then gradually add to the yolk mixture. Strain back into the saucepan, poach over hot water, until it coats the back of a spatula. Remove the vanilla pod, whisk the mixture immediately, until it doubles in volume and is completely cold. Fold in half of the whipped cream. Use as required.

Pâte à bombe (Syrup method)

Cube sugar	150 g
Water or fruit pulp	120 g
Egg yolks	6
Cream	6 dl

Produce a syrup with the water or pulp, 28° Baumé. Add to yolks, whisking until cold. Fold in the cream. Use as required.

Pâte à bombe (Bain-marie method)

Castor sugar	150 g
Water	120 g
Egg yolks	6
Cream	6 dl

Produce a syrup using the water, sugar and any desired flavour. Add to the yolks. Cook as for sauce anglaise method.

Lining and filling of bombes glaces

Basically bombes are composed of two different flavoured fillings in bombe moulds. They can be decorated, just before serving, using whipped cream, fresh fruits, etc.

Chill the moulds. Using a spoon, line the inside of the mould with an even layer of the prepared appareil. Allow to set in the freezer. Fill the centre with another flavour and colour, return to the freezer to set. To demould, chill the dishes to be used for serving. Dip the mould into warm water, for a few moments. Insert a small knife into the ice cream and twist, pulling out at the same time, place on the prepared dish. Decorate as required.

Bombes: Line (chemiser) the chilled bombe or plombières moulds with one flavour ice cream and fill with another. Decorate appropriately.

PLOMBIÈRES GLACES
Proceed as for pâte à bombe using plombière moulds.

PLOMBIÈRES GLACES

Name	Flavour to line	Flavour to fill
Abricotine	apricot	kirsch pâte à bombe and layers of apricot jam
Africaine	chocolate	vanilla
Aida	strawberry	kirsch
Alhambra	vanilla	strawberry
(surround the base with strawberries marinaded in kirsch)		
Andalouse	apricot	vanilla
Bresilienne	pineapple	vanilla and rum
(decorate with diced pineapple)		
Diable rose	strawberry	kirsch
(decorate with candied cherries)		
Diplomate	vanilla	maraschino
(decorate with candied fruits)		

Name	Flavour to line	Flavour to fill
Duchesse	pineapple	pears and kirsch
Espagnole	coffee	vanilla
(decorate with praline)		
Esperanza	orange	kirsch and praline
(decorate with red bar-le-Duc currants and vanilla ice)		
Fanfreluche	vanilla	tangerine
Fedora	orange	praline
Florentine	raspberry	praline
Formosa	vanilla	strawberry
(add large fresh strawberries)		
Frou-frou	vanilla	rum
(decorate with candied fruits)		
Georgette	praline	kirsch
Grand Duc	orange	Benedictine
Hilda	hazelnut	chartreuse
(decorate with praline and hazelnuts)		
Hollandaise	orange	curaçao
Jamaique	pineapple	orange and rum
Japonaise	peach	tea-flavoured mousse
Javanaise	coffee	chocolate
Jeanne d'Arc	vanilla	chocolate and praline
Jocelyn	peach	maraschino
Madrilene	coffee	vanilla and praline
Maltaise	blood orange	tangerine-flavoured whipped cream
Marie-Louise	chocolate	vanilla
Mascotte	peach	kirsch
Mignon	apricot	hazelnut and praline
Mikali	pineapple	kirsch
(decorate with red bar-le-Duc currants)		
Mousseline	Strawberry	whipped cream masked with strawberry sauce
Nelusko	praline	chocolate
Odette	vanilla	praline
Otéro	apricot	blackcurrants
Othello	praline	peaches
Pompadour	asparagus	grenadine
Printaniere	strawberry	strawberry mousse and fruits
Succes	apricot	kirsch-flavoured whipped cream and diced apricots
Tosca	apricot	maraschino and fruit
(decorate with lemon ice cream)		

Name	Flavour to line	Flavour to fill
Trocadero	orange	diced orange peel
(add rosettes of ice cream, slices of genoise marinaded in kirsch, decorated with orange peel)		
Tutti-frutti	strawberry	lemon
(decorate with dice candied fruits)		
Tzigane	praline	pistachio
(decorate with sliced grilled almonds)		
Venitienne	vanilla	strawberry
(fill with maraschino ice cream)		
Zamora	coffee	curaçao

Chartreuse glace aux fruits

Chemiser (line) savarin moulds with lemon-flavoured jelly. Decorate the inside with poached fruit, as desired. Fill the mould with jelly, which could be of another colour and flavour. Allow to set. Turn the fruit jelly out onto a chilled serving dish, fill the centre with roches of ice cream, flavour as desired. Decorate with fresh whipped cream and more fresh fruit.

Various chartreuse can be produced using fruits and ice creams, or sorbets of choice.

Ice cream soufflés, *Soufflés glaces*

Pâte à bombe mix is poured into a paper-lined soufflé dish, with the paper raised 2½–3 cm above the mould. Place in the freezer. When required, remove the paper, place either roasted cake crumbs or roasted almonds on the side. Decorate the top with whipped cream, glacé cherries, angelica, etc. If a liqueur is used, it should be added before folding in the cream and Italian meringue.

SOUFFLÉ GLACE COINTREAU

Produce the basic pâte à bombe recipe incorporating 200 g of Cointreau instead of the water. Proceed as previous recipe.

Other liqueurs can be used instead of Cointreau, following the same method.

Baked ice cream soufflé, *Omelettes soufflé surprises*

To make baked ice cream soufflés, use either the basic meringue (p. 164) or meringue Italienne (p. 164).

OMELETTE SOUFFLÉ ALASKA

Place an oval-shaped base geniose on the centre of oval dish well in advance, store in the freezer. Neatly arrange a small block of ice cream on the chilled base. Cover with the prepared meringue, using a piping bag and a small palette knife, to form a roche shape. With the remaining meringue decorate with a piping bag, forming a suitable pattern. Finish the decoration with previously prepared diced glacé cherries and angelica. Dust the surface with castor or icing sugar. Place in a very hot oven, 250 °C, to glaze. Serve immediately.

OMELETTE SOUFFLÉ MY LADY

Prepare the base as for the previous recipe. Before adding the ice cream, arrange one half poached peach per portion round the sponge base. Place the ice cream in the centre and continue as above. Compote of peaches can be served separately, if desired.

OMELETTE SOUFFLÉ MY LORD

Prepare as for soufflé My Lady, using pears instead of peaches.

Omelette soufflé Alaska

OMELETTE SOUFFLÉ NAPOLITAINE

Chill a large round silver dish. Place in the centre a sponge base 10–12 cm in diameter, chill. Saturate with Marsala and stand on it a bombe made with three coloured ice creams in layers (strawberry, vanilla and pistachio). Place a small (150 ml) mould on top, return to the freezer to set. Prepare three coloured Italian meringues. Pipe alternate colours of meringue, starting from the base of the bombe to the rim of the mould, decorate with more piped slices of glacé cherries and angelica. Dredge with icing sugar. Place in the oven to glaze. Serve immediately, by pouring a small amount of brandy in the mould and ignite in front of the customer.

Granite

Ideal for a nouvelle cuisine service, especially favourable after a fish course. Care and judgement is necessary in the preparation, the 14° Baumé reading should be maintained, which is very difficult when sugar is required. It may be necessary to add colour to enhance the appearance.

LES GRANITÉS

Follow the sorbet method, using one litre of fruit juice or pulp, and adding 500 g of sugar. Prepare the syrup, (wines can be used to make up the litre), density 14–15° Baumé.

Serve in wine glasses. The granite mix should have a frothy and grainy texture.

BURGUNDY GRANITÉ
Use one bottle of Burgundy 3 dl stock syrup (14° Baumé) and soft fruit of choice.

CLARET GRANITÉ
As for Burgundy granite, using claret.

CHAMPAGNE GRANITÉ
As for Burgundy granite, using champagne, with the addition of white grapes as decoration.

GRANITÉ AU CAFÉ
Prepare one litre of strong coffee, add 500 g of granulated sugar and 100 g of Tia Maria. Freeze on a large tray. Scrape off when ready for serving in glasses, sprinkle more Tia Maria on top.

Biscuits glacés

Using pâte à bombe mixture, fill the biscuit glacé moulds. For this dessert the appareil is just poured into the chilled mould, then placed back into the freezer. When demoulded the ice cream is cut into the required portions and decorated accordingly. Layers of various flavours and colours can be used in the assembly of the dish, freezing each layer before adding the next.

PARFAITS
Basically a pâte à bombe mixture is used with a combination of fruit pulp and whipped cream.

NAPOLITAINE
Chill the moulds, place alternate layers of biscuit glacé mix of three colours and flavours (vanilla, strawberry and pistachio). Decorate with fresh cream and a pistachio nut on top.

ITALIENNE
Chill the moulds, place alternate layers of biscuit glace mix consisting of strawberry, vanilla, pistachio. Decorated with rosettes of full cream with a fresh strawberry on top.

TORTONI
Use two layers of biscuit glacé mix: vanilla and pistachio.

MONT BLANC
Use two layers of biscuit glacé mix: chestnut with rum flavoured ice cream and vanilla.

BISCUIT GLACÉ COINTREAU
One mix of biscuit glacé, flavoured with Cointreau.

BISCUIT GLACÉ AU CHOCOLAT
One mix of biscuit glacé, flavoured with chocolate.

BISCUIT GLACÉ MERINGUE
One layer of vanilla biscuit glacé, when turned out, pipe a rope of meringue Italienne on top.

BISCUIT GLACÉ TIRAMISU
Set on a sponge base, moistened with Tia Maria. Use a half mix of coffee flavoured biscuit glace, half mix of Tiramisu cheesecake mix (p. 52). Dredge bitter cocoa powder on top before cutting.

BISCUIT GLACÉ MOCHA
One mix of biscuit glacé, coffee flavour and Tia Maria.

BISCUIT GLACÉ FORÊT NOIRE
Two layers of biscuit glacé mix, one chocolate flavoured with rum, the other vanilla flavoured with kirsch. Decorate with whipped cream and black cherries marinaded in kirsch.

BISCUIT GLACÉ ROTHSCHILD
One mix of biscuit glacé, made with a salpicon of fruit soaked in curaçao.

■ COUPES AND SUNDAES

The composition of these two dishes is similar, they differ only in presentation. The coupes are served in silver coupes and sundaes on plates of various shapes and sizes.

For first class service the timbale is normally used, this is a silver double container, one fitting inside another. The advantages are that crushed ice can be placed in the larger one, which will help in keeping the inner dish chilled for serving.

Coupes and sundaes are made of ice cream, fruit, sauce, whipped cream, liqueur, and decoration (such as nuts, almonds, crystallised fruits, violets, cherries), and are customarily served with some sort of biscuit. All fruit used must be skinned and pitted, decorated simply and tidily presented – preferably prepared at the last possible moment. Always keep the coupes in the storage compartment of the freezer box, to have a chilled container to scoop the ice cream in.

COUPE ALEXANDRA
Fill with macedoine of fruit, add syrup and kirsch and roches of strawberry ice cream. Decorate with a rosette of cream and a crystallised violet.

COUPE ANDALOUSE
Fill with orange segments marinaded in curaçao, coat with apricot glaze and two roches of lemon sorbet. Decorate with whipped cream and a segment of orange.

COUPE ANTIGNY
Fill with two roches of strawberry ice cream, dress with half a peach, mask with apricot sauce, decorate with a rosette of whipped

cream, finish with spun sugar on top.

COUPE BÉBÉ
Fill with two roches of raspberry ice cream, pineapple slices and fresh strawberries. Decorate with a rosette of whipped cream and crystallised violets.

COUPE BRÉSILENNE
Fill with an arrangement of pineapple, sugar marinaded in maraschino, add two roches of lemon sorbet. Decorate with a rosette of whipped cream, add cherries and angelica.

COUPE CARDINAL
Fill with pears, peaches and strawberries and two roches of vanilla ice cream, then mask with raspberry sauce, decorate with grilled almonds.

COUPE CÔTE D'AZUR
Cut oranges into a basket shape, add tangerines, fill with macedoine of fruit marinaded in curaçao and two roches of orange ice cream.

COUPE DAME BLANCHE
Fill with two roches of almond-milk ice cream, fill half a peach with Bar-le-Duc white currants. Place it upside down covered with lemon ice cream.

COUPE EDNA MAY
Fill with two roches of vanilla ice cream, add compote of cherries, decorate with a rosette of whipped cream and raspberry sauce.

COUPE ELIZABETH
Fill with cherries marinaded in kirsch and cherry brandy. Decorate with a rosette of whipped cream, add cinnamon and spices.

COUPE EMMA CALVÉ
Fill with two roches of vanilla ice cream, add praline and compote of cherries marinaded in kirsch, mask with raspberry sauce.

COUPE GRESSAC
Fill with two roches of vanilla ice cream, add

three small macaroons marinaded in kirsch. Place a peach upside down filled with bar-le-Duc red currants. Decorate with whipped cream.

COUPE HÉLÈNE
Fill with two roches of vanilla ice cream, add fresh fruit. Mask with chocolate sauce, decorate with a rosette of whipped cream, arrange in the middle chocolate shavings and crystallised violets.

COUPE JEANNETTE
Fill with two roches of pistachio ice cream, add strawberries. Mask with cream sauce, add wild strawberries and crystallised violets.

COUPE JACQUES
Fill with macedoine of fruits marinaded in kirsch, add a rosette of lemon ice cream and another of strawberry ice cream. Decorate with one black grape.

COUPE JAMAÏQUE
Fill with diced pineapple marinaded in rum, add two roches of coffee ice cream and a little coffee essence.

COUPE MELBA
Fill with two roches of vanilla ice cream, decorate with peaches, pears, nectarines, mask with melba sauce.

COUPE MEXICAINE
Fill with two roches of tangerine ice cream and diced pineapple.

COUPE MONTE CRISTO
Fill with macedoine of fruit marinaded in kirsch mask with two roches of pistachio ice cream.

COUPE MONTMORENCY
Fill with cherries marinaded in brandy and two roches of vanilla ice cream.

COUPE MONTREUIL
Fill with two roches of vanilla ice cream, mask half a peach with apricot sauce and decorate with whipped cream.

COUPE NEBULE
Fill with two roches of chocolate ice cream, add cherries and mask with kirsch-flavoured raspberry sauce. Decorate with a rosette of whipped cream, finish with praline and crystallised violets.

COUPE NIÇOIX
Fill with macedoine of fruits marinaded in curaçao, mask with two roches of orange ice cream.

COUPE SAVOY
Fill with macedoine of fruits marinaded in anisette, with one roche of coffee ice cream and another of violet flavoured ice cream.

COUPE SARAH BERNHARDT
Fill with two roches of pineapple ice cream, mask with strawberry mousse and curaçao.

COUPE TETRAZZINI
Fill with two roches of pistachio ice cream, dressed with half a peach, mask with raspberry mousseline sauce. Decorate with whipped cream and orange segments.

COUPE TUTTI-FRUTTI
Fill with one roche of strawberry ice cream, add salpicon of fruit marinaded in kirsch, add one roche of pineapple and one of lemon ice cream, decorate in layers.

COUPE VENUS
Fill with two roches of vanilla, add a small peach with a strawberry on top of it. Decorate with whipped cream.

COUPE VICTORIA
Fill with macedoine of fruits marinaded in champagne, add one roche of strawberry ice cream and one of pistachio ice cream.

25 ICE CARVING

Flowers set in ice

Although very intricate ice carvings require a great deal of artistic ability, for basic shapes only minimal skill is needed. Ice carvings have been used to adorn food displays for many years. In traditional buffet presentations, ice carvings are used for show-casing frozen desserts, ice cream, drinks, etc. They can be placed on pedestals as centrepieces which will enhance any cold buffet display.

Occasionally ice sculptures are made by freezing water in moulds, but professionals tend to use this method only to make small sections of a larger sculpture. Traditional techniques involve 'hewing' the ice with a series of sharp tools. Not only does the sculpture require considerable skill, but very ex-

Ice carving with flowers, and bombe rubané

pensive equipment is also needed. Despite the beauty and appeal of ice sculpture, it is rarely executed because of the considerable work, time and skill required to create something that will last only a few hours. Carvings are also extremely heavy, and are cumbersome to carry and store. Large freezers are required to store the ice blocks as well as the sculptures when finished.

◼ EQUIPMENT

Three basic tools are essential for ice carvings: chisel, chipper and saw. But there are many more tools available, which are essential only to the artisan who aims for more elaborate pieces.

Callipers and dividers

Callipers and dividers are useful once the carving is taking shape. For instance, when carving the neck of a swan the thickness is indicated on the template, and can be measured against the thickness being carved in the ice. Handles of pitchers and flower baskets can also be measured with these tools.

Chippers – six-point

The six-point chipper is a must for ice carving of all kinds. It is used for marking out from a template, reducing the block to the rough figure and when adding character to the sculpture. Try to purchase a chipper that has hardened steel points set into a cast base; these points are much sharper and can be sharpened on a stone. A chipper with cast points cannot be sharpened and the points are more likely to bend and break.

Chipper – one-point

The one-point chipper is basically an ice pick used for chipping very small pieces, drilling out small holes or scoring lines on the surface of the ice. A hardened steel chipper is best, because it can be sharpened and will not break or bend.

Chisels

Angle chisel: cuts a V-shape groove in the ice. It is ideal for outlining a form on the surface of the ice. Used for feathering on wings of swans and grooves on bowls or vases. Sizes range from a quarter inch to one inch.

Flat chisel: a chisel used by carpenters will do quite well. Normal sizes range from a half inch to two inches wide. The narrow size is good for scoring and chipping and shaping small areas, the wide blades are good for smoothing flat surfaces. The better the quality of the chisel the longer it will retain its edge. Flat chisels made especially for ice carving are

Equipment for ice carving

much more expensive than the conventional carpenters chisel. They are highly tempered and hold a good edge for a long time. Three and a half inches is the widest available.

Round gorge chisels: with blades shaped like a crescent moon, round chisels are useful for carving features of living creatures, also for grooving a display piece such as a side of a dish.

Normally the chisel handle would be 4–5 inches long. Extensions can be attached to the handles of chippers and chisels, the ideal length would be 18–24 inches. An extended handle helps protect knuckles when working.

Drill

Hand operated brace drills can be used for marking and starting holes. Electric hand drills are excellent for marking holes to hold flower stems or releasing pressure in the ice,

for instance when carving out the canopy in a gondola. This also prevents the ice from cracking. If the drill is forced it will crack the ice, so care must be taken.

Chain saw

While this is not necessary, it is a very quick and useful tool for trimming off large sections of ice, also for relieving pressure in the centre of the ice by using the tip only, and for final shaping.

Hand saw

Some kind of hand saw is essential. Hand saws provide the cheapest method of cutting, but the process is long and tedious. There are many different types of teeth and lengths to choose from. Generally a 12–24-inch large-toothed saw will suit most purposes. A hand saw places less strain on the ice than a chain saw, as the latter causes vibrations. I would recommend that the novice ice carver should use a hand saw first then progress to a chain saw.

Other items used for ice carving are: waterproof marking pens, set squares, yard sticks, tongs, wood rasps or surforms (plane), hacksaw blades, and one must always have flat and round stones for sharpening. Many of these tools are not essential for the beginner, but the majority are probably accessible any way.

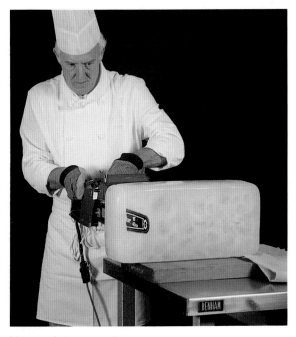

Using a chain saw on ice

■ ICE PREPARATION

In America a standard block of ice weighs approximately 300 lb. It measures $25 \times 50 \times 100$ cm. When ordering a block of ice you must remember that approximately 50% of ice is lost during chipping and carving to get the required shape for display. On occasions large blocks are bonded together to achieve the right size for very large displays. These blocks are very expensive, and the cost is of course passed onto the customer.

With care and attention you can prepare your own blocks. Look around your pastry room and you will find the necessary equipment to make ice blocks of the size that you require.

Preparing the blocks

The ice blocks must be frozen several days in advance, especially if large blocks are required. The length of freezing time will depend on the temperature of the freezer. But in general 24–72 hours is required for complete freezing.

Several methods can be used, but whatever method you choose, be careful that the blocks are well formed and do not contain cracks or large air pockets. Remember water starts to expand once it starts to freeze; this must be considered when selecting a container for the block. As water starts to freeze it will freeze from the outside in. This is a problem, because when the centre starts to freeze it expands and causes cracks. For this reason it is necessary to break up the outer section of the ice from time to time during the freezing process.

Here are some ideas of how blocks of ice can be made in your pastry section with very little expense to you.

METHOD ONE

Choose a suitable container, fill with cold water and place in a refrigerator overnight so that the water is cold as possible. Put in the freezer, but do not place directly on the floor. If it has to be on the floor, protect the bottom with several cake racks and cardboard; this will help prevent the bottom from freezing too quickly. Regularly check the water to make sure it is not freezing too quickly. When the ice starts to form on the surface break it up with an ice pick. If a block of water is freezing, it will probably be necessary to break up the ice after the first eight hours, and then six to eight hours after that. Plan to break it up three or four times while it is freezing. Approximately 48 hours will be required to freeze a block of $60 \times 30 \times 20$ cm at 20 °C.

METHOD TWO

Put thin sheets of water on clean flat trays in the freezer. When frozen break up the ice and fill your container with the broken ice, then top up with very cold water to the desired level and proceed as for method one. This method has an advantage over the first, as the ice block only needs to be broken up once as it freezes, and it is also much quicker.

METHOD THREE

Fill your container with ice cubes, proceed as for method two. If you have a blast freezer or chiller very cold water can be obtained from

these which will also hasten the freezing process.

METHOD FOUR

Some pastry chefs like to add salt of potassium nitrate to the water before freezing. This provides a softer ice for carving but there are two disadvantages to this method. Ice containing salt will freeze at a lower temperature so therefore it takes longer to freeze the block; also when carved and presented, salted ice will melt more quickly. Use 5 g of salt or potassium nitrate to one litre of water. Boil with water before placing in the very cold water – this is to ensure even distribution.

Plant-produced ice or can ice

The cans of water are lowered into brine tanks which are filled with a calcium chloride solution of sufficient concentration to keep the brine from freezing at minus 9 °C. The brine is

Prawn boat

chilled by expansion pipes which run through the brine tanks. The coolant used is ammonia in the expansion pipes, this draws heat out of the brine solution.

To obtain a good clear block of ice for carving, air is bubbled into the can of carving ice as the ice freezes. The purpose of this is to equilibrate the temperature of the water as it freezes. It also prevents the formation of large air bubbles, and aids the extraction of water impurities thus rendering a clear piece of ice.

When the blocks of ice are nearly frozen they are removed from the brine solution. The centre of the block will be very dark in colour, due to all the impurities that the air bubbled method has pushed to the centre of the block. A hole is bored in the centre and the dark cloudy water is drained out. It is refilled with fresh clear cold water and the cans are returned to the brine tub for complete freezing without the aid of pumped in air.

By this method ice blocks are frozen at minus 9 °C in brine solution and allowed to temper to minus 3 °C in holding rooms for 24 hours before carving commences. The ice will be less prone to cracking at minus 3 °C.

Because ice has a tendency to become brittle as it ages it is best to carve soon after it is made. Delivery problems may force you to purchase more than is immediately needed, therefore storage is required. When storing the ice try to avoid temperature fluctuation. If the temperature fluctuates between minus 4 °C and minus 12 °C the ice will expand and contract, which weakens the ice bonds and can lead to cracks.

■ MAKING A TEMPLATE

A template is simply a silhouette of the design you plan to carve. You would generally need only one template for each ice carving, most often the side view.

After selecting your design and the size of the carving, make sure your template fits the block of ice to be used. Greaseproof paper is the cheapest material for a template, but it can only be used once as it will freeze onto the side of the ice block and will tear when removed. If you want to use the same template again a good idea is to cut it out of a thin sheet of plywood. Plywood templates are easier to hold against the block of ice and chiselling round for the basic shape.

Sketching the design

1 CROSS-HATCH METHOD
Draw a square grid across the face of the design by ruling 2 cm spaced lines across your picture, then 2 cm spaced lines down it, On a large sheet of greaseproof paper rule a grid of 10 cm squares. Copy the small lines of the picture freehand on the larger template square by square. The template will be five times larger than the original. Cut around the template, at this stage it is a good idea to make two or three more paper templates in case the first tears. One template should always be kept in storage for later use or even transferred onto a plywood template.

2 OVERHEAD PROJECTOR
This method requires equipment not readily available to all. If you have a drawing available make a photocopy on an acetate sheet for a transparency. Tape a sheet of greaseproof paper the size of the ice block to the wall. Place your transparency on an overhead projector and focus the image onto the sheet of paper. Trace the image and cut out for a completed template. Detailed lines may have to be added at a later stage. Do not forget to make two or three templates. This method has an advantage over the first method as the template can be easily enlarged or decreased in size to fit the size of the block.

Ice boat with flowers

3 FREE HAND

If you have an artistic ability this method may be the easiest. I suggest you cut the sheet of paper to the size of the ice block first, before starting to sketch.

Always remember that a base is required for any ice carving, this will give height and sturdiness. The base can be included as part of the template or can be carved separately and bonded onto the carving when it is finished.

Starting to carve

Examine the block of ice to see if it is symmetrical. Look for cracks or chips, if there are any try to place them on the least visible side of the carving. Choose the best side of the block and designate it for the first outline of the sculpture. Square off the base of the ice block whether the block will be standing up or lying down. Always check with a steel square to see if the bottom of the carving is square. This will ensure that the carving is stable. Place the block of ice on a wet towel or sack and place onto a cutting board, this will prevent the block from sliding. It also elevates the block of ice from the working surface, which will help you cut down to the bottom of the block and score round your template. Score round the template, remove it and groove with a V-shaped chisel ¼ inch deep. Remove large chunks with a chain or hand saw to gain the basic shape. During this operation try to keep the floor as dry as possible – for safety reasons.

Carve from the top down

If you do not carve from the top to bottom you might end up breaking large pieces of ice. To remove large pieces that cannot be reached with a saw, use a six-pointed chipper.

Always think ahead about eliminating internal ice pressure, to decrease the likelihood of the ice breaking. For example, when carving out the handle of a basket relieve the pressure by removing a section within the arch, or by cutting an X underneath the handle loop with the point of the chain saw. This will help prevent the handles from breaking later in the carving process. After cutting the X, use a chipper to remove the ice, aiming as many strokes as possible towards the centre of the block. This will minimise the stress on the area. If small cut-outs are required a drill can be used.

Always try to carve a little larger than required. The basic shape can be done two or three days before use. The final shaping should be performed as close to presentation as possible. Do not waste time in creating very intricate detailed work on your piece, as it may be removed from the freezer two hours prior to the service. At this stage every chip of the chisel increases the risk of breaking your masterpiece. And of course the ice will begin to melt immediately. The melt rate varies depending on the temperature of the display area, and on the starting temperature of the ice. On average, under normal circumstances, the ice will melt at a quarter to half an inch per hour.

Working in detail is only done when the item is intended as a single service piece. If the carving is served to a guest always make sure to use very sharp tools for finer detail, and that the ice is well frozen before serving.

Melting effects

Melting changes the structure of the ice as it sits during carving. If the ice remains in a warm location for too long the surface begins to flake, and therefore becomes nearly impossible to carve.

Another melting problem arises when the piece is displayed. For instance, the ice on top of a swan's head will melt first. The water runs down the beak and will drop onto the swan's chest and could change its appearance.

Always bear melting effects in mind when preparing the template, and try to make the template a little larger than required to allow for this.

Using the three basic tools

SAW

Place the teeth of the saw along the line to be cut. Make full strokes with the saw, but never force it. If you find it hard to move through the ice you have one of two problems. Either the set of the teeth on the saw is wrong or the teeth are blunt. If ice dust clogs up the saw, the teeth are set too small. Always try to use a large toothed saw.

CHIPPER

This is used to make the rough carving. Hold the handle of the chipper in the palm of your hand, this position gives maximum leverage and helps quick removal of ice. For roughing out work use a poking action – quick, short jerks of the hand, striking the ice at an angle. If using a long-handled chipper the tips should strike the ice at an approximately 30° angle and the chipper is pushed across the ice. This is a much more controlled method, also it places less stress on the ice as the carving begins to take shape. If the chipper does not bite into the ice, the angle could be wrong or the tips could be blunt.

CHISELS

Use short and long-handle chisels much as you would use the chipper. The chisel is most useful for smoothing surfaces and cutting grooves. There should be no impact action. Holding it at a 30° angle to the surface of the ice and sliding it across will give you the best results. When putting the finishing touches to the carving always work with the chisel carving into the centre of the piece, this lessens the chance of breakages.

For final smoothing of the sculpture, hacksaw blades and surforms are used, even the heat from your hands can help give a very good smooth surface.

What if it breaks?

This is a fear that every carver has. If you exercise caution, care and attention during your work the ice should not break. Breakages are caused by a blow, or rushing to get the job done, or ice temperature fluctuation (possibly caused by working in sunlight), from carving a dimension too small and from moving the sculpture too often.

If a piece does break off all is not lost. Simply fit the piece back onto the point at which it broke to see whether it is a clean break (as most are). Remove the broken piece, dust it with table salt and hold it back in position. If the ice is cold enough it will bond together in about two minutes. Wear rubber gloves when holding it in place. Do not move the ice once it is in position. If your first attempt fails wash off the salt, resalt the broken piece and try again. While holding the broken piece in place ask someone else to pack snow or ice chippings around the break, which will help the bonding. Dry ice or carbon dioxide could be used to hasten the bond – but only as a last resort.

If all else fails, drill a hole in the large part of the carving, a small hole in the broken piece and plug with a clear plastic dowel. Proceed as above with the salt bonding method.

Storage

Place the carving on pieces of wood on the floor of the deep freeze. This will stop the carving from freezing to the floor. Remember the carving will be fragile and should be placed where it is not likely to be damaged.

26 SUGAR CONFECTIONERY, *TRAVAIL DU SUCRE*

Sugar work may be considered the most artistic part of patisserie. The production of high standard boiled sugar displays requires various difficult techniques, but with good guidance and perseverance, these can be learned. Sugar (sucrose) is a disaccharide which dissolves in about half its own weight of water. Its solubility increases as the temperature rises; by prolonging the boiling, moistures are evaporated and the sugar viscosity increases. On hydrolysis the sugar undergoes a physical change, the two-molecule structure breaks into separate molecules – glucose and fructose (monosaccharides). The mixture of the two is known as invert-sugar. On heating dissolved sugar has a tendency to revert to its original nature, that is to say, grain or crystallise. As the crystallisation may be too rapid for the purpose on hand, it is necessary to introduce an extra quantity of non-crystalline or invert-sugar, glucose. Alternatively the crystallised sugar can be turned into invert-sugar by adding tartaric acid.

When introducing either glucose or tartaric acid, care must be exercised not to use too much, as too large a percentage of either would result in the boiling solution refusing to grain at all.

Crystallised sugars, despite the introduction of glucose, quickly grain if worked or stirred; for best results do not agitate or disturb the crystals during the boiling process.

It is important to observe the condition of vessels used for boiling: copper is considered the best, as it has a smooth surface, can be easily kept clean and is a good conductor of heat, this is very necessary for sugar boiling.

Certain stages of the boiling process can be checked, either by the use of a sugar boiling thermometer, or testing a little of the boiling solution in cold water.

Cube or granulated sugars are always preferred for boiling purposes. It is even better to use sugars from small packages, which are more likely to be free from impurities (500 g packets).

Glucose syrup

Glucose syrup is a colourless viscid fluid principally made from starchy foods, such as maize, potatoes and wheat starch. The production consists of mixing starch, water, and a small amount of sulphuric acid. When the starch has hydrolysised, the mixture no longer turns blue when tested with iodine. To the solution chalk is added, the acid is neutralised and the insoluble salts are allowed to settle. The upper liquid is separated and concentrated to the syrup consistency, comprised of dextrose, maltose, and dextrins.

Confectioners use liquid glucose mainly for sugar boiling purposes. It aids hydrolysis, inverting the sugar solution and slowing down the crystallisation. The glucose is added when the solution reaches the boiling stage.

Cane and beet sugars

Sugars are found in almost every plant structure, fruits, stems, and trunks of trees. The

AVERAGE QUANTITIES OF SUGAR OCCURING IN FRUITS.		
Fruits	Sucrose type	Glucose type
Apricots	6.04	2.74
Pineapples	11.33	1.98
Figs	0.00	11.55
English cherries	0.00	10.00
Strawberries	6.33	4.98
Raspberries	2.01	5.22
Oranges	4.22	4.36
Apples	5.28	8.72
Pears	0.35	8.42
Grapes	0.00	17.26

1 Sucrose ($C_{12}H_{22}O_{11}$). The principal members of the group are cane and beet sugar.
2 Glucose ($C_6H_{12}O_6$), the principal members are dextrose or grape sugar. And laevulose or fruit sugar (found in honey).

Stock syrup

Syrup for sugar boiling can be prepared by boiling sugar, water and glucose to various densities, according to the temperature reached.

Granulated or cube sugar	1 kg
Water	1 ℓ
Glucose	200 g

Bring all the ingredients to the boil, allow to continue on low heat, occasionally removing any surface scum and any crystals forming on the sides of the vessel. An instrument called a saccharometer can be used for measuring the density, or appropriate degrees Baumé. The saccharometer is placed into the prepared liquid, standing upright; the scale marked in degrees reads the depth at which it floats.

Stock syrups are part of everyday mise-en-place, used for ice creams, confits, water ices, sorbets, soaking of savarins, fresh fruit salads, etc.

raw materials for the manufacture of sugar are usually sugar-cane or sugar-beet. These belong to the group of compounds known as carbohydrates, which constitute the largest division under the name of sugar.

Sugar is considered an important nutritive food. Only two types of sugar are valuable for commercial purposes, classified into two groups:

DEGREES BAUMÉ AND USES		
Solution	Degrees	Uses
1 kg sugar + 5 dl water	14 to 15	granite
1 kg sugar + 9 dl of water	16 to 17	water ices
1 kg sugar + 112 dl of water	20	compotes of fruit, babas, savarins
1 kg sugar + 115 dl of water	28	pâte à bombe, ice cream
1 kg sugar + 118 dl of water	34	crystallisation of fruits, liqueur chocolates, bon-bons
	36	fruit confits
	38	glazing of fruits, chestnuts

TESTING FOR DEGREES

100 °C = Boiling Point	Hand testing methods
107 °C Thread	Place a dry finger on the surface of the syrup, join finger to thumb and a thread should be formed.
112 °C Strong thread	Test as before, the thread is thicker.
118 °C Soft ball	Test by chilling the fingers in cold water. By rolling the fingers together, the syrup sets into a soft ball shape.
125 °C Hard ball	The syrup sets firmer.
140 °C Soft crack	The sugar will harden when immersed in water.
150 °C Crack	When cold, the sugar will break crumbling.
155 °C Hard crack	When cold, the sugar will crumble and will have a very slight tinge (amber).

USES

Thread degree	Stock syrup
Strong thread	Stock syrup
Soft ball	Fondant, marzipan, fudge, pastille à menthe
Hard ball	Italian meringue, nougat
Soft crack	Italian meringue, nougat Montelimar (hard type)
Hard crack	Dipped fruits and deguises, pulling, blowing, modelling, moulding, piping, rock sugar, spun sugar.

EQUIPMENT REQUIRED FOR SUGAR BOILING

Copper sugar boiler
Bowl for cold water
Vegetable oil
Metal scraper
Scissors
Triangles
Saucepan for thermometer
Marble slab
Palette knife
Sugar thermometer
Large knife
Heat lamp

Basic boiled sugar

Cubed or granulated sugar	500 g
Water	100 g
Glucose	60 g
(or cream of tartar, pinch)	
Lemon juice	

Place the sugar and water into the boiler. Place over the heat. Heat gently to boiling point. While the initial boiling is in progress, remove any scum that appears. Add the glucose or diluted cream of tartar. Allow to boil rapidly, until the required consistency is attained. Wash the sides of the saucepan while boiling, using fingers dipped into cold water. A clean brush may be used. When the required temperature is reached, remove from the heat and place the base of the saucepan into cold water to arrest the cooking for a few seconds. Rest the saucepan on a triangle on the working surface, allow the bubbles to subside. Use as required. For pulling purposes add only 15 ml of lemon juice for 500 g sugar, by shaking it into the boiled liquid.

■ POURED SUGAR, *SUCRE COULÉ*

Many different designs, figures and display items can be easily made by pouring. Elaborate pieces are used decoratively at cold buffets or other exhibited work, or simply for the presentation of petits fours. As the sugar does not have to be pulled, items can be made quite quickly, which is very useful for the busy pastry chef.

It may be necessary to prepare stencils for the intended items, using cardboard or actual stencil cards. For example, rabbits, swans, cartoon figures, flowers, etc. Place the stencil on rolled marzipan or plasticine about 5 mm thick. Cut round and remove the inner shape. Alternatively a similar outline can be made out of a rubber matt, which can then be permanently kept for other occasions. Place on a slab of marble, lightly oil inside the shape. Boil the sugar to 155 °C, allow to stand

An example of poured sugar work

2–3 minutes for the bubbles to subside. Pour gently into the prepared base, starting from the centre pouring towards the edge, at a thickness of 2–4 mm, depending on the size of the item being prepared. When cold, gently remove the border, ease the sugar piece free with a palette knife, assemble or decorate as required.

For welding pieces together use either liquid boiled sugar or heat the pieces over a small flame. Wipe the oil off the pieces to be welded first, otherwise they may not stick together. Royal icing can then be used for adding detail to the design.

Fine ornamental work can also be produced by piping the boiled sugar, using a silicone paper cornet, making decorative shapes over a sketch drawn directly onto the marble slab.

Croquante, *Nougat noire*

Boil the sugar as described to 165 °C, or to a very light caramel colour. Using a spatula stir in nibbed, flaked or whole almonds, in a quantity half the weight of sugar used. Pour the mixture on the oiled surface, maintaining the desired shape. As it begins to set, turn the piece over using a palette knife, at this stage it can be pressed thinner, if necessary.

It can be further moulded using fingers. If it becomes too cold to work, soften in a warm oven for a few moments, on a tray lined with silicone paper. For moulding insert the cut croquante into a lightly oiled mould or basin. Weld the pieces together in the same manner as poured sugar. Decorate the completed item with royal icing.

Almond toffee, *Praline*

Praline is an almond toffee produced by first making a croquante, then pounding it down to a powder form. Traditionally skinned hazelnuts are used instead of almonds.

Praline can be stored in sealed containers and kept in the dry store, as part of the pastry mise-en-place. It is used in ice cream, butter cream, chocolate ganache, crème beau-rivage, gâteau, pastries, petits fours, etc.

■ SPUN SUGAR, *SUCRE FILÉ*

Boil the sugar to 150 °C, remove from the heat and dip the base of the sugar boiler in cold water for a couple of minutes to arrest the boiling. Place on a triangle and allow the saucepan to stand longer to thicken further.

It is important to have all the necessary utensils prepared well in advance, including the floor lined with paper or a couple of large baking trays, and two or three broom handles hanging out over the edge of a table. Holding the sugar boiler in the left hand, dip the whisk in the boiled sugar, raise and shake the whisk backwards and forwards over the broom handles. The sugar will fall across the handles in long threads. Continue the operation until enough spun sugar is obtained. Wait a few moments for the sugar to cool, then lift it by placing two hands under the sugar and place as much as possible on a clean surface. Roll up very lightly. Use immediately produced to decorate ice cream dishes, croquenbouche, croquante dishes, gâteaux, Saint Honoré, etc.

Spinning sugar

Sucre rocher

Lump sugar	500 g
Water to saturation	
Royal icing	30 g
(No lemon juice)	

Boil the saturated sugar to 138 °C. Make sure the saucepan is kept clean by washing down the sides. Remove from the heat and stir in the royal icing with a wooden sppon. Cover the saucepans with a tight fitting lid and return to a very low heat for the mixture to rise. Immediately tip onto a dish and allow to cool before breaking up for use. Colour can be added just before the royal icing.

■ FONDANT

Fondant is mostly bought ready made, as it hardly pays to make it yourself, because of the time involved and the difficulties achieving uniform texture and colour.

Granulated or cube sugar	5 kg
Glucose	750 g
Water	3 dl

Boil the sugar as described on page 187. Boil until the solution reaches 118 °C (soft ball stage). Arrange the marble slab surrounded by four iron bars, keeping the corners well closed. Sprinkle the slab with cold water, and pour the fondant on it. Sprinkle all over with cold water to prevent a skin forming, allow to cool.

Work the sugar with a palette knife in one hand and a scraper in the other. Keep on working until white, creamy and set. Scrape the completed fondant into a container with a tight fitting lid, store and use as required.

Using fondant

Rewarming fondant for covering gâteaux, pastries or petits fours, is a very sensitive operation. Even in the best circumstances the covered item can quickly lose its gloss. It is important, for that reason, not to prepare the intended items too far in advance. Also if it is overheated, the gloss will disappear, leaving the fondant dull in appearance and with a hard texture. Only warm the quantity required, placing the fondant in a saucepan, warming over a very low heat while stirring with a wooden spatula. As the fondant begins to melt add a small amount of stock syrup. When the correct temperature is reached, remove from the heat and continue stirring until smooth, creamy and well blended. If more syrup is required, add a little at a time. Do not overbeat as this will introduce air pockets and spoil the coated surfaces.

Colour may be used for very light shades. Add the colour slowly, in small increments, to prevent an overcolouring. Fondant can also be flavoured with compounds, essences, liqueurs and orange or rose-flower water.

All fondant coating work is done using draining wires with a tray underneath. The wires are made in all sizes and stand raised to facilitate the flow of the fondant, and to avoid crumbs mixing with it. Pour or spoon over the prepared item with a continuous movement, allow to set for 10 minutes, before removing the coated item.

For chocolate fondant it is necessary to add extra syrup when warming the fondant, as chocolate tends to thicken it.

The left-over fondant is simply scraped back into the saucepan, the sides of the saucepan are cleaned down, and water is poured in to flood the top – this will prevent a skin forming. Keep for further use, pouring away the water and rewarming the fondant when needed.

27 COCOA AND CHOCOLATE

Couverture is made from cocoa, sugar and cocoa-butter. These ingredients are used in varying proportions, and ground to varying degrees of smoothness according to the price paid.

◼ COCOA

Cocoa is derived from the crushed beans of the cacao tree. This is the chief ingredient and the component from which the product takes its name. As far as can be ascertained, it was first introduced in Europe from Mexico, by the Italian explorer Christopher Columbus in the early 16th century. It seems to have been used only in Spain for over a century, where the cocoa beans were roasted and named 'chocolatl'. At first it was mainly used as a drink, flavouring dishes and later in the making of sweets. Eventually the fashion spread all over Europe, the first 'chocolate house' was opened by a Frenchman in London in the middle of the 17th century.

The cacao tree's botanical name, *Theobroma cacao*, means 'the food of God'. It is now cultivated in South America, Trinidad, Ceylon and on the Gold Coast of Africa. The tree grows to about 20 feet, and produces fruit from about four years old, bearing two crops every year. When ripe the pods are cut from the branches, opened and the beans are extracted. At this stage the beans are white and very moist. Each pod yields 20–40 beans. The beans contain proteins, carbohydrates, fibres, sugar and mineral salts.

In order to prevent germination the beans are sweated in boxes, allowing the moisture to drain away and air to circulate. They are then dried, either in the sun or artificially, reducing the moisture content to 5%. The drying process can last about a week, depending on the crop quality.

Further treatment is applied after shipment to the cocoa manufacturers. The beans are cleaned, roasted to produce the characteristic flavour, broken and dehusked to obtain the 'nibs'. The nibs are milled in revolving stones, and the heat generated during this grinding causes them to melt, resulting in a mass of dark viscous liquid known as cocoa-mass or crude chocolate.

COUVERTURE
Sugar, cocoa, and cocoa-butter are used for manufacturing couverture. It should have good flavour and rich colour. By law it has to contain a minimum of 31% cocoa-butter, before it can be classified as chocolate, and it is the cocoa-butter that assists in the smoothness and melting quality of the chocolate.

MILK CHOCOLATE
Fresh milk cannot be added to chocolate, mainly because milk contains a large percentage of water. Milk is added to the crude chocolate in a crumb form, made from condensed milk. Good quality milk chocolate should consist of 40% sugar, 35% cocoa-butter and 25% condensed milk.

COCOA-BUTTER
This is extracted from the cacao beans after milling. It is expressed from the crude choco-

late when cocoa is made. It is very brittle and pale yellow in colour.

■ CHOCOLATE, *CHOCOLAT*

There are two types of chocolate available; plain and milk. The highest quality of chocolate must contain at least 31% cocoa-butter. The quality of chocolate is directly related to the calibre and amount of cocoa-butter used. Cocoa-butter contributes to the richness, smoothness, and melting point of the chocolate.

Plain chocolate is manufactured from cocoa-butter, sugar, and cocoa-mass. *Milk chocolate* also contains milk solids and milk fats.

Preparation and tempering

It is because of the cocoa-butter that care must be taken when tempering chocolate. Beyond a certain temperature, cocoa-butter melts and separates. This means that chocolate has to be worked close to the point of setting, otherwise the chocolate will not set hard again. If tempering is omitted or incorrect the fat sets slowly into a crystalline form, and the chocolate sets with a streaky and dull appearance.

Cleanliness is paramount when handling chocolate, all the working surfaces and utensils to be used have to be washed, dried well and free from grease.

The working conditions should be between 18 °C and 25 °C. Below this the chocolate will cool too quickly. It is also important that no moisture comes into contact with the chocolate. Steam or any water near the melted chocolate is to be carefully avoided. Spoiled chocolate cannot be tempered or used for any chocolate work. It can, however, be used in sauces or the making of ganache.

The two methods of tempering are as follows.

1   Chop the couverture into small pieces and place in a clean, dry bowl or tempering kettle. Allow to melt very slowly. If using a double saucepan make sure the water does not exceed 49 °C. Stirring constantly, melt to 47 °C. Remove from the heat. Place bowl in cold water, again stirring until thoroughly cool, approximately 27 °C, or until it *just* begins to set. Replace the bowl in the warm water and allow the temperature of the chocolate to rise to 30 °C, stirring constantly. It is ready for use. If the temperature of the chocolate is allowed to rise above 30 °C it must be cooled again to 27 °C and reheated to 48 °C.

2   *Slab method.* Melt as above, at 45–48 °C, stirring thoroughly. Pour about three-quarters of the chocolate onto a clean and dry marble slab. Work the chocolate to and fro using a palette knife and a scraper, until it begins to thicken. Quickly transfer it back into the saucepan and stir thoroughly; the temperature should reach 30 °C. It is then ready for use.

The same methods can be used for milk chocolate, but the temperature must be two degrees lower, i.e., 28 °C.

If the tempered chocolate is too cool, it can be warmed slightly, so that it again reaches 30 °C for plain or 28 °C for milk. If the couverture is overheated, the cocoa-butter will break down again and it will have to be retempered.

TESTING
Before using the tempered chocolate, it is best to test it to see if the tempering has been successful. This can be done by spreading a little of the melted couverture on a piece of paper to cool at room temperature. Within 8–10 minutes the chocolate, using a small

knife, should roll up like a cigarette, or, if put in a refrigerator for longer, when set the chocolate should snap when broken.

Chocolate compound

This is available in either milk or plain. It is of similar composition to couverture, except the cocoa-butter has been removed and replaced with vegetable fats on a stabiliser (lecithin). Because of the type of fat present, no bloom can develop, so tempering can be omitted altogether. Melt the plain compound to 55 °C and 52 °C for milk compound.

Ganache

Ganache can be used both as a filling or as a topping. To obtain a good smooth texture only couverture should be used.

Chocolate	1 kg
Cream	750 g
Castor sugar	50 g

Bring the cream to the boil with the sugar, whisk into the melted couverture, pouring in very gradually. Flavour with vanilla if required, or rum can be added to taste. Store the prepared mix for further use in a bowl until the following day. For coating just cool to the required consistency.

Chocolate for piping

The chocolate has to be as cool as possible, the texture can be achieved by adding just few drops of water to a small amount of melted chocolate (of the same temperature), stirring thoroughly. Best results are achieved using a few drops of glycerin, again until a piping consistency is reached.

The paper cone should be previously prepared, fitted with a suitable tube, and the piping done immediately.

Cigarettes

Prepare a clean and dry surface (if a marble slab is available it would be an advantage). A palette knife and scraper, and a tray for placing in the pieces made, also should be at hand.

Spread a very small amount of melted chocolate, about 50 g, on the surface with the palette knife, scrape back up and spread again, repeat the process until the chocolate sets thinly on the surface. Holding the scraper slightly raised, start at one end pushing forward, the chocolate should roll evenly into a cigarette shape. Place in the prepared tray, use as required. The pieces can be stored well covered in the refrigerator, as part of the mise-en-place in the pastry.

CHOCOLATE SHAVINGS, *COPEAUX DE CHOCOLAT*

Proceed as for cigarettes, scraping the set chocolate into flakes, large or small.

Chocolate cut-outs

For this purpose the chocolate has to be tempered. Spread the chocolate on a tray lined with greaseproof paper, allow to set (not in the refrigerator as it will curl up). Cut into the required shape, either using a knife or a cutter, slightly warmed. The cut-outs can be traingles, squares or rounds and used for decorations on gâteaux, pastries and petits fours.

Modelling chocolate

This is practically as versatile as marzipan and is very useful for making decorations. The paste can be made with either plain or milk chocolate.

Chocolate couverture	*1 kg*
Liquid glucose	*1 kg*

Melt the glucose with the couverture to about 35 °C. Mix together thoroughly. Place the mixture in a bowl and keep for 24 hours in an air-tight container or polythene bag. Knead well before using.

Work the chocolate paste to a pliable texture, avoid overmixing, as this will give an oily surface. Roll out the paste as thinly as desired, depending on the use, placing a small amount each time in between silicone paper or in a polythene bag. This method can be used for smoothing out rose petals, leaves, daffodils; strips can be cut and curved into ribbon and bows; or it can be used to cut out presentation caskets, etc.

28 SWEETMEATS, *PETITS FOURS*

The term petits fours was adopted to identify a large variety of small confectionery cakes and biscuits. The literal interpretation is 'little oven-baked goods'. Petits fours are consumed in one or two mouthfuls, the size should be approximately 3 cm, and served two per portion.

The first sweetmeats were made of fruit preserves, using honey. Recipes for these can be traced back as far as Greek and Roman times. Later, in the middle ages, sticks of candy and sugar fancies were available for children, as sugar became cheaper when it was no longer taxed. It also gained popularity as a remedy for ailments. A further development was coating seeds, spices and fruits in hard sugar syrup. These were mainly sold by pedlars. Famous pâtissiers introduced the term 'petits fours' in the early 18th century. Today these sweetmeats are considered an important production of the pâtisserie, and should be part of daily mise-en-place.

Petits fours are normally served with the coffee, to complete the meal. They are also served with ice creams, sorbets, mousses, fruit fools, bavarois and sabayons.

ALTERNATIVE TERMS
Friandise – Daintiness, delicacy
Gourmandise – Greediness (of tit-bits)
Sucrerie – Sweet candy
Delice de dame – Ladies' delight
Mignardise – Small delicacy

■ TRUFFLES, *TRUFFES*

These are produced from ganache, as described on page 193. One kilogram of prepared ganache will produce approximately 100 petits fours.

Chocolate rum truffles, *Truffes au chocolat*

| Chocolate ganache |
| Rum |
| Chocolate vermicelli |

Warm the previously prepared ganache, add sufficient rum or rum compound to suit the required taste. Allow to set in the refrigerator. Ball to the required shape, about the size of a large olive, allow to set. Roll the prepared balls in a shallow dish of melted couverture and immediately roll in chocolate vermicelli, allow to set. Place in paper cases for serving.

WHISKY TRUFFLES, *TRUFFES AU WHISKY*
Proceed as for rum truffles, replacing the rum with whisky.

Cinnamon truffles, *Truffes à la canelle*

| Chocolate ganache |
| Cinnamon powder |
| Icing sugar |

Warm the previously prepared ganache, add cinnamon powder to taste, allow to set in the refrigerator. Ball to the required shape, allow to partly set, roll in a mixture of icing sugar and cinnamon powder. Place in paper cases for serving.

Hazelnut truffles, *Truffes aux aveline*

Warm half of the amount of ganache (500 g) and add 500 g of hazelnut powder. Allow to set in the refrigerator. Using a small amount, ball up, enclosing a skinned hazelnut in the centre. Allow to partly set, dip in tempered couverture. Decorate the top with a spiral of piped chocolate. When set place in paper cases for serving.

Orange truffles, *Truffes à l'orange*

Warm half the amount of the prepared ganache (500 g), mix in 500 g of very finely diced crystallised orange peel and 100 g of orange liqueur (Grand Marnier, Cointreau, curaçao). Allow to set, ball to the required size, when set dip in tempered chocolate couverture. Decorate the top with a spiral of piped chocolate. Place in paper cases for serving.

Autumn truffles, *Truffes d'automne (au marrons glacés)*

Method 1: Warm half the amount of ganache (500 g), add 500 g of broken crystallised chestnuts and 50 g of rum. Allow to set in the refrigerator. Ball up to size, roll in a mixture of icing sugar and cocoa powder. Place in paper cases for serving.
Method 2: Dip a crystallised chestnut in tempered couverture, allow to set. Wrap in a small amount of marzipan, allow to set. Dip again in tempered couverture, allow to set. Place in paper cases for serving.

Chocolate cherries, *Cerises au chocolat*

Marinade the cherries in maraschino, allow 3–4 cherries per piece. Drain and dry the cherries well on a clean white cloth. Using a dipping fork drop one cherry at a time in tempered chocolate and place 3–4 in a heap fashion on greaseproof paper. Allow to set.

CHOCOLATE MORELLO BITTER CHERRIES, *GRIOTTES AU CHOCOLAT*
Proceed as above, using morello cherries.

Orange-peel chocolates, *Écorces d'oranges confites enrobées du chocolat*

Slit the skin of the oranges lengthways and remove. Place peel in boiling water for five minutes, immediately run cold water over to cool quickly (this helps remove the bitter taste). Drain well then place the peel in syrup and bring to the boil, allow to simmer very gently for ten minutes, place aside until the following day. Repeat the process daily for 4–5 days, until the syrup reaches 32–34 °Baumé. Drain the peel well, cut the crystallised peel in strips 5 cm in length and 5 mm wide. Dip the strips in tempered chocolate, place on greaseproof paper to dry.

Almond chocolates, *Amandes au chocolat*

Place whole almonds on a baking tray, add icing sugar, shake together to coat the almonds, remove the surplus sugar. Place the tray in a hot oven, 220 °C, for a few minutes to roast the almonds thoroughly. As soon as roasted, shake the almonds in a sieve, spread out and allow to cool. Dip the almonds in tempered chocolate, using 3–4 almonds per piece.

■ CHOCOLATE FONDANTS

Casting centres in starch

The most familiar centres are those of fondant cream, these being cast in starch impressions made with suitable moulds. The moulds are of various shapes: round, square, oval, heart-shaped, etc. Fine dry starch is sifted into a tray about 3 cm deep, until the starch is slightly higher than the sides. It is then struck off level with the sides of the tray by a long ruler. The starch must not be compressed, otherwise excessive displacement will disturb the clarity and regular shape of the impressions as each row is formed.

The impressions are made by moulds securely glued to stout sticks. Take both ends of a stick between the thumb and first two fingers of each hand and hold the remaining two fingers on the edge of the tray. Press the moulds into the starch, starting at one end, then lift with a clean vertical movement and continue until the whole tray is covered.

FONDANT CENTRES
Warm sufficient fondant, preferably using a double saucepan, adding 150 g of stock syrup to each kilogram of fondant. Work the fondant continually, using a wooden spatula, to a temperature of about 46–48 °C. If it is allowed to heat above this temperature, the fondant centres will be gritty in texture. Add colour and flavour as desired.

Warm a funnel and stick in hot water, so that both are warmed through. Stand the funnel in an upright position in a jar or similar receptacle. Put in the stick to bung the funnel and two-thirds fill with the prepared fondant cream. The impressions are now filled by holding the stick with the right hand, and the funnel with the left. The funnel should be raised 3–4 cm above the starch. Lift the stick a little to allow sufficient fondant to pass to fill the impression, shutting off the flow just before the impression is full by pressing down the stick. Continue until all the impressions are filled level with the surface of the starch. Any fondant setting on the sides of the funnel must be scraped out and re-

warmed, and the funnel warmed again.

As each tray of impressions is filled, they can be placed on top of each other and put aside to set. It may be an advantage to leave the trays in a warm place overnight. Twelve hours is usually long enough for the centres to set, if left longer they could become too hard. Remove the centres using the point of a small knife and brush off any surplus starch, before dipping.

DIPPING
It is essential that the chocolates dry quickly, to obtain a good gloss. For best results, the heat of the room should not exceed 21 °C. Problems such as streaky, dull and grey covering can be traced directly to the dipping room being too hot. In the summer it may be extremely difficult to both dip and store chocolates under ideal conditions.

Temperature for dipping: The temperature of the chocolate should be maintained at 23 °C. The use of a double saucepan is vital for maintaining the temperature of both chocolate and water.

Method for dipping: The items to be dipped are placed on the left of the saucepan, the operator in front, and the prepared papered tray or cards on the right.

Take a few centres in the left hand and drop one face down into the couverture. With the fork in the right hand draw a film of couverture over it to cover, place the fork underneath, remove from the couverture, tap the fork lightly and wipe off surplus chocolate on the edge of the pan. Lift over the paper, turn the fork with a quick twist of the wrist to drop the chocolate onto the paper. The chocolate can be marked by placing the prongs of the fork on the still wet couverture and drawing away.

Dipped chocolate fondants in a display box made from modelling chocolate (p. 193) and two chocolate figures

FINISHING THE CHOCOLATE

Many types of decoration are available for topping chocolates: crystallised violets, roses, mimosa, walnuts, hazelnuts, imitation flowers, marzipan leaves. Alternatively a spiral of chocolate can be piped on top when set.

Place the dipped chocolates in petits fours paper cases for serving.

■ GLAZED PETITS FOURS, *PETITS FOURS GLACÉS*

All petits fours glacés are served in petits fours paper cases, always on the same day of preparation.

Fondant dips, *Petits fours glacés au fondant*

> *Pain de genes or victoria sponge*
> *Apricot jam*
> *Butter cream (optional)*
> *Marzipan*
> *Fondant*

Remove the crust from the sponge, cut lengthways to about 1 cm thick and moisten with a mixture of stock syrup and liqueur. Spread lightly with apricot jam and butter cream if needed. Roll the marzipan thinly on silicone paper or a large board, cut to the size of the sponges, brush over the marzipan with boiled apricot jam and place the sponges on top, jammed side down, press down lightly. Cut evenly in various desired shapes (squares, oblongs, lozenges, circles) using a cutter. Place the cut pieces with the marzipan face up on draining wires in tidy rows, about 2 cm apart from each other. (The wires should be put on a clean surface, so that the surplus fondant can be scraped off later. Warm the fondant to 37 °C, colour and flavour as desired, add stock syrup to correct the consistency – it should be quite soft.

Pour the prepared fondant over the pieces, to coat completely. If difficulties are experienced, it is advisable to pour the fondant over each with a large spoon. Place the glazed petits fours in paper cases, decorate the tops by piping softer fondant of any desired colour, complete with crystallised violets, roses, mimosa, glacé cherries or angelica.

■ MIGNONETTES

Slice the pain de genes to a 5 mm thickness, moisten and cut out using an oval cutter (15 mm × 25 mm). Place the cut pieces on a draining wire in the refrigerator to harden, for about 10 minutes. Immediately glaze with apricot jam. Pipe a small rosette of butter cream on top, flavoured with a desired liqueur. Place in the freezer for a further 10 minutes to set the cream. Cover with fondant, decorate as above.

AMANDINE
Prepare the pain de genes as for mignonettes, placing a whole almond on top of the butter cream. Glaze with fondant, decorate as desired.

MONTMORENCY
Cut rounds 2 cm in diameter from the moistened pain de genes, pipe a rosette of butter cream flavoured with kirsch, place a glacé cherry on top, glaze with fondant and decorate as desired.

MASCOTTE
Proceed as for montmorency, using coffee-flavoured butter cream. Place a walnut on top, glaze with coffee flavoured fondant, decorate.

Glazed chestnuts, *Marrons glacés*

Remove the first skin of each chestnut, without damaging the second. Place in a saucepan with enough water to completely flood the chestnuts. Bring to the boil, decrease the heat and continue boiling very slowly, to prevent the chestnuts from breaking. After about 20 minutes, depending on the size and quality of the chestnuts, change the water, replacing with clean boiling water. This is important, as it prevents the original dark water from tanning the skin. Repeat the process twice more until the chestnuts become white. Test with the point of a small knife, if it enters easily they are cooked. When cold remove the second skin.

Centrepiece made from piped sugar (p. 188) and a selection of glazed petits fours

Prepare a syrup of 3 kg to one litre of water and flavour with vanilla. Add about 1.5 kg of prepared chestnuts to the boiling syrup, simmer for two hours. On no account allow it to boil. Repeat daily for two to three days, so that by gentle evaporation for two hours each day, with the syrup reaching 35–36 °Baumé, the chestnuts will gradually crystallise. Place the glazed chestnuts on a draining wire. Any that are broken can be used by mixing with melted chocolate. When well drained, the chestnuts can be rolled in castor sugar or dipped in melted chocolate.

Glazed Cape gooseberries, *Physalis glacés*

These fruits are normally available in January, February and March. Mustiness is quite common, so a thorough examination is essential.

Pull the outer covering leaves back and twist to expose the berry. Dip the berry in prepared warm fondant, flavoured with coffee and Tia Maria (if desired). Place onto a sugar-dusted surface, allow to set.

Glazed strawberry fondants, *Fraises aux fondant glacés*

Select firm, fresh strawberries of equal size. Do not remove the hull and leaves. Place onto a draining wire for an hour to dry. Holding the fruit by the hull, three-quarters dip into prepared, strawberry-flavoured, warm fondant, adding strawberry liqueur if desired. Place onto a surface dusted with icing sugar, allow to set.

Glazed pineapple pieces, *Ananas glacés*

Select firm pineapples, remove the skins. Slice the fruit into 2 cm rings. Prepare the syrup as for glazed chestnuts, bring to the boil, place in the slices of pineapple, gently for two hours. Place aside until the following day, leaving the fruit in the syrup. The process can be repeated twice more. Drain the fruit onto draining wires. Cut in 2 cm wedges, rolled in castor sugar. The wedges can be partly dipped in chocolate, wrapped in marzipan and also dipped in chocolate, or left just glazed.

■ GLAZED APRICOTS, *ABRICOTS GLACÉS*

Choose firm fresh apricots, cut in half, remove the stone, proceed by glazing as for pineapple. When glazed slice in half again, and complete as for pineapple.

Marie Louise

Line small barquette moulds with sweetpaste. Allow to rest, bake to a light brown colour. Produce chestnut ganache by creaming equal quantities of chestnut purée and butter cream. Pipe a small amount of apricot jam in the bases of the baked barquettes. Using a palette knife, fill with the prepared butter cream, place in the freezer to set firm, coat with warm white fondant, decorate with broken glazed chestnut.

Malakoff

Line small barquette moulds with sweetpaste, pipe some apricot jam in the centres, fill with frangipane, bake to a brown colour. When cold, coat with coffee-flavoured fondant. Pipe a small rosette of coffee-flavoured butter cream on top, decorate with a marzipan coffee bean.

Piedmontais

Prepare square shortbread biscuits. Using a palette knife, shape chestnut purée into pyramids on top, add a hazelnut, place in the freezer to set. Glaze with coffee-flavoured warm fondant. Decorate the top as desired.

Japonaise

Sandwich light almond biscuits with apricot jam and pistachio butter cream. Coat with pistachio-flavoured fondant, coloured pastel green. Decorate with a pistachio nut on top.

Olga

Using macaroon biscuits, pipe kummel-flavoured butter cream on top, place in the freezer to set. To glaze pour over warm fondant, flavoured with kummel. Allow to set, decorate as desired.

À l'orange

Using shortbread biscuits, pipe a rosette of butter cream, flavoured with orange and curaçao. Glazed with warm orange-flavoured fondant, decorate as desired.

Harlequin

Using vanilla-flavoured shortbread biscuits, pipe a ring of white butter cream, then a pyramid shape into the centre with chocolate butter cream. Allow to set in the freezer for ten minutes. Coat with chocolate fondant, and with white fondant pipe a white line across the middle.

Coconut kisses

Warm the fondant in a sauteuse, to make it easier to shape. To one kilogram of fondant add 600 g of desiccated coconut, add any colour, liqueur or flavour desired. Beat well using a wooden spatula. Using two teaspoons dipped in hot water, shape into ovals by passing the mixture from one spoon to the other, two to three times. Drop onto grease-proof paper, allow to set. Partly dipped in melted chocolate if desired.

Coconut nougatine

Coconut	500 g
Fondant	750 g
Praline	200 g
Tia Maria (optional)	100 g

Line a swiss roll tin with rice paper. Warm the fondant in a saucepan, add the coconut, praline and Tia Maria, mix well together, using a wooden spatula. Pour the mix into a prepared tin, to about 2 cm thick. Cover with rice paper, roll a rolling pin over, to flatten down. Allow to set. Remove from the tin to a chopping board, cut into cube shapes, place in paper cases for serving. If cut slightly smaller, they can be dipped in melted chocolate if desired.

Marzipan petits fours, Petits fours d'amande

KIDNEY MARZIPAN, *ROGNON D'AMANDE*
Roll the marzipan to a long sausage shape, cut into pieces, roll each piece to 5 cm in length. Turn to form crescent shapes, egg-wash, place onto wires, allow to dry for about an hour, or longer if possible. Dredge the surface with icing sugar, glaze under the salamander.

AMANDINES
Mix 100 g of nibbed almonds in 500 g of marzipan. Roll out the prepared paste, using a rolling pin, to 1½ cm thick. Cut out pieces, using a 2½ cm plain cutter. Place the cut pieces on wires, allow to dry for about an hour. Dredge with icing sugar, glaze under the salamander.

STUFFED CRYSTALLISED FRUIT, *FRUITS FARCI OR MARZIPAN DEGUISES*
Dates: Select firm dates, cut in half and remove the kernel. Roll out the marzipan of any flavour or colour in a sausage shape. Cut into

A variety of marzipan petits fours

small pieces, insert each piece into the cavity of the half date, roll in the palm of the hands to smooth. Mark the marzipan with a small knife, making 3–4 marks on the sides. Roll in castor sugar.

Cherries: Cut the crystallized cherries in half. Ball equal-sized pieces of marzipan, place two half-cherries on either side and roll in castor sugar.

Prunes: Proceed as for dates.

Pistachio: Mix 100 g of pistachio nuts in 500 g of marzipan. Roll to a sausage shape, cut into pieces, ball to form ovals, roll in castor sugar.

Hazelnuts: Roughly chop the hazelnuts, mix 100 g of nuts to 500 g of marzipan, roll into a sausage, cut into pieces, ball into spheres, roll in castor sugar.

Praline: Mix 100 g of praline into 500 g of marzipan, roll into a sausage, cut into pieces, ball into spheres, roll in crushed praline.

Marzipan is a very versatile paste; many more marzipan fruits can be produced by the methods outlined above.

Modelling fruits and vegetables

Prepare the marzipan by colouring and flavouring according to the intended item. Roll out to a sausage shape, and cut into equal-sized pieces. Mould each piece of marzipan, with the palms of the hands to give it the basic form of the fruit or vegetable to be represented, then further shape with marzipan modelling tools. Colour can be added with an air brush, if available.

Gum arabic can be used for glazing of marzipan shapes. This is bought in a powder form, to be dissolved in water or orange- or rose-flower water. Alternatively, for the busy pâtissier, marzipan rollers are now on the market. These tools are designed to produce perfect uniformity. The rollers are ideal for bulk production. Very little else needs to be done, except a touch of colouring using the air brush or dusting powder. Serve in paper cases.

■ BOILED SUGAR PETITS FOURS (FUDGE), *PETITS FOURS AU SUCRE BOUILLI*

Soft chocolate caramels (Fudge), *Caramels mous au chocolat*

Cube sugar	250 g
Double cream	3 dl
Couverture (melted)	50 g
Glucose or honey	80 g

Place all the ingredients into a clean saucepan (not copper, as cream is being used). Boil to a fierce heat, 120 °C, washing down the sides of the saucepan occasionally. Oil a marble slab or a 15 cm flan ring. Pour the cooked mixture onto the slab or ring, allow to cool completely, cut into small cubes.

SOFT COFFEE CARAMELS (FUDGE), *CARAMELS MOUS AU CAFÉ*
Proceed as above, replacing the chocolate with concentrated coffee.

SOFT VANILLA CARAMELS (FUDGE), *CARAMEL MOUS VANILLE*
Proceed as for chocolate caramels, replacing the chocolate with vanilla flavour, added when the sugar has reached the required temperature and stopped boiling.

CHOCOLATE FUDGE
Proceed as for vanilla fudge replacing the vanilla with sufficient melted couverture to obtain adequate colour and flavour.

COFFEE FUDGE
Proceed as for vanilla fudge, replacing the vanilla with sufficient coffee concentrate to obtain adequate colour and flavour.

BRAZIL NUT FUDGE

Proceed as for vanilla or coffee fudge, adding 150 g of skinned Brazil nuts just before pouring out.

Hard caramels, *Caramels durs*

Cube sugar	500 g
Glucose	250 g
Milk	3 dl
Double cream	3 dl
Butter	125 g
Vanilla to taste	

Dilute the sugar with the milk, melt over low heat to a syrup, then bring to the boil. Add the glucose, boil to 120 °C, add the cream gradually, continue boiling. Remove from the heat, add the butter and vanilla, stirring gently. Boil again, until it reaches 148 °C. Pour onto an oiled marble slab, allow to just set, cut into cubes. If it is possible to use cocoa-butter instead of butter, the result will be caramel of much greater firmness.

HARD CHOCOLATE CARAMELS, *CARAMELL DURS AU CHOCOLAT*

Proceed as for vanilla caramels, adding 200 g of melted couverture instead of the butter.

HARD COFFEE CARAMELS, *CARAMELL AU CAFÉ*

Proceed as for vanilla caramels, replacing the vanilla with concentrated coffee.

Candy cushions (pulled straw sugar), *Berlingots (Sucre paille)*

Boil the sugar, following the basic sugar boiling recipe (p. 187). As soon as it reaches 154 °C, remove from the heat, allow the bubbles to subside. Add 10 ml of pure lemon juice and any colour or flavour, shake in well. Pour the mixture onto an oiled marble slab, leave for a few minutes to slightly settle, fold in the edges, wait again, and again fold in the edges. At this stage the sugar should be sufficiently firm to be lifted with both hands, and stretched to twice its length, fold together, pull again, repeat the process about six times. The sugar at this stage should resemble a thick ribbon. Close up to form a tube, sealing in the air. Pull the sugar again to double its length, fold again and continue until you have several tubes together. Either cut the cushions immediately to the required size, using a sharp knife, or allow to cool, then cut using an old knife heated and wiped as necessary with a damp cloth.

Dipped fruits

DIPPED ORANGES

Select good quality fruit, slit the skins, blanch in boiling water. Remove the skin and divide the segments. Space on a draining wire and allow to dry for at least two hours. Using a dipping fork, dip the segments into boiled sugar (hard crack), then place onto an oiled surface to cool.

DIPPED GRAPES

Select good quality fruit. Divide the grapes into pairs. Allow to dry. Using tweezers to hold the pairs together, dip the grapes into boiled sugar (hard crack), and place onto an oiled surface to cool.

FRUITS DEGUISES

Select good quality dried fruit or nuts, for example, prunes, glacé cherries, dates, almonds, walnuts, etc. Cut in half if large. Fill the cavities or coat with marzipan and allow to dry. Using a dipping fork dip the fruit into boiled sugar (hard crack), place onto an oiled surface to cool.

CROQUANTS

Boil the sugar to hard crack, remove from the heat, place the saucepan on the working surface resting on a triangle. Using a spatula stir in 100 g of almonds (flaked, nibbed or whole) or skinned hazelnuts. Pour the mixture onto an oiled surface. Cut into squares.

Nougat montelimar

Cube sugar	I kg
Water	2 dl
Glucose	250 g
Honey	200 g
Egg whites	120 g
Almonds	200 g
Pistachio nuts	200 g
Hazelnuts	200 g
Glacé cherries	200 g

Boil the sugar following the method for basic sugar boiling (p. 187). Add the liquid glucose and continue boiling to about 120 °C. Add the honey and again boil to 140 °C. At this stage the egg whites should have been whisked to a point, using a mixer. Very gradually pour in the boiled sugar, while whisking, until all the boiled sugar and honey has been added. Replace the wisk with a beater, and continue beating until nearly cold, at a slower speed. At the last stage add the nuts and cherries, avoid overmixing. Spread the mixture on rice paper, place another sheet of rice paper on top, flatten using a rolling pin and allow to set. Cut to the required shapes.

Peppermint pastilles, *Pastilles de menthe*

Cube sugar	500 g
Water	I dl
Icing sugar	130 g
Oil of Peppermint to taste	
Colour (optional)	

Boil the sugar following the basic sugar boiling recipe. Sieve the icing sugar, warm the funnel and stick. When the sugar has reached 123 °C, remove the saucepan to the work surface, on a triangle. Allow the bubbles to subside, stir in the icing sugar, peppermint and colour, using a small whisk. Pour the mixture into the warm funnel stopped with the stick. Holding the funnel with the left hand and raising the stick with the right hand, allow the mixture to drop evenly onto a clean marble slab (oil is not necessary, as the sugar will contract on setting and is easily removed).

Other flavours and colours can be used instead of peppermint. The pastilles are normally placed onto dishes without paper cases.

Marshmallow I

Gum arabic	750 g
Cube sugar	750 g
Water	I ℓ
Egg whites	I ½ dl
Glucose	250 g
Orange-flower water	I dl

Place the gum to soak overnight in three-quarters of the water. The soaking will be greatly facilitated if warm water is used and the container allowed to stand in a warm place (such as the prover). Boil the sugar with the remaining water, using a copper sugar boiler large enough to hold all the liquids. Add the glucose and boil to 123 °C. It is important that the egg whites are whisked just as the sugar reaches the required degree, and the gum should be lightly warmed to dissolve. Add the orange-flower water to the gum and amalgamate with the sugar solution. Keeping the whisk going, add the boiled solution, gradually, as for making Italian meringue. Continue beating until the mass is white, light, and spongy. Spread in swiss roll tins lined with icing sugar. When cold, cut into pieces using a damp knife, roll in icing sugar. Alternatively, fill prepared starch-impression trays, for dipping when set in melted chocolate.

Marshmallow 2

Cube sugar	750 g
Water	6 dl
Egg whites	4 dl
Leaf gelatine	35 g
Cream of tartar, pinch	
Flavour and colour as required (orange, lemon, peppermint)	

Soak the gelatine in half of the water, leave in a warm place to dissolve. Boil the sugar with the remaining water and a pinch of cream of tartar, to 130 °C. Simultaneously whisk the egg whites, when the sugar reaches the required degree, pour gradually into the egg whites while still whisking, forming a light Italian meringue. Continue whisking adding flavour and colour as desired. Spread in swiss roll tins, allow to set. Complete as above.

Turkish delight (Gelatine type)

Cube sugar	I kg
Water	50 dl
Honey	150 g
Leaf gelatine	75 g
Flavour as required (orange, lemon, etc.)	

Soak the gelatine in half of the cold water. Boil the sugar to 110 °C in the remaining water, using a copper sugar boiler large enough to hold all the liquids. Add the honey, continue boiling to 123 °C. Warm the gelatine and water to dissolve, gradually pour in the boiled sugar, add the flavour and colour. Pour the mixture into swiss roll tins, allow to set. To remove, lightly warm the base of the tin,

turn the set mixture out on a bed of icing sugar. With a damp knife, cut the delight to the required size, roll in plenty icing sugar.

Turkish delight (Starch type)

Cube sugar	1.25 kg
Leaf gelatine	60 g
Potato starch or arrowroot	125 g
Glucose	60 g
Water	5 dl
Flavour as required	

Dilute the starch with half the water. Use the remaining water to saturate the sugar, and boil to 123 °C. Add the diluted starch, flavour and colour, reboil and proceed as above.

■ PÂTE À CHOUX PETITS FOURS

Pâte à choux

Water	3 dl
Butter	125 g
Flour	250 g
Castor sugar	60 g
Salt	10 g
Eggs	6–7
(Makes 100 pieces)	

Bring the water, sugar and butter to the boil. Add the sieved flour, stir with a wooden spatula, and return to the heat to gelatinise the flour. Add the eggs gradually. The completed mixture should have a creamy texture.

Petits choux grillés

On greaseproof paper form a bed of nibbed almonds. Using a 1 cm plain piping tube, pipe little balls, about the size of an olive, onto the prepared nibbed almonds, producing a few at a time then rolling to completely cover with almonds. Place slightly apart on greased baking tray and bake at 200 °C until well dry. When cold fill with whipped cream, dust with icing sugar.

SALAMBÔ

Pipe round shapes on greased baking trays, bake at 200 °C. When cold, fill with apricot jam, coat the top with boiled sugar (hard crack).

SALOMÉ

As for previous recipe, placing a pistachio nut on top.

VELOUTÉ

The choux is piped into finger shapes. When baked and cold fill with vanilla pastry cream. Brush boiled apricot jam on top, dip the tops in grated couverture.

CAROLINE AU CHOCOLAT/CAFÉ

Pipe finger shapes. When baked and cold fill with chocolate or coffee crème pâtissiére. Dip in chocolate or coffee fondant.

CAROLINE GLACÉ

Pipe finger shapes. When baked and cold fill with vanilla pastry cream. Coat the top with boiled sugar (hard crack).

RELIGIEUSE

Pipe pear shapes. When baked and cold fill with praline-flavoured pastry cream, dip the tops in chocolate fondant.

ALEXANDRA

Line small tartlet moulds with sweetpaste, place a small spoonful of raspberry jam in the centre. Mix equal parts of choux paste and pastry cream (flavoured with orange-flower water). Half fill the moulds with mix and bake at 200 °C until well dry. When cooked lightly dust with icing sugar.

ROGNONS

Pipe crescent shapes. When baked and cold fill with pastry cream, glaze with white or pink fondant.

HELIEYETTE

Pipe round or finger shapes. When baked and cold, fill with pastry cream flavoured with rose-flower water. Dip in pastel pink fondant, pipe a spiral of the same fondant on top.

À L'ORANGE

Pipe round shapes. When baked and cold fill with orange-flavoured crème pâtissiére and curaçao. Dip in pastel orange fondant. Pipe a spiral on top using the same fondant.

■ DRY PETITS FOURS, *PETITS FOURS SEC*

Macaroon and almond biscuits, *Biscuits d'amandes et macarois*

Almonds are frequently used in the preparation of petits fours. Confectioners always stock a selection of almonds; ground, chopped, shredded, cut into fillets, nibbed and whole. For the best results it is essential to use good quality almonds. Other nuts containing less oil, like cashews or peanuts can be ground and used in place of almonds, but biscuits made from these will have a tight texture and poor appearance.

Macaroons

Biscuits made from almonds were first brought to England by the Romans. They were mainly served to visitors with sweet wines. Because of the absorbing properties of the almonds, the biscuits were believed to have a sobering effect.

Ground almonds	500 g
Granulated sugar	750 g
Ground rice	50 g
Egg whites	3 dl
(Makes 50)	

Mix together the ground almonds, sugar and ground rice, add the egg whites, thoroughly beat for five minutes. Pipe the mixture onto baking trays lined with rice paper or silicone paper, into rounds about the size of a 50 pence piece. Dredge with castor sugar, place a whole or split almond on top of each biscuit. Bake at 180–190 °C, until dry and lightly coloured.

A selection of dry petits fours

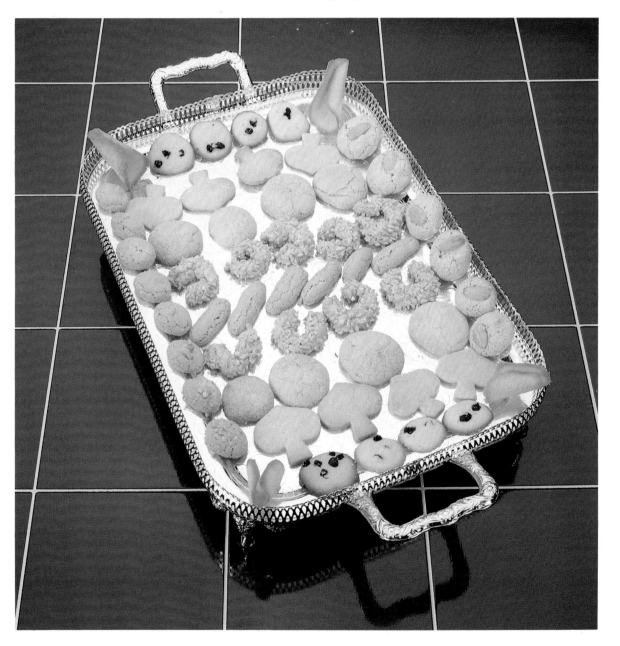

Light macaroons

Ground almonds	250 g
Castor sugar	250 g
Granulated sugar	250 g
Ground rice	50 g
Egg whites	4
(Makes 50)	

Whisk the egg whites until stiff, fold in the castor sugar, forming a firm meringue. Mix together the almonds, ground rice and granulated sugar and fold into the meringue, maintaining volume as much as possible. Extra almond flavour, compounds, or rum can also be folded in. Pipe the mixture onto baking trays lined with either rice or silicone paper, to about the size of a 50 pence piece. Dredge with castor sugar, place a whole or split almond on top of each biscuit, bake at 180–190 °C, until a light brown in colour.

Chocolate macaroons, *Macarois au chocolat*

Ground almonds	375 g
Castor sugar	500 g
Vanilla flavour to taste	
Cocoa powder	100 g
Egg whites	7–8

Proceed as for rich macaroon mix, adding the cocoa powder to the almonds and sugar prior to mixing in.

RATAFIA BISCUIT

Proceed as for light macaroons, adding ratafia flavour.

ORANGE MACAROONS, *MACAROIS À L'ORANGE*

Prepare a light macaroon mixture adding the zest of two oranges and 100 g of finely chopped orange peel. Roll the almond paste to a sausage shape, cut into 3 cm lengths. Roll the sweetpaste to a large square, about 2–3 mm thick. Cut the rolled paste into 5 cm squares, egg-wash the surface, place the rolled pieces of almond paste in the centre of the squares, fold over, seal and roll to resemble croissants. Place the prepared pieces on lightly-greased baking trays, bake at 204 °C.

Parisienne balls, *Boules Parisiennes*

Egg whites	5
Cube sugar	300 g
Ground almonds	100 g
Flaked almonds	200 g
Flavour as required (vanilla, chocolate, coffee, etc.)	
(Makes 50)	

Produce an Italian meringue, boiling the sugar to 120 °C. When cold fold in the almonds. Using two teaspoons dipped in warm water, form roches and drop onto a bed of flaked or nibbed almonds, roll to coat all over, place on tray lined with silicone paper, bake at 130 °C, until dry.

Walnut delights, *Délices de noix*

Flour	750 g
Butter	500 g
Castor sugar	250 g
Ground walnuts	75 g
Baking powder	15 g
Eggs	2
(Makes 50)	

Cream the butter and the sugar to a light texture. Add the eggs gradually, mix in the flour, baking powder, and ground walnuts, to form a smooth paste, allow to rest in the refrigerator for 15 minutes. Roll out the paste to about 2–3 cm thick, egg-wash all over, place walnut halves on top, in tidy rows. Cut out using a small oval cutter with a walnut at the centre of each, place on a lightly-greased baking tray. Bake at 204 °C to a light brown colour.

Mock Holland biscuits, *Biscuits Hollandais simulé*

Castor sugar	250 g
Ground almonds	250 g
Egg whites	5
Mixed peel	150 g
(Makes 25)	

Produce a meringue with the egg whites and sugar, fold in the ground almonds and mixed peel. Spread the mixture into two greased baking trays, bake in a cool oven, 170–180 °C, until well dry. Sandwich together with apricot jam, cut into small squares.

Ladies palette biscuits, *Palettes des dames*

Castor sugar	200 g
Butter	200 g
Eggs	5
Flour	250 g
Currants as required	
(Makes 50)	

Cream the butter and sugar to a light texture, add eggs gradually. Add the flour. Using a small piping tube, pipe discs about the size of a 10 pence piece onto a greased baking tray, about 5 cm apart. On top of each place 2–3 currants. Bake in the oven at 210 °C, to a very light brown colour. Remove from the baking tray immediately (if this is not done, they will continue baking).

Champagne biscuits, *Biscuits champagne*

Eggs	5
Castor sugar	200 g
Flour	200 g
(Makes 200)	

Produce a sponge mixture as for genoise (p. 142), by warming and whisking the eggs to a ribbon stage. Fold in the sieved flour, maintaining the volume. Pipe the mixture onto silicone paper lined baking trays, as for finger biscuits. Dredge generously with castor sugar, holding the tray and paper at one end, shake off the surplus sugar. These biscuits can be baked as for finger biscuits or allowed to stand for 2–3 hours then dredged again, left overnight, when the process can be repeated before baking.

Gazelle's horns, *Cornes de gazelle*

For the sweetpaste:	
Flour	300 gaf29
Butter	100 g
Icing sugar	100 g
Orange-flower water	20 ml
For the almond paste:	
Ground almonds	100 g
Cube sugar	20 g
Glucose	20 g
Water	50 g
Kirsch	50 g
(Makes 100)	

Melt the butter in a saucepan, stir in the sieved flour, add the orange-flower water, turn the paste onto the working surface, smooth out and allow to rest for 15 minutes.

For almond paste, saturate the sugar with the water, add the glucose, boil to 120 °C. Using a wooden spatula, stir in the ground almonds, add the kirsch. Turn the paste onto the working surface, allow to cool.

Dutch macaroons, *Macarois Hollandaise*

Ground almonds	500 g
Icing sugar	1.5 kg
Egg whites	12
(Makes 40)	

Mix all the ingredients together in a bowl to a smooth paste. Pipe ovals onto silicone paper lined trays using a plain 1½ cm tube. Allow to stand overnight in a dry, ventilated area. Using a sharp implement make a cut across the tops to slit the surface. Bake at 180–185 °C, to a golden brown colour. When cold sandwich two together using any desired jam.

Parisien rout biscuits

Ground almonds	200 g
Icing sugar	200 g
Egg whites	50 g
(Makes 40)	

Mix the ground almonds and sugar together, add the egg whites and continue mixing to form a smooth paste, quite firm in texture. Using a large star tube, pipe various shapes onto trays lined with rice or silicone paper. Decorate the tops with bits of glacé cherries, angelica, nuts or almonds. Allow to stand overnight, or at least for six hours. Bake in a very hot oven, 240–245 °C, until the rims of the biscuits have obtained a brown tinge. To glaze, brush the surfaces with a prepared solution of gum arabic.

Cat's tongues, *Langues des chats*

Butter	200 g
Castor sugar	200 g
Egg whites	6
Flour	200 g
Vanilla flavour	
(Makes 50)	

Cream the butter and castor sugar to a light texture, lightly whisk the egg whites, stir gently into the butter, fold in the flour and flavour. Using 1 cm piping tube, pipe little finger shapes, about 3 cm long, onto a greased baking tray, 5 cm apart. Bake in the oven at 210 °C to a very light colour. Remove from the tray immediately to avoid over cooking.

CIGARETTES

Proceed as for cat's tongue, using a 1 cm plain piping tube, pipe round shapes, the size of a 10 pence piece, well spaced out. Bake only few as they tend to dry very quickly once cooked. Immediately take out of the oven, remove from the tray one at a time, using a palette knife and rolling up to form a cigarette shape.

MARQUIS

Produce and bake a cat's tongue mixture. Sandwich two biscuits with chocolate butter cream flavoured with rum. Using the same butter cream, pipe 'marquis' on top of each.

LOOKING GLASS, *MIROIR*

Using a 5 mm piping tube, pipe nougatine parisienne in ovals (3 × 2 cm) onto greased baking trays. Fill the centres with frangipane, lightly sprinkle with chopped flaked almonds, bake at 204 °C. When baked, coat the centres with boiled apricot jam.

By using smaller moulds, or quantities of paste to each item, petits fours can be made from other recipes, including: friands, pigs ears, tartlets and barquettes, almond tiles, piped shortbreads, scotch shortbreads and finger biscuits.

29 DECORATIVE ICINGS

■ MARZIPAN

Marzipan was first produced in the middle ages. It came originally from Italy, and was known as 'St Marc's bread'. It later found its way to England (called March-pane), and was mainly used as a decorative item for tarts and fruit dishes.

Commercial marzipan is now made by using sugar and almonds ground together with rollers to form a smooth and pliable paste. A true marzipan must contain not less than 23½% of almond.

Boiled marzipan, *Pâte d'amande*

Granulated or cube sugar	I kl
Water	2 dl
Glucose (liquid)	150 g
Egg yolks	200 g
Ground almonds	750 g
Yellow colour	

Boil the saturated sugar and glucose to 120 °C. Immediately pour in the sieved ground almonds and stir to a smooth texture using a spatula. Quickly stir in the egg yolks, adding a little yellow colour if desired, then tip out onto a clean surface. Allow to cool, turning over occasionally to prevent a skin forming. Store in a sealed container or polythene bag. Marzipan can be used for covering cakes, in petits fours, modelling, biscuits, etc.

■ TRAGACANTH

Tragacanth is also known as 'gum dragon'. It is a gum obtained from several species of *Astragulas*, particularly *Astragulas gummifer*. This is a small shrub flourishing in west Asian deserts. The gum may be bought in either a powder or flake form, the flake being superior, but very tough and difficult to powder. The powder is more readily available, but it is sometimes adulterated and thus of poor quality, because of the high price of tragacanth.

Tragacanth possesses strong adhesive properties; it is used as a thickening agent for sauces, as a preservative in cream and ice cream manufacture, and as a binding agent for sugars in the production of gum paste.

Gum tragacanth (gum paste), *Gomme adragante (pastillage)*

METHOD I

Icing sugar	500 g
Cornflour	50 g
Water	40 g
Tragacanth powder	30 g
Royal icing	25 g
Blue colour	

Soak the tragacanth in the water for at least 18 hours, in a clean, covered container, in the refrigerator during warm weather (as it tends to deteriorate quickly). When soft and jelly like in consistency, pass through a muslin, silk or nylon. Two or three drops of blue colour can be added, if the paste is to be kept white – the blue will enhance the whiteness. Add the sieved icing sugar and cornflour in stages, mixing continually to a smooth pliable paste. Work in the royal icing, again mix to a smooth and malleable paste, without being at all sticky. If the paste does not appear to be dissolved, place in a basin, in a bain-marie of warm water, work the paste until all the specks have disappeared. Store the paste in a double polythene bag until required.

Only use an amount sufficient for the work in hand, keep the rest well wrapped, as it tends to crust very quickly. All trimmings should be placed immediately back in the bag.

METHOD 2

Icing sugar	500 g
Cornflour	50 g
Water	40 g
Leaf gelatine	10 g
Royal icing	25 g
Blue colour	

Soak the gelatine in cold water. Sieve the cornflour and icing sugar onto a clean surface, make a large bay. Drain the gelatine thoroughly, place in a small saucepan, add the water and colour (if used), warm gently over low heat, to dissolve the gelatine. Pour into the bay, draw in the icing sugar and mix to a smooth paste, continue as in method one.

Working with tragacanth

Stencils for the intended work must be prepared in advance. Use as little cornflour as possible for dusting purposes; small bags of muslim filled with cornflour can be useful. Roll out the paste evenly, turning it round constantly, to a thickness of 3–4 mm, depending on the size of the piece being rolled or moulded. Using the prepared stencils, cut out with a clean and damp small knife, place the cut pieces immediately onto a clean surface – a board or glass can be used.

Leave to dry for at least one hour, then turn the pieces over. Turn again after another hour. If the pieces are not turned the edges

Working with tragancanth and some complete examples

will curl up. Leave overnight. Before sealing the pieces together, remove any particles of cornflour on the surface with a soft brush, as the dust will prevent the pieces from adhering.

If the pastillage begins to dry, work in a small amount of royal icing.

For making flowers, add a small amount of white fat to the pastillage. An equal amount of sugar paste worked into the pastillage will make a very good flower paste.

Pastillage is used for celebration cake tops, plaques, shields, extended border work, vases, mounted pieces for table decoration, flowers, caskets, cake pillars, etc.

■ SUGAR PASTE

Sugar paste has many uses including the covering of cakes and gateaux, modelling, decorations and frills.

Icing sugar	1 kg
Egg white	55 g
Liquid glucose	100 g

Sieve the icing sugar into a bowl. Warm the liquid glucose. Make a bay in the sugar, add the egg white, then add the warm glucose. Mix thoroughly, using one hand and a scraper in the other, until smooth. Add colour if desired. Add a very small amount of fat if needed. Wrap in polythene to avoid crusting. Only prepare the amount needed at one time.

Rolling out

Brush the cake or dummy lightly with egg white, pipe with gel or apricot glaze. If the fondant has 'rested', knead again to warm and soften it before using. Roll the fondant out on an oiled plastic sheet or between two thick sheets of plastic, until large enough to cover the cake (at least one inch larger than the cake) and approximately quarter of an inch thick. Pick up the fondant on a rolling pin and place over the cake, smoothing with the hands. Work quickly as this fondant dries rapidly and you have only a short time to smooth it. Trim off the excess with a knife. Dry for at least 24 hours before decorating, except when crimping or inserting ribbon.

This recipe will cover a 9-inch cake but can be halved or doubled as required. The fondant will keep in an air tight container for several weeks in a cool place. It may be stored in the refrigerator if kept for a longer period. (It should then be returned to room temperature before using.) After storage the fondant must be kneaded well and may require a little water to bring it back to the correct consistency. The recipe will require adjusting in certain climates; when it is very dry, add a little more water or glycerine. Alternatively, a little crisco (1–2 tablespoons) may be added just before application. The latter will give a slightly different, shinier finish and help to prevent the fondant from drying as quickly, giving you longer to work or crimp it.

■ SUGAR PASTE CAKES (Australian cake decorating)

Australian cakes start with a rich fruit cake, covered with marzipan then with rolled fondant icing (sugar paste). The cakes have to be well proportioned and trimmed to a perfect, flat finish. Pastel colours are used in the icing. Flowers, either piped or hand modelled from gum paste, are added discreetly (never in masses or heavy clusters). Two of the most striking characteristics of the sugar pasted cakes are extension work using fine strands of icing to build 'shelves', and dainty embroidery work, including 'flood' work, where an outline is piped directly on the cake and then filled in.

Sugar paste cake and detail of paste work

With the addition of lace work, crimping patterns, brush embroidery, ribbon insertion, frills and flounces, embossing, filigree design and flowers, their is much scope for artistic flair when icing with sugar paste.

■ **FLOWER PASTE** *(FOR MOULDING FLOWERS)*

Icing sugar	500 g
Tragacanth powder	10 g
Gelatine leaves	10 g (or 3)
Water	5 g
White fat	8 g
Liquid glucose	15 g
Egg white	25 g

Place icing sugar and tragacanth in a mixing bowl and mix together. Add the water, glucose and fat to the sugar. Add the egg white, mix together by hand to a crumbly texture. Mix thoroughly by machine for 4–5 minutes, to a smooth pliable paste. It should not be sticky. Store in a polythene bag and place in a refrigerator to set for a couple of hours before use.

When preparing flower paste, follow these rules.
1 Only use the amount needed at one time, keep the rest well sealed.
2 Only use a very small amount of cornflour to dust fingers and surfaces.
3 Always store the finished items in a dry place. Do not attempt wiring them until thoroughly dry.
4 Use clean utensils and equipment to produce and to handle the paste.
5 If the paste gets too dry, add a very small amount of white fat to soften.

Wedding cake (Basic recipe)

Butter	1.50 kg
Soft brown sugar	1.50 kg
Eggs	1.5 kg
Flour (Medium grade)	1.50 kg
Ground almonds	25 g
Spice (mixed)	100 g
Currants	4 kg
Sultanas	3 kg
Glacé cherries (diced)	750 g
Mixed peel	1 kg
Zest and juice of lemons	4
Rum or brandy	200 g
(Makes a 15 kg cake)	

The above recipe is sufficient for a 3 tier wedding cake with a base of 30 cm, middle tier 25 cm, and top tier 15 cm.

Although not important, it is an advantage to place all the fruit, juice and spirit in a sealed container for a few hours, or overnight, for the fruit to absorb the flavours.

Cream the butter with the sugar to a light texture. Beat in the eggs gradually. Add the ground almonds, and the previously sieved flour and spice. Stir in. Add the fruit. Mix all ingredients together.

Baking

Line the cake tins with well-greased greaseproof paper. Divide the mixture between the tins. Place the tins on a baking tray in the oven. Bake at 160 °C, until the surface of the cake has a spongy texture. Remove from the oven and turn the cakes over immediately on greaseproof paper. Allow to get cold and for the tops to flatten.

Storage

When cold, the cakes should be wrapped in greaseproof paper, then in tin foil, and stored in a cool, well-ventilated cupboard to ripen before use. A lengthy storage period will assist in ripening the texture of the cake crumb, more so if occasionally the cake is moistened with more rum or brandy, then re-wrapped. Do not use sherry or any sweet wines, as it may activate fermentation in the cake, whilst in storage.

*Where a batter curdles, the texture will not be so even. Sometimes the mixture will curdle through the eggs being added too quickly or if the ingredients are of uneven temperature. The butter will slip and slide about, and will not amalgamate with the other ingredients. Where possible, cakes should always be baked in fairly large batches, the door of the oven should be kept closed until they are baked. A metal container half filled with water and placed at the bottom

A completed wedding cake

Detail of Royal icing rosettes

of the oven, will produce steam. This will assist in maintaining moisture within the cake's structure.

■ ALMOND PASTE *(see recipe page 31)*

Only good quality and smooth almond paste or marzipan should be used for covering cakes. Because of the high price of almond pastes it is very important to follow certain precautions. Use a good reputable brand of paste. Avoid storing paste incorrectly wrapped, as it quickly crusts. Avoid unnecessary trimmings.

For the confectioners who may wish to make their own home-made almond paste, it can be simply produced by mixing equal quantities of ground almonds, icing sugar and castor sugar. This is made pliable by using either whole eggs or egg whites. As an average guide it requires approximately half the weight, in almond paste to the weight of the cake to be covered. Alternatively, 250 g of almond paste is also sufficient for every 5 cm of the cake to be covered. If a cake measures 30 cm it requires ½ kg of almond paste. It is common practice to use more for the top of the cake than for the side, probably 2 kg for the top and 1 kg for the side. Place the cake on a cake board about 3–4 cm larger than the cake, with the cake top side up (*not with the skin on the board*). Brush the top with boiled apricot jam. Roll out the amount of almond paste sufficient for the top, using castor sugar to prevent it from sticking. The use of a marble slab is also an advantage. Turn the cake over on the rolled paste. Using another cake board, press down lightly and make sure it is level. Push the surplus paste into the remaining gaps, using a palette knife (so not to damage the working surface). Trim away the surplus paste. Turn back over on the board. Brush the side with the boiled jam.

Roll out the remaining paste in a long strip and trim to fit the height of the cake. Roll it up loosely. Unroll on the jammed side, pressing lightly to make it stick, but avoiding any indentures as this will cause air pockets when placing the icing on the cake. Allow the cake to dry for at least 24 hours, otherwise the oils from the ground almonds will show through the icing, and this is sometimes impossible to rectify.

Coating the cake with almond paste

■ ROYAL ICING

Reconstituted albumen is better for producing royal icing than egg whites. It gives the icing a smoother consistency and stable texture.

The use of acid (i.e., lemon juice) may be an advantage for setting the icing, especially for 'run-out' work, as it helps keep the icing white. But it can also make the icing brittle and has the added danger that when colour is added to the icing sugar, it may dissipate. Glycerine prevents the icing from becoming hard and flinty.

Egg whites	2½–3
Icing sugar	500 g
Lemon juice	½ teaspoon
Glycerine	1 teaspoon

USING PURE ALBUMEN OR SUBSTITUTES

Albumen crystals	15 g
Water	150 ml
Icing sugar	1 kg
Lemon juice	½ teaspoon
Glycerine	1 teaspoon

Place egg whites or diluted albumen into a mixing bowl, add a small amount of blue colour to enhance the whiteness. Add the icing sugar, mix to a smooth paste using a clean spoon. Beat the icing until the correct texture is achieved, adding the lemon juice and glycerine if needed. Store the royal icing in a sealed container or keep covered with a clean damp cloth.

For best results when preparing royal icing, remember the following points.

1 All utensils should be first washed in boiling water, as the smallest amount of grease will prevent the icing from becoming stiff.

2 Under-beating produces a runny icing, unsuitable for piping and which will not set.
3 Over-beating will give a coarse texture, difficult to pipe or to spread smoothly.
4 If fresh egg whites are used they should be at room temperature, this achieves a greater volume.
5 Pure fine icing sugar should be used. I personally never recommend sieving the sugar, as it increases the likelihood of incorporating grease. A good quality sugar and commonsense purchasing should be sufficient.

■ ICING THE CAKE

It is extremely important, when handling royal icing, that all utensils are free from grease. The presence of even the smallest amount can prevent the royal icing reaching a firm and smooth consistency, essential for coating the cakes. One needs to purchase good quality icing sugar. Packets or bags should have a springing back effect when handled. Lumpy and hard sugar should be avoided and not recommended for producing royal icing. As I have mentioned before, I do not favour sieving icing sugar, unless the sieve used is solely for this purpose. It is well worth the expense. During the icing process, keep the required amount of royal icing in a china or glass bowl (not plastic, as it attracts grease) covered with a damp clean cloth, to prevent a crust forming on top. Leave for at least one hour before using. This will then clear air pockets caught in the icing. I strongly disagree with the practice of paddling the royal icing on a working surface, to exclude air pockets, as this again encourages absorbtion of grease and any other unhygienic matter. Adjust the consistency with egg whites if the royal icing was made with egg whites, or water if a substitute was used. A small amount of glycerine will prevent the icing from drying too hard.

Coating method for round, heart- and oval-shaped cakes, horseshoe

Rub an implement, such as a scraper or palette knife over the marzipan cake to remove any obstacles.

Icing the top

Put the cake (on a board) on a turntable. Using a palette knife, place a quantity of icing on top. With a paddling motion and at the same time revolving the turntable, spread the icing evenly over the top only, slightly going over the edge. Remove the cake keeping the cakeboard underneath. Place onto the working surface, holding slightly tilted up. With a flat blade, longer than the top of the cake, draw the blade towards the opposite side of the cake, leaving a fine film of icing over the surface. The process should be done in one go; if repeated, more icing may have to be added. Place the cake back on the turntable and using a small scraper, remove the surplus icing from the side of the cake. Allow the top to completely dry before icing the side of the cake.

Icing the side

Using the side of the palette knife, spread sufficient royal icing on the side of the cake, holding the palette knife in a vertical position. This will spread the icing evenly from the base to the top. Using a scraper place the edge against the slightly raised side and in one movement simultaneously rotate the cake against the scraper, keeping the scraper stationary. The process can be repeated if necessary. The scraper can be removed by easing it away gently from the cake. During the process some royal icing will travel over the top. This can be removed with a clean palette knife as the top icing will be dry. This will result in a clean and sharp edge. Again allow the side to dry completely. As described, the basic technique is to ice the top and side alternately, waiting for one stage to dry com-

Smoothing the icing over the top

Icing the side of the cake

pletely before attempting the next. To have an adequate coating of royal icing cakes should have four layers for the top and three for the sides. The edge of the board can also be iced, using a slightly softer, textured royal icing, and allowed to dry before decorating the cake.

Coating method for square, hexagonal, oblong, diamond shapes

Follow the same procedure as for the previous shapes, making sure the corners have sufficient icing to complete the overall width of the cake.

For the sides it is sufficient to give a coating similar to the round cake. When dry, coat two alternate sides, then allow to dry before coating the other two sides. Following this operation will result in a cake with very sharp edges. It is important to allow either the top or sides to dry completely before attempting the next stage.

Piping techniques

In order to acquire a high degree of skill, it is imperative to practice repeatedly until a stage of self-confidence is reached. Paper cornets have to be made, particularly for fine work, where very small tubes are used. Ensure that all surfaces are dry before piping, so that if a mistake should be made, it can be cleaned off with ease. The cornet should be only half-filled with the icing. Holding the paper cornet in the left hand, fold the top over enough to thoroughly seal in the icing. Placing the cornet in the right hand, with the thumb over the folded flap, squeeze out the icing under pressure from the thumb and forefinger. At the same time support the tube with the forefinger of the left hand. Always use two hands when piping. Raise the end of the cornet to about 3 cm to allow the thread of

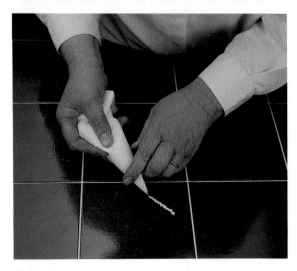

Making paper cones

icing to drop, this is especially useful when piping lines. If coloured icing is to be used, ensure that it is well matched with the prepared design and intended colour scheme. Make sure sufficient coloured icing is prepared to complete the work in hand.

Scroll work

Shells, ropes, rosettes or twisted ropes can be piped, using a star tube and by holding the piping bag at a slight angle, just above the surface of the cake. Squeeze with the right hand and balance the tube with the left. Continue squeezing until the correct size and shape is formed. Stop squeezing and pull the tube away. Move to the next position and repeat the process until the cake is fully decorated. The piping should be done when the surface of the cake is thoroughly dry.

Run-out techniques

A run-out is a shaped piece of icing such as a plaque, flower, leaf, lettering work, numbers, figures or collars piped to a size to fit round the iced cake. It is then extended out and decorated, with fine filigree work, dots etc. It is important that the icing is made using either fresh egg white or dry albumen and at least 24 hours in advance, to eliminate any air pockets. It should not contain any glycerine. The icing is then thinned down with either more egg white or dry albumen. Using a pencil, draw the outline on a board or cardboard, cover with waxed paper, making sure that the waxed side is uppermost, hold in position sticking it down with icing. Using a No 2 piping tube, pipe a continuous line of icing following the outline of the shape. The icing should be of a firm texture. When the piped border is dry, using another cornet with a No 3 piping tube and the thinned down icing, flood the inner space of the pattern. When complete, place in a warm place, about 20 °C, to dry. This may take 2 to 3 days. To remove the run-out, pull the paper downwards, sliding the run-out toward you at the same time. Place on the cake and stick down with firm icing.

Run out work

225

GLOSSARY

Abaisse – sheet of dough
Abaisser – to roll out
À la pôche – piped
Alcooliser – to add liquor
À porter – to carry, to take away
Appareil – mixture of ingredients
Apprêt – final rising (dough)
Aromats – flavourings

Bain-marie – cook in a water bath
Balance – scales
Bande – strip or band
Barquette – boat-shaped tartlet
Bassin – bowl
Bâton – stick shape
batterie de cuisine – kitchen equipment
Battre – to whip or beat
Bavarois – bavarian cream
Beignet – fritter
Berlingots – pulled sugar candy
Beurre noisette – brown butter
Beurre manie – butter flour thickening
Beurre – butter
Blanchir – to blanch
Bombe – ice cream (bombe shaped)
Bonbon – sweet, comfit
Bouchee – mouthful (small vol-au-vent)
Bouillir – to boil
Boulangerie – bakery
Boule – ball shape
Bouler – to roll into balls
Boulet – ball stage in boiling sugar
Brosser – to brush
Brosse a Dorere – pastry brush
Brioche à tête – cottage loaf
Buffet chaud – hot buffet
Buffet froid – cold buffet

Braconner au four – to poach in the oven
Brûler – to burn
Bruee – steam, vapour
Brûlée – burned

Cacao – cocoa
Café – coffee
Caillé – curdled, clotted
Candi – candied, crystallised
Candir – to crystallise
Canne à sucre – sugar cane
Cannelle – cinnamon stick
Caramelise – to caramelise
Cartouche – round piece of paper
Cerner – to mark edge of pastry
Châtaigne – chestnuts
Chaud – hot
Chausson – turnover
Chemiser – to line (as in a mould)
Chinois – conical strainer
Chiqueter – to flute, to crimp edge
Cocotte – small fire-proof dish
Coler – to thicken
Compôte – stewed fruit
Confiserie – confectionery
Confits – crystalised fruit
Copeaux – shavings (of chocolate)
Couleur – colour
Coulis – basic preparation of fruit pulp and juice
Couper le gâteau – cut the cake
Couronne – crown
Couteau d'office – small knife
Crème anglaise – egg custard sauce
Crème fouette – whipped cream
Crème glacée – ice cream
Crème pâtissiére – pastry cream

Crêpe – pancake
Cristallisé – crystallised
Croquante – crunchy (as in praline)
Croquenbouche – crisp or hard (sweet)
Croûte – crust
Croûter – to crust
Cuiller – spoon
Cuire – to cook
Cuire à feur – copper pan

Damier – cheese board pattern
Dariole – mould (creme caramel)
Décanter – to pour off
Décercler – to remove flan rings
Décorer – to decorate
Décrouter – to remove crust
Défourner – to remove from the oven
Déglacer – to deglaze
Dégourdir – to warm
Déguiser – to fill with marzipan
Délayer – to mix with liquid, thin down
Démouler – to unmould
Demi – half
Demi-feuilletage – half puff paste
Densité – density
Denteler – to indent, serrate
Dérobé – blanched
Dérober – to blanch (almonds)
Dessecher – to dry
Détrempe – mixing of flour and water for making a paste
Développer – to rise
Diminuer – to reduce
Dissoudre – to dissolve
Diviser – to divide
Dore – coloured golden
Dorer – to glaze (to give a sheen)
Dorure – glaze (eggwash)
Douce – sweet
Douille – piping tube
Doux – sweetish
Douce-amère – bitter-sweet
Dragée – almond covered (hard sugar)

Eau – water
Eau chaude – warm water
Eau-de-vie – brandy
Eau froide – cold water
Ébouillir – to boil away
Ébouillante – dipping in boiling water
Échaude – scalded
Écorce – peel, rind
Écourter – to shorten, to trim
Écrémage – creaming, skimming
Écremer – cream
Ecume – froth, scum
Effiler – to strip, to shred
Émincer – to slice
Emporter – to carry away, to cut off
Émulsionner – to prepare an emulsion
Enfourner – to put in the oven
Entremets – sweet course
Entrober – to coat
Enveloper – to seal
Épaissir – to thicken
Éponge – sponge
Épicé – spiced
Éplucher – to peel, trim
Équeuter – to stem
Étaminer – to filter
Été – summer
Étoile – star, star-shape
Étuver – to warm, cook covered
Evaporation – evaporation

Façon – preserving fruit
Faire – to make, to do
Farcir – to stuff
Farinaçe – farinaceous
Farine – flour
Fariner – to flour
Fermenter – to ferment
Fermentation – fermentation
Feuillantine – small puff pastry
Feuilletage – making of puff paste
Feuilleté – laminated
Feuilleter – to roll and fold
Flamber – to flame

Fleuron – small puff paste crescent
Foissoner – to whip (vigorously)
Foncer – to line with pastry
Fonds – pastry basis or stock
Fontaine – flour well
Fouetter – to whip/to beat
Four – oven
Four doux – low oven
Four modère – moderate oven
Four moyen – medium oven
Fournée – pastry for the day
Four vif – brisk oven
Frapper – to chill suddenly
Friandise – small delicate – (petit four)
Frigorifié – freezing, frozen
Frire – to deep fry
Friture – frying
Froid – cold

Ganache – mixture of chocolate and cream
Garnir – to garnish
Gâteau – cake
Gaufrette – wafer, biscuit
Gelée – Jelly
Glacé – iced, glazed
Glacer – to glaze
Glucoser – to add glucose
Grainer – to become grainy
Gourmand – greedy
Grainer – to become grainy
Grillage – shape of lattice of trellis

Hacher – to chop
Homogénéité – Homogeneousness
Huiler – to oil

Infuser – to infuse
Inverti – to invert

Julienne – finely diced strips of peel
Jus – Juice

Lait – milk
Laver – to wash

Lever – to rise
Levure – yeast
Lier – to bind
Lisser – to smooth
Lit – bed, layer
Losange – diamond shape

Macédoine – diced mixture
Macérer – to macerate
Madère – madeira
Manie – soft butter
Manier – to work
Marbrer – to marble
Masquer – to mask, to coat
Masse – mixted
Maturation – to ripen/develop
Mélangé – mixing
Mélanger – to mix together
Mélasse – treacle
Meringuer – to decorate with meringue
Mesurer – to measure
Met au four – put in the oven
Miel – honey
Millefeuilles – 1000 leaves
Mise-en-place – advance preparation
Modeler – to shape/form
Monte – worked up
Monte au fouet – worked up with a whisk
Monter – to work up
Mouiller – to moisten
Moule a baba – baba mould
Moule a charlotte – charlotte mould
Mouler – to mould
Moule a brioche – brioche mould
Moulin – mill
Mousser – to froth/to foam
Muscade – nutmeg

Nappé – coated
Napper – to coat
Noël – Christmas
Noir – black
Noisette – hazelnut
Nouilles – noodles

Nouillettes – small noodles
Noix – walnut

Pain – bread
Pain blanc – white bread
Pain bis – brown bread
Paillette d'or – cheese straw
Palmier – puff paste biscuit
Panache – mixed colours/flavour
Paner – to dress with breadcrumbs
Panier – basket
Parer – to trim
Parfumer – to flavour
Passé – passed, strained
Pasteuriser – to pasturise
Pâte – paste
Pâte à beignets – fritter paste
Pâte à brioche – brioche paste
Pâte à choux – choux paste
Pâte feuillette – puff paste
Pâte à foncer – lining paste
Pâte à frire – batter
Pâte à l'eau – water paste
Pâte à pate – pie paste
Pâte à nouilles – noodle paste
Pâte brissée – short paste
Pâte demi-feuillette – half puff paste
Pâte d'entremets – fruit pies
Pâte lever – raised paste
Pâte sucre – sweet paste
Patisserie – pastry department
Paton – block of pastry dough
Peler – to peel
Peser – to weigh
Pétrir – to knead
Poché – poached
Poche – piping bag
Pocher – to poach
Pointage – rising/fermentation
Pousse – expansion
Pralin – almond toffee
Praliné – decorated with praline
Praliner – to coat with cooked sugar
Printanier – of the spring

Rabattre – to fold over
Raffermir – to stiffen
Rafraîchir – to cool/to refresh
Raper – to grate
Réduire – to reduce
Refrigérant – refrigerating/freezing
Rix – rice
Roche – rock-shape (using two spoons)
Rognures – trimmings
Rompre – to push down
Roule – rolled
Roulette – wheeled cutter
Ruban – ribbon
Rubané – ribboned
Russe – mould/saucepan

Sabler – to break up
Salpicon – chopped fruit filling
Sans sucre – sugar-free
Sécher – to dry
Sirop – syrup
Siroper – to soak in syrup
Sorbet – flavoured water-ice
Steriliser – to sterilise
Sucre – sugar
Sucré – sugared
Sucrer – to sugar
Sucre cristallise – granulated sugar
Sucre en poudre – castor sugar
Sucre en tablettes – cubed sugar

Tamis – sieve
Tamiser – to sift
Tartine – slices of bread and butter
Tartelette – tartlet
Timbale – silver double container
Tiere – to pull
Tourer – to turn (paste)
Tourner – to turn/shape yeast dough
Tranche – slice
Tremper – to soak

Viennoiserie – viennese pastries
Voiler – to veil
Vol-au-vent – puff paste case

APPENDICES

■ CONVERSION TABLES

WEIGHT	
Ounces	Grams
.04	1
.07	2
.11	3
.14	4
.18	5
.21	6
.25	7
.28	8
.32	9
1	28.35
2	56.70
3	85.05
4	113.40
5	141.75
6	170.10
7	198.45
8	226.80
9	255.15

WEIGHT	
Pounds	Kilograms
2.20	1
4.41	2
6.61	3
8.82	4
11.02	5
13.23	6
15.43	7
17.64	8
19.84	9
1	.45
2	.91
3	1.36
4	1.81
5	2.27
6	2.72
7	3.18
8	3.63
9	4.08

CAPACITY

Pints	Litres
1.76	1
3.52	2
5.28	3
7.04	4
8.80	5
10.56	6
12.32	7
14.08	8
15.84	9
1	.57
2	1.14
3	1.70
4	2.27
5	2.84
6	3.41
7	3.98
8	4.55
9	5.11

CAPACITY

Gallons	Litres
.22	1
.44	2
.66	3
.88	4
1.10	5
1.32	6
1.54	7
1.76	8
1.98	9
1	4.55
2	9.09
3	13.64
4	18.18
5	22.73
6	27.28
7	31.82
8	36.37
9	40.91

CONVERSION CHART

Approximate figures

Liquid Pts	Weight Lbs Ozs	Linear Ft Ins	Temperature Fahrenheit °F	Millilitre ML / Grams G / Millimetre MM / Centigrade °C
0	–	–	32	0
–	–	¼	43	6
–	–	½	50	10
–	–	¾	68	20
–	1 oz	1″	80	28
1/16	–	–	100	40
–	–	–	120	49
–	2 oz	2″	125	(56.70 g) 60
1/8	–	–	160	70
–	–	3″	175	80
–	3 oz	–	195	90
–	–	4″	212	100
–	–	–	230	110

CONVERSION CHART

Approximate figures

Liquid Pts	Weight Lbs Ozs	Linear Ft Ins	Temperature Fahrenheit °F	Millilitre ML / Grams G / Millimetre MM / Centigrade °C
–	4 oz	–	250	120
–	–	5"	266	130
–	–	–	285	140
¼	5 oz	6"	300	150
–	–	–	340	170
–	6 oz	7"	355	180
–	–	–	378	190
–	7 oz	–	390	200
–	–	8"	400	204
–	–	–	430	220
–	–	–	455	235
–	8 oz	10"	480	250
–	–	–	500	260
–	9 oz	–	–	270
–	–	11"	–	280
½	10 oz	–	–	300
–	–	1 ft	–	305
–	11 oz	–	–	320
–	12 oz	–	–	340
–	13 oz	–	–	370
–	–	1 ft 3"	–	3??
–	14 oz	–	–	400
¾	15 oz	–	–	430
–	–	–	–	450
–	1 lb	1 ft 6"	–	460
–	–	–	–	500
1pt	–	–	–	568

* All equivalents are listed in the far right-hand column.

OVEN TEMPERATURE COMPARISONS

Gas mark	°Centigrade		Possible uses
	80– 90	very cool	Meringues
¼	115–116	cool	
½	130–131	slow cooking	Japonaise
1	142–144		
2	155–156		
3	165–168	moderate	Biscuits
4	178–181		Sponges, biscuits
5	190–193	hot	
6	200–204		Flans, tarts, pies
7	218–220	hot	Scones, yeast goods, puff paste
8	228–230	very hot	Swiss roll
9	240–244		Bread rolls, breads
10	258–260		

APPROXIMATE MEASURES

1 litre	equals	1¾ pints
1½ litres	equals	2 pints
1¾ litres	equals	3 pints
2 litres	equals	3½ pints
1p	coin weighs	5 g
2p	coin weighs	10 g
5p	coin weighs	2½ g
10p	coin weighs	15 g
20p	coin weighs	5 g
50p	coin weighs	15 g
£1.00	coin weighs	10 g
1 pinch	equal to	1 g

TEMPERATURE CONVERSION FORMULA

To convert Centigrade (Celsius) into Fahrenheit: Multiply by 9, divide by 5 and add 32.

For example, to change 204 °C into Fahrenheit.

$$204 \times \frac{9}{5} + 32 = 399.2 \ (400 \ °F).$$

To convert Fahrenheit into Centigrade: subtract 32, multiply by 5 and divide by 9.

For example, to change 400 °F into Centigrade.

$$400 - 32 \times \frac{5}{9} = 204.44 \ °C$$

LITRE MEASURES

10 ml = 1 centilitre
10 cl = 1 decilitre
10 dl = 1 litre
10 l = 1 decalitre

■ PATISSERIE EQUIPMENT

SMALL PASTRY EQUIPMENT

Pastry wheel	*Pâtisserie roulette*
Pastry nippers	*Pince à pâtisserie*
Savarin mould	*Moule à savarin*
Sugar boiler pan	*Poêlon*
Charlotte mould	*Moule à charlotte*
Dariole mould	*Moule dariole*
Small saucepan	*Russe*
Copper bowl	*Bassin en cuivre*
Rolling pin	*Pâtisserie rouleau*
Baking sheet	*Plaque à pâtisserie*
Pancake pan	*Poêle à crêpe*
Omelette pan	*Poêle à l'omelette*
Frying basket	*Panier à friture*
Boat shape mould	*Moule à barquette*
Tartlet mould	*Moule à tartlette*
Flan ring	*Moule à flan*
Raised pie mould	*Moule à pate*
Wooden triangle	*Triangle bois*
Lemon presser	*Messe au citron*
Grater	*Râpe*
Ladle	*Louche*
Piping tube	*Douille*
Piping bag	*Poche*
Cooling wire	*Grillea pâtisserie*
Funnel	*Entonnoir*
Sugar shaker	*Boite à sucre*
Cutters	*Coupe pâte*
Knife	*Couteau*

STATIC EQUIPMENT

Stove electric, gas ring	*Rechaud*
Refrigerator	*Réfrigérateur*
Cool room	*Chambre froide*
Deep freeze	*Congélateur*
Ice machine	*Turbine à glaces*
Refrigerated table	*Tour frigori fique*
Prover	*Étuve*
Steamer	*Four à vapeur/ autoclave*
Mixing machine	*Mélangeur – batteur*
Grill	*Salamandre*
Sink	*Plonge*
Draining board	*Égoutoir*
Deep fryer	*Friteuse (électrique)*
Chocolate kettle (electric thermostat)	*Bac à température réglable*
Table, wood	*Tour en bois*
Table, marble	*Tour marbre*
Table, stainless steel	*Table en acier inoxydable*
Pastry rolling machine	*Laminoir*
Tray rack	*Échelle à plaques*
Grinding mills (almond)	*Broyeuse*

A selection of pastrywork equipment

■ FRUITS IN SEASON

JANUARY

Fruit	Source
Apricots	South Africa
Chinese gooseberries	New Zealand
Cranberries	Holland; USA
Custard apples	Madeira
Dates	Tunis
Lychees	South Africa
Mandarines	Morocco; Japan; Spain; Italy; South Africa
Mangoes	Morocco; Japan; Spain; Italy; South Africa
Nectarines	Morocco; Japan; Spain; Italy; South Africa
Passion fruit	Madeira
Peaches	South Africa
Plums	South Africa
Rhubarb	Home-grown
Seville oranges	Spain

FEBRUARY

Fruit	Source
Apricots, peaches	South Africa
Chinese gooseberries	New Zealand
Cranberries	Holland; USA
Custard apples	Madeira
Dates	Tunis
Golden berries; Cape gooseberries (physalis)	Kenya
Limes	Kenya
Lychees	South Africa
Mandarines	Morocco
Mangoes, passion fruit	Kenya
Nectarines	South Africa
Ortaniques	Jamaica
Plums	South Africa

MARCH

Fruit	Source
Golden berries; Cape gooseberries (physalis)	Kenya
Cumquats	Morocco
Limes	Kenya
Mangoes	Kenya
Nectarines	South Africa
Ortaniques	Jamaica
Passion fruit	Kenya
Peaches	South Africa
Persimmons	France
Plums	South Africa
Rhubarb	Home-grown, forced and outdoor

APRIL

Fruit	Source
Limes	Kenya; Trinidad
Mangoes	Kenya
Ortaniques	Jamaica
Peaches	USA; Belgium
Persimmons	France
Plums	Argentina; South Africa
Rhubarb	Home-grown
Strawberries	Greece; Holland; Cyprus; France; USA

MAY

Fruit	Source
Apricots	Spain
Cherries	France; Italy; Spain
Limes	Kenya
Mangoes	India
Nectarines	Belgium
Peaches	Belgium
Persimmons	France
Plums	Spain
Raspberries	France
Rhubarb	Home-grown
Strawberries	Guernsey; Greece; Holland; Home-grown; France

JUNE

Fruit	Source
Apricots	Spain
Bilberries	Poland
Blackcurrants	Home-grown
Cherries	Italy; Spain; Home-grown; France
Gooseberries	Home-grown
Greengages	Spain
Peaches	Spain; Home-grown; Italy; France
Plums	Italy; Spain
Raspberries	France; Home-grown
Redcurrants	Home-grown
Rhubarb	Home-grown
Strawberries	Jersey; France; Home-grown

JULY

Fruit	Source
Apricots	Spain; Hungary
Blackberries	Home-grown
Blackcurrants	Home-grown
Cherries	Home-grown
Gooseberries	Home-grown
Greengages	Spain; Home-grown
Limes	USA
Loganberries	Home-grown
Mangoes	India; USA
Nectarines	Home-grown
Peaches	Spain; Home-grown; France; Italy
Plums	Spain; Italy; Home-grown
Raspberries	Home-grown
Redcurrants	Home-grown
Strawberries	Home-grown

AUGUST

Fruit	Source
Apricots	Spain; Hungary
Bilberries	Poland
Blackberries	Home-grown
Blackcurrants	Home-grown
Cherries	Home-grown
Damsons	Home-grown
Loganberries	Home-grown
Naartjes	South Africa
Nectarines	Home-grown; USA
Peaches	France; Italy; Home-grown; Greece
Persimmons	France
Plums	Home-grown; Bulgaria; Hungary
Raspberries	Home-grown
Redcurrants	Home-grown
Strawberries	Home-grown

SEPTEMBER

Fruit	Source
Blackberries	Home-grown
Chinese gooseberries	New Zealand
Damsons	Home-grown
Figs	France
Peaches	Italy; Greece
Plums	Home-grown; Bulgaria; Hungary

OCTOBER

Fruit	Source
Blackberries	Home-grown
Chinese gooseberries	New Zealand
Damsons	Home-grown
Dates	Tunis; Iraq
Figs	France; Greece
Peaches	Canada
Plums	Bulgaria; Hungary
Pomegranates	Spain; Israel
Quinces	Home-grown

NOVEMBER

Fruit	Source
Chinese gooseberries	New Zealand
Dates	Tunis; Iraq
Figs	Turkey; France; Greece
Mandarines	Morocco; Spain
Medlars	Home-grown
Persimmons	France
Pomegranates	Spain; Israel

DECEMBER

Fruit	Source
Apricots	South Africa
Chinese gooseberries	New Zealand
Dates	Tunis; Iraq
Figs	Greece; Turkey
Mandarines	Spain; Morocco
Nectarines	South Africa
Plums	South Africa
Rhubarb	Home-grown (forced)

FRENCH NAMES FOR FRUIT

Les Fruits (m, f)	Fruits
Pomme (f)	Apple
Abricot (m)	Apricot
Banane (m)	Banana
Mûre sauvage (f)	Blackberry
Cerise (f)	Cherry
Groseille à grappes (f)	Currant
Airelle (f)	Cranberry
Groseille cassis (m)	Blackcurrant
Groseille rouge (f)	Redcurrant
Prune de damas (f)	Damson
Figue (f)	Fig
Groseille à maquereau (f)	Gooseberry
Raisin (m)	Grape
Une grappe de raisin (f)	Bunch of grapes
Nèfle (f)	Medlar
Melon (m)	Melon
Pastèque (f)	Water melon
Mûre (f)	Mulberry
Brugnon (m)	Nectarine
Noisettes (f. pl.)	Hazelnuts
Noix du Brésil (f)	Brazil nut
Châtaigne (f) Marron (m)	Chestnut
Cacahuète (f)	Peanuts
Aveline (f)	Cobnut
Coco, noix de coco (m)	Coconut
Aveline, noisette	Filbert
Noix (f)	Walnut
Orange (f)	Orange
Pêche (f)	Peach
Poire (f)	Pear
Ananas (m)	Pineapple
Prune (f)	Plum
Pruneau (n)	Prune
Framboise (f)	Raspberry
Rhubarbe (f)	Rhubarb
Fraise (f)	Strawberry
Orange de Tanger (f)	Tangerine

The items Hazelnuts, Brazil nut, Chestnut, Peanuts, Cobnut, Coconut and Filbert are grouped together under the heading Nuts.

■ MINCEMEAT

It is customary to use mincemeat mainly for mince pies. But it has many other uses; it can be used as fillings for tarts, rolls, Danish pastries, and steamed puddings. It is called mincemeat because it was first made with actual minced meat, steak and tongue were originally the principle ingredients, dried fruit was then added. Brandy was also added to preserve the meat. The recipe has since been altered, for unknown reasons, to replace the meat with suet and adding apples for moisture. It is now mainly used for the production of sweets and pastries.

As for Christmas pudding, mincemeat is better if prepared well in advance, and allowed to mature. Preferably it should be made at least a week before use.

Mincemeat can be stored in jars with tight fitted lid. It will also freeze very well.

moisture is well distributed. Store and use as required.

MINCE PIES

Mince pies can be produced with sweet paste or puff paste (see pp. 30, 35). Traditionally they were supposed to be eaten on each of the 12 days of Christmas, this was intended to ensure 12 happy months ahead. Originally they were oval in shape, to represent the crib in which Jesus was laid, and the spices represented the gifts the Three Kings brought.

Basic mincemeat

Sultanas	500 g
Currants	500 g
Raisins	500 g
Mixed peel	500 g
Suet	500 g
Mixed spice	50 g
Nutmeg	25 g
Rum	50 g
Brandy	50 g
Cooking apples	750 g
Dark sugar	500 g
Oranges (juice and zest)	2
Lemons (juice and zest)	2
Cooking apples	750 g

Wash and dry the dried fruit well in advance. Add the peel, suet, finely diced apples, zest of oranges and lemons and spices. Dilute the sugar with the liquids and add to the fruit, mix well to ensure the

■ MENU PLANNING FOR THE PATISSIER

Menus first appeared as long ago as 400 years. Catherine De Medici is said to have begun to teach the French the art of Italian hospitality and new and exciting ways of preparing food. The French applied their new found skills and abilities to their own culinary tastes, making improvements on the Italian method of food preparation and in time, such skills became fashionable in court circles.

The art of menu planning has often been relegated to the bottom of the list of catering tasks, despite its importance. Regardless of whether planning should be on a daily or longterm basis, menus in any establishment, canteen to first class hotel, must be given some considerable thought.

The pâtissier, on choosing the sweets for the menu, has to include as much variety as possible and consider factors such as texture, colour, decoration and portion control and cost. Full use should be made of all fresh food, particularly fruit in season, when it is at its highest quality and lowest price. Shopping and catering are easier if the menu is planned a few days in advance. A menu must also take into account the nature of the occasion: it may necessitate discussion with the client. The origins of the dish should be adhered to and repetition of terms avoided where possible. It has been said that a menu should 'tell a story' rather than appear as a rigid plan. Proper descriptions and imaginative wording will prevent the appearance of a boring menu and are also likely to sell more food.

Classical dishes are often based on original Italian or French cuisine. Many names are used to honour or commemorate a battle, an outstanding event, or a famous personality. These types of dishes have very distinctive methods of preparation and appearance.

■ HISTORICAL EXPLANATIONS OF SWEETS AND PASTRY DISHES

A host of dishes and their origins is outlined below.

Some of the names are of little importance to the patissier in the context of production of food. However, the regional, national and international origins are listed here for the sake of interest and historical background.

Abernethy Dr John Abernethy, surgeon to St. Bartholomew's hospital 1815–27. *Abernethy biscuits* – digestive biscuits (wheatmeal).

Aboukir A French general of the Napoleonic Army, also Battle of Aboukir, 1801, where Napoleon defeated the Turks. *Bombe Aboukir* – bombe mould lined with pistacchio ice cream, and filled with almond ice cream and chopped pistacchio.

Aida Herione of the well-known opera, by Giuseppe Verdi (1813–1901). First performed in Cairo in 1871. Verdi was born in Italy at Roncole, near Busseto. *Bombe Aida* – bombe mould lined with strawberry ice cream and filled with kirch-flavoured vanilla ice cream.

Aiglon Young eagle. After Napoleon Francis Joseph Charles, Duke of Reichstadt, son of the Emperor Napoleon I and Marie Louise. *Fruit Aiglon* – fresh fruit on vanilla ice cream covered with spun sugar and crystallized violets.

Alaska Territory of the United States of America. *Omelette soufflé Alaska* – ice cream on sponge base, coated with meringue, glazed in the oven, served immediately.

Albemarle George Thomas, 6th Earl of Albemarle (1799–1891). British general, served in the Campaign of Waterloo. *Pouding Albemarle* – almond souffle pudding, made with sweet and bitter almonds.

Albufera A lake near Valencia, Spain. Marshal Suchet, Duke of Albufera. After the battle of Vittoria in 1813, he lost the domaine but kept his title. *Pouding Albufera* – semolina soufflé pudding, with chopped chestnuts and currants, served with raspberry sauce. *Glace Albufera* – vanilla ice cream mixed with chopped chestnuts, maraschino cherries.

Alexandra   Queen Alexandra (1844–1925) was Consort of Edward VII, King of Great Britain. Dishes created by Escoffier. *Coupe Alexandra* – fresh fruit salad and strawberry ice cream.

Alhambra   An ancient palace and fortress of the Moorish rulers of Granada, Spain. Founded in the thirteenth century. *Bombe Alhambra* – bombe mould lined with vanilla ice cream and filled with strawberry ice cream.

Alice   Princess Alice Maud Mary, Grand Duchess of Hess, third child of Queen Victoria. *Bavaroise Alice* – vanilla bavarian cream, mixed with chopped roasted almonds, coated with cream and streaked with red currant jelly. Set on a puff paste base.

Alma   A river of Russia. Lends its name to a famous allied victory gained over the Russians on the 20th September 1854, in the Crimean War. Dishes were created based on the scarlet uniform using cherries as fillings. The stand of the British Infantry became famous as 'The Thin Red Line'. *Alma pudding* – steamed pudding with cherries, and cherry sauce.

Alsacienne   Alsation style. The French province of Alsace. *Flan Alsacienne* – apple flan with egg custard.

Antoinette   Marie Antoinette, Queen of France (1755–93). *Pouding Antoinette* – egg custard dish with cherries and cherry sauce.

Aremberg   Charles Victor, Prince d'Aremberg of Belgium. The dishes were created by Albert Chevalier. *Poire d'Aremberg* – poached pear on sponge base, coated with cream sauce. Add a spiral of red currant jelly.

Baumé Antoine   French chemist (1728–1804). Inventor of the saccharometer used to measure the density of liquids.

Baba   Turkish for 'father'. A rich, fermented dough introduced to France by King Stanislas Leczinski of Poland and based on the tale Ali Baba and the Forty Thieves. Popularized in Paris by the Polish chef,

Sthorer at Rue Montgeuil, who also added the currants. *Baba au rhum* – sweetened yeast dough, baked in moulds, soaked in syrup and flavoured rum.

Balmoral   Jelly mould with bold flutes for moulding jellies. The flutes are large enough to take fruit.

Battenburg   A family of German Counts which died out in 1314 but was revived in 1851. Prince Henry of Battenburg was born in October 1858 and married Princess Beatrice of England in 1885. Maurice of Battenburg was killed in action near Ypres in October 1914. *Battenburg cake* – a lattice pattern of pink, yellow and chocolate sponge, encased with marzipan.

Belle Hélène   Sister of the Duc d'Orleans, queen of Romania. Subject of the opera by Offenback, produced in 1864. *Poire Belle Hélène* – vanilla ice cream poached pear, served with hot chocolate sauce.

Brillat Savarin   (1755–1826) A noted French Gastronome and author, famous for 'La Physiologie du Gout'. The sweet *Savarin aux fraises* was named after him.

Cardinal   The highest dignitary of the Roman Catholic church after the Pope, wears a distinctive scarlet dress and scarlet cap. The kitchen term stands for a dish of that colour. *Poire Cardinale* – vanilla ice cream, poached pear, coated with Melba sauce, sprinkled with roasted almonds.

Careme Antoine   (1784–1833) Chef of King George IV and later with an Austrian Emperor, Francis IV, and Russian Czar, Alexander I. Famous Chef of the 19th century and author of many culinary works. He created and perfected butter cream and was noted for his extravagant decorations.

Carmen   Star role in the opera of the same name, by Bized and first produced in Paris in 1875. *Charlotte Carmen* – line charlotte mould with wafers and fill with strawberry bavarois, mixed with chopped ginger.

Caroline Amelia Elizabeth (1768–1821). Queen of George IV, known as Caroline of Brunswick. *Carolines* – little éclairs used for petits fours.

Chantilly City and district of France, famous for its rich cream. It was first served to Prince de Condé in 1668. *Crème Chantilly* – whipped cream.

Chateaubriand Viconte de Chateaubriand, Ambassador to the Court of St. James. French author and gourmet, his favourite dish, a double fillet steak, is named after him. *Bombe Chateaubriand* – line the mould with apricot ice cream and fill with vanilla ice cream.

Charlotte Princess of the Palatinate, known as Charlotte Liese-lotte and daughter-in-law of Louis XIV, King of France. *Charlotte Russe* – vanilla bavarois, encased with sponge fingers.

Chartreuse The convent known as 'La Grande Chartreuse' near Grênoble in France. The resident monks, originally strict vegetarians, invented various vegetarian and fruit dishes, using moulds and pudding basins. *Chartreuse aux fruits* – line a chilled mould with cold jelly. Line with slices of soft fruit, and fill with bavarian cream.

Châtelaine This mistress of a castle. Ususally the châtelaine carried the keys suspended from her girdle. *Fruit Châtelaine* – place chestnuts or apples on the base of a dish and coat with crème pâtissiére. Sprinkle with crushed macaroons and glaze under salamander.

Emma Calvé (1866–1942) French operatic singer *Coupe Emma Calvé* – praline ice cream, cherries, raspberry sauce.

Conde Prince Louis de Conde (1530–1569) Poire conde – set rice pudding in mould or dish, poached pear, glaze with apricot glaze, and add cream.

Congress It usually applies to gatherings of professional people. In 1647 there was a meeting of delegates, for the purpose of peace negotiations. They were assembled at Osnabruck and Munster and the term 'congress' was evolved. It was at this congress that a mixture of sugar, almonds and egg whites baked in a light pastry and finished with a cross, made from the same paste, was first introduced to the Pope and bishops assembled there.

Colbert (1619–1683) Colbert Jean Baptiste, diplomat during the reign of Louis XIV and patron of the arts. *Abricot Colbert* – two half apricots. Sandwich with rice condé and fry in deep frier.

Créole Originally the name of persons born in the West Indies of Spanish parents. *Ananas créole* – thickened rice mixture set with gelatine and cream covered with pineapple and glazed.

Cyrano de Bergerac Savinien. French writer, born in Paris in 1620. Spent most of his life involved in duels and quarrels, chiefly because of his writing. *Gâteau Cyrano* – genoese sponge sandwiched with jam, coated with meringue and glazed in the oven.

Escoffier (1847–1935) Auguste Escoffier, the celebrated Chef of the Savoy. Father of modern cookery. Author of several cookery books. Collaborated with the development of many of the large hotels of London: the Ritz, Savoy, Carlton, for example. His talent attracted fashionable ladies, after whom he created and named many dishes. They have become part of the classic repertory of all time.

Dame Blanch Dame is the British legal designation of the wife or widow of a Baronet or Knight. Only dishes white in colour should bear this name. Title of the comic opera by Boieldieu, from the novel by Walter Scott. *Pêche Dame Blanche* – almond ice cream, white peach, coated with lemon ice cream and whipped cream.

Grissini Italian breadsticks invented by Antonio Brunero in 1679.

Gênes The battle of Gênes in the nineteenth century. The origin of *Pain de Gênes* and created in honour of Massena, a French Marshall. A sponge mixture containing ground almonds.

Josephine (1763–1814) Marie Josephine Tasker de la Pagerie, first wife of Napoleon. *Bombe*

Josephine – line the mould with coffee ice cream and fill with pistacchio ice cream.

Knickerbocker   Herman Jansen Knickerbocker (1650–1716). Dutch colonist of New Amsterdam (New York). The name has become synonymous with ice cream dishes and drinks. *Knickerbocker Glory* – using a tall glass, place in Melba sauce, vanilla ice cream, scarlet berries, Melba sauce, pineapple ice cream, slices of peaches or apricots, Melba sauce, strawberry ice cream, Melba sauce, top with whipped cream, chopped nuts, a cocktail cherry and a large scarlet berry.

Lucullus   Lucius Licinius, surnamed Ponticus (110–56 BC). A wealthy Roman General. *Souffle Lucullus* – soak a savarin and fill the cavity with a fruit soufflé mixture. Place in the oven to cook and serve immediately.

Medici   Famous Italian family. Catherine de'Medici, who married Henry II of France. *Bombe de Medici* – line the bombe mould with brandy-flavoured ice cream, fill with raspberry ice cream.

Melba   Dame Nellie. British operatic soprano. Her real name was Helen Porter Mitchell. She adopted the name Melba because she was a native of Melbourne, Australia in 1865. *Melba sauce* – boil together strawberry and raspberry jam. Pass through a fine strainer.

Meringue   The name originates from the northern Italian village, Marengo, where the famous battle of Marengo took place in June 1881 between Napoleon and the Austrians. In honour, both the meringue and chicken sauté were invented by Napoleon's cook.

Mousseline   Derived from mousse, which stems from muslin, a fabric named after the city of Mosul on the river Tigris. *Sauce mousseline* – cream sauce.

Normande   In the style of Normandy, northwestern province of France. *Flan Normande* – apple flan.

Othello   Shakespeare's tragedy first produced in 1604. *Othello* – a pastry composed with sponge biscuits, crème pâtissiére and coated with fondant.

Pithiviers   Town in France, well noted for its speciality, lark pie, and pastries. *Gâteaux Pithiviers* – puff paste rings, filled with frangipane.

Prasline Duplessis   Personal Chef to Marechal Duc de Choiceul. The inventor of *praline* – nuts coated with boiled sugar and crushed to a crumb texture.

Pompadou   Jeanne Antoinette Poisson le Normant d'Etroles, Marquisse de Pompadour, mistress of Louis XV of France. Very influential with the politicians of the time. *Gateaux Pompadour* – cream gâteau, decorated with cornets on top in a fan shape.

Ratafia   Believed to stem from the Malay Gafia, a spirit or liqueur made from cane sugar with a slightly bitter almond flavour. There are many varieties.

Rothschild   Family noted for the magnitude of financial transactions. Most famous was Nathan Mayer, born in 1777. *Pouding soufflé Rothschild* – vanilla-flavoured soufflé with diced confits.

Sarah Bernhardt   Famous Parisian actress, born in Paris in 1845. *Gâteau Sarah Bernhardt* – fresh cream gâteaux with fresh strawberries.

Suzette   Said to be the name of a very important person at the end of the nineteenth century. During her visit to a high class Parisian cabaret club, the Chef, Henri Charpentier, created the *Crêpe Suzette*.

Tatin   An apple tart, made famous by the Tatin family from Sologne, France.

Tosca   Title of a famous Italian opera. *Bombe Tosca* – line the bombe mould with apricot ice cream, fill with lemon ice cream.

Victoria   Queen of the United Kingdom, Ireland and Empress of India. Born in Kensington Palace on 24th May, 1819 she came to the throne in 1837 and died in 1901. *Coupe Victoria* – fresh fruit salad with strawberry and pistacchio ice cream.